ALLUSION AS NARRATIVE PREMISE IN
BRAHMS'S INSTRUMENTAL MUSIC

Musical Meaning and Interpretation
Robert S. Hatten, Editor

A Theory of Musical Narrative
Byron Almén

Approaches to Meaning in Music
Byron Almén and Edward Pearsall

Voicing Gender: Castrati, Travesti, and the Second Woman in Early Nineteenth-Century Italian Opera
Naomi André

The Italian Traditions and Puccini: Compositional Theory and Practice in Nineteenth-Century Opera
Nicholas Baragwanath

Debussy Redux: The Impact of His Music on Popular Culture
Matthew Brown

Music and Embodied Cognition: Listening, Moving, Feeling, and Thinking
Arnie Cox

Music and the Politics of Negation
James R. Currie

Il Trittico, Turandot, and Puccini's Late Style
Andrew Davis

Neil Young and the Poetics of Energy
William Echard

Psychedelic Popular Music: A History through Musical Topic Theory
William Echard

Reconfiguring Myth and Narrative in Contemporary Opera: Osvaldo Golijov, Kaija Saariaho, John Adams, and Tan Dun
Yayoi Uno Everett

Interpreting Musical Gestures, Topics, and Tropes: Mozart, Beethoven, Schubert
Robert S. Hatten

Musical Meaning in Beethoven: Markedness, Correlation, and Interpretation
Robert S. Hatten

Intertextuality in Western Art Music
Michael L. Klein

Music and the Crises of the Modern Subject
Michael L. Klein

Music and Narrative since 1900
Michael L. Klein and Nicholas Reyland

Musical Forces: Motion, Metaphor, and Meaning in Music
Steve Larson

Is Language a Music? Writings on Musical Form and Signification
David Lidov

Pleasure and Meaning in the Classical Symphony
Melanie Lowe

Breaking Time's Arrow: Experiment and Expression in the Music of Charles Ives
Matthew McDonald

Decorum of the Minuet, Delirium of the Waltz: A Study of Dance-Music Relations in 3/4 Time
Eric McKee

The Musical Topic: Hunt, Military, Pastoral
Raymond Monelle

Musical Representations, Subjects, and Objects: The Construction of Musical Thought in Zarlino, Descartes, Rameau, and Weber
Jairo Moreno

The Rite of Spring at 100
Severine Neff, Maureen Carr, and Gretchen Horlacher

Meaning and Interpretation of Music in Cinema
David Neumeyer

Deepening Musical Performance through Movement: The Theory and Practice of Embodied Interpretation
Alexandra Pierce

Expressive Intersections in Brahms: Essays in Analysis and Meaning
Heather Platt and Peter H. Smith

Expressive Forms in Brahms's Instrumental Music: Structure and Meaning in His Werther Quartet
Peter H. Smith

Music as Philosophy: Adorno and Beethoven's Late Style
Michael Spitzer

Death in *Winterreise*: Musico-Poetic Associations in Schubert's Song Cycle
Lauri Suurpää

Music and Wonder at the Medici Court: The 1589 Interludes for *La Pellegrina*
Nina Treadwell

Reflections on Musical Meaning and Its Representations
Leo Treitler

Debussy's Late Style: The Compositions of the Great War
Marianne Wheeldon

ALLUSION AS NARRATIVE PREMISE IN BRAHMS'S INSTRUMENTAL MUSIC

Jacquelyn E. C. Sholes

Indiana University Press

Publication of this book was supported by the AMS 75 PAYS Endowment of the American Musicological Society, funded in part by the National Endowment for the Humanities and the Andrew W. Mellon Foundation.

This book is a publication of

Indiana University Press
Office of Scholarly Publishing
Herman B Wells Library 350
1320 East 10th Street
Bloomington, Indiana 47405 USA

iupress.indiana.edu

© 2018 by Jacquelyn E. C. Sholes

A version of chapter 2 was published as "Lovelorn Lamentation or Histrionic Historicism? Reconsidering Allusion and Extramusical Meaning in the 1854 Version of Brahms's B-Major Trio" in *19th-Century Music* 34/1 (2010): 61–86. This material appears here in accordance with the copyright agreement with the University of California Press.

All rights reserved

No part of this book may be reproduced or utilized in any form or by any means, electronic or mechanical, including photocopying and recording, or by any information storage and retrieval system, without permission in writing from the publisher. The Association of American University Presses' Resolution on Permissions constitutes the only exception to this prohibition.

Manufactured in the United States of America

Cataloging information is available from the Library of Congress.

ISBN 978-0-253-03314-7 (cloth)
ISBN 978-0-253-03315-4 (paperback)
ISBN 978-0-253-03316-1 (ebook)

1 2 3 4 5   23 22 21 20 19 18

To my parents,
Barbara and Joseph Sholes,
and in loving memory of my grandmothers,
Ruth Stella Coran Sholes (1918–2013) and
Evelyn June Kagan (1907–2014)

Contents

	Acknowledgments	*ix*
	List of Musical Instrument Abbreviations	*xiii*
	Introduction	*1*
1	The Notion of Allusion as Narrative Premise in Brahms's Instrumental Music	*11*
2	Lovelorn Lamentation or Histrionic Historicism? Reexamining Allusion and Extramusical Meaning in the B-Major Piano Trio, op. 8	*68*
3	Musical Memory and the D-Major Serenade, op. 11	*103*
4	A Historical Model, an Emerging Soloist, a Young Composer in Turmoil: The Piano Concerto in D Minor, op. 15	*133*
5	A Later Example: Tragic Antiquarianism in Brahms's Fourth Symphony	*179*
	Conclusion	*227*
	Bibliography	*233*
	Index	*249*

Acknowledgments

I WOULD LIKE to thank the numerous colleagues, friends, mentors, and family members who generously gave of their time and expertise and provided much encouragement and support during the period in which this book came into being. I begin by thanking acquisition editors Janice Frisch and Raina Polivka, series editor Robert Hatten, the editorial board of Indiana University Press, and the manuscript reviewers for their enthusiasm about this project, for their expertise and insight, which were invaluable as I made final revisions to the text, and for guiding me so smoothly through the review and publication process with my first book. Thanks also to those on the production teams at Indiana University Press and at Ninestars who helped to prepare the project for publication, particularly Nancy Lightfoot and Narasimhan, and to Benjamin Ayotte for typesetting the musical examples. I send most profound thanks to Christopher Reynolds for his encouragement and his support of this project and for his detailed, thoughtful feedback on the manuscript. Many thanks to Margaret Notley for her editorial work for *19th-Century Music* on my article on Brahms's op. 8 Trio, as well as to Lawrence Kramer and the journal's editorial board for their helpful feedback on the article, on which Chapter Two of this book is based; both the article and the chapter are the stronger for their work.

I will be forever grateful to my dissertation advisor, Allan Keiler, for his thoughtful readings of early versions of some of the material presented here and for his guidance not only in developing this material, but in developing as a thinker and a writer. I am also deeply grateful to the other members of my dissertation committee, Eric Chafe and Daniel Beller-McKenna, whose feedback on early drafts was, similarly, delivered with much insight and much kindness. I am thankful to all three for remaining so steadfastly supportive of my work and my career over the past several years.

I am deeply thankful as well to the American Musicological Society for two generous publication subventions from the AMS 75 Pays Endowment, funded in part by the National Endowment for the Humanities and the Andrew W. Mellon Foundation, which helped to cover costs related to the preparation of this book. I am grateful to the American Brahms Society for the award of a Geiringer Scholarship in Brahms Studies, which helped to support my research in its early stages—and also to the Graduate School of Arts and Sciences and the Music Department at Brandeis University for supporting my work with a Phyllis G. Redstone Dissertation-Year Fellowship, a Herbert and Mildred Lee Fellowship, and a four-year doctoral fellowship.

In my current position in Boston University's Department of Musicology & Ethnomusicology, I have been extremely grateful for the advice and support of department chairs Victor Coelho and, before him, Jeremy Yudkin, and for the collegiality of current and former fellow department members Marié Abe, Michael Birenbaum-Quintero, Sean Gallagher, Brita Heimarck, Miki Kaneda, Thomas Peattie, Joshua Rifkin, Andrew Shenton, and Rachana Vajjhala. I am grateful to Jeremy Yudkin and Lewis Lockwood, co-directors of the Center for Beethoven Research at Boston University, for the opportunity to serve as Scholar in Residence at the Center in 2017–18. I would also like to thank current and former mentors, colleagues, and research and administrative staff in the music departments and libraries of Boston University, Brown University, Wellesley College, Williams College, Harvard University, and Brandeis University, including Jennifer Bloxam, Pamela Bristah, Marci Cohen, Vera Deak, Marion Dry, Claire Fontijn, Dana Gooley, Marjorie Hirsch, Sarah Hunter, David Kechley, Robert Levin, Michael McGrade, Holly Mockovak, Jessie Ann Owens, Eric Rice, Darwin Scott, Laura Stokes, and Anthony Sheppard.

I am grateful to Roger Moseley for sharing with me the contents of his article on Brahms's B-Major Piano Trio just prior to the article's publication in the *Journal of the Royal Musical Association* and to Paul Berry for discussing with me in detail the contents of his book *Brahms among Friends* in advance of the book's publication in 2014. Thanks also to Scott Burnham, David Ferris, Nancy Reich, the late Joel Sheveloff, and Boston University German Studies scholar William Waters for responding quickly and thoroughly to questions related to their respective areas of expertise.

I would like to thank several other fellow Brahms scholars not yet mentioned for welcoming me so warmly into their ranks in the early years of my career, for their collegial support and, in some cases, for their feedback on work published elsewhere. Sincerest gratitude and admiration to Styra Avins, George Bozarth, David Brodbeck, Robert Eshbach, Walter Frisch, Valerie Goertzen, Virginia Hancock, William Horne, Karen Leistra-Jones, Marie Sumner Lott, Laurie McManus, Heather Platt, Daniel Stevens, and many other members of the "Brahms community" and the broader musicological community with whom I look forward to future conversations.

Thanks are in order, as well, to the teachers who helped me to prepare for graduate work and ultimately a career in musicology, most especially Susan Schoonmaker, Eric Delson, Julia Hawkins, and Wellesley College faculty members Martin Brody, Charles Fisk, Vincent Jay Panetta, and the late Arlene Zallman. Without the knowledge they shared with me during some of my most formative years, and without the skills they helped me to develop, I could never have hoped to succeed as a professional musicologist. I will always be grateful to them for the roles they played in enabling me to pursue a career in this field.

I would also like to thank all of the students I have taught over the past several years—at Boston University, Brown University, Wellesley College, Williams College, the University of Massachusetts Boston, Harvard University, and Brandeis University, as well as my private piano students—for serving as constant reminders of why I chose to join this field, for allowing me to share with them what I love and what I have to give, and for helping me to grow as a teacher and as a person while learning more about my field and while refining my ideas and their presentation. I also thank my current and former teaching assistants at Boston University and Brown University—namely Melody Chapin, Brett Kostrzewski, Shaoying Ho, and Kristen Edwards—for their help, which resulted in my being able to devote to research and writing more time than would otherwise have been available.

My heartfelt thanks go to other colleagues and to friends and family who provided general advice, moral support, and professional encouragement, or feedback on partial drafts—or who otherwise served as "sounding boards" for some of the ideas I present in the following pages. Thanks in particular to John Aylward, Bruce Alan Brown, Will Butts, Michael Cuthbert, Dana Dalton, Joan Gaylord, Tracy Gleason and Dave Kaiser, Cathy Gordon, Melissa de Graaf, Erin Jerome, Elizabeth Joyce, Kevin Karnes, Erinn Knyt, Benjamin Korstvedt, Daniel Libin, Carolyn Lyons and Chris Dangel, Rebecca Marchand, Katarina Markovic, Alexandra Sholes McLeod and Chris McLeod, Becky Miller, Joseph Morgan, Adriana Ponce, Sam Rechtoris, Margarita Restrepo, Douglas Shadle, Adam and Linda Sholes and family, Daniel Sholes, Jason Silver, Alexander Stefaniak, and Bennett Zon. I also thank Liza Wachman Percer for her helpful advice on the publishing process.

Last but not least, I am inexpressibly grateful to Leif Gibb for his profoundly kind and sensitive encouragement and love and to my parents, Barbara and Joseph Sholes, whose enduring love and support have made the completion of this book, along with so many other things, possible.

Musical Instrument Abbreviations

Fl. = Flute

Ob. = Oboe

Cl. = Clarinet

Bsn. = Bassoon

C. Bsn. = Contrabassoon

Hn. = Horn

Tpt. = Trumpet

Tbn. = Trombone

Pf. = Piano(forte)

Vln. I = Violin I

Vln. II = Violin II

Vla. = Viola

Vc. = (Violon)cello

Cb. = (Contra)bass

(For transposing instruments, the key is indicated in parentheses, e.g., Hn. (C) designates horns in C.)

ALLUSION as NARRATIVE PREMISE in BRAHMS'S INSTRUMENTAL MUSIC

Introduction

THIS BOOK PRESENTS a fresh look at an aspect of Brahms's music that has been noted frequently from the nineteenth century to the present: Brahms's employment of references to works of earlier and contemporaneous composers, whether through thematic allusion or the use of structural or stylistic models from the past. The main premise of the book, which distinguishes this study from earlier examinations of Brahms's historical references, is that such references may be understood to play an important role in Brahms's handling of the musical and narrative relationships between the different movements of works in which they appear. Thus, Brahms's concern with the music of others, and especially historical works, affects his musical conception in a more global sense, rather than manifesting itself merely in isolated thematic reminiscences. In this book, I will demonstrate how Brahms's employment of historically referential material in specific works may be read not as the result of a need for inspiration, nor even simply a desire to pay homage to composers he revered or friends he admired, but as generative of movement-spanning connections that suggest things about Brahms's more nuanced, and sometimes conflicted, attitudes toward the material to which he alludes as he establishes and defines his own historical position in relation to his predecessors.

Scholars and critics from Brahms's own time to the present have heavily underscored Brahms's historical consciousness, identifying apparent references to earlier composers in most of his works. But even in studies that focus specifically on allusion in Brahms, the musical and dramatic relevance of each historical reference is often assumed to be limited to a particular passage, theme, or movement. It is frequently the case, however, that a historical reference in one movement of a work resonates meaningfully, musically, and dramatically, with material in other movements in ways not previously recognized. As we will observe, Brahms indeed appears, in many instances, to weave one or more such references into broad, cross-movement narratives that culminate in the decisive realization, transformation, or abandonment of the historical element(s). In this way, Brahms's acute historical consciousness, so frequently and consistently emphasized in the existing scholarship, seems to take on an additional, as-yet-unappreciated dimension as an important factor in his construction of intermovement form and drama. The works in this sense represent expressive outlets for Brahms's complicated orientation toward the music of others—music which, it is clear, inspired and in some cases burdened him as he emerged with his own, unique artistic voice and established his own place in music history.

The main intention here is not merely to identify specific allusions to earlier composers, but to suggest that we explore how such references may function structurally and expressively in Brahms's music. With few exceptions, the historical references discussed here have long been observed and are widely accepted by the scholarly community as allusions to the music of others. (The two main exceptions are discussed in chapters 2 and 5, where I argue for the presence of previously undetected references in the 1854 version of Brahms's Trio in B-Major, op. 8, and in the Fourth Symphony, respectively.)

The formation of Brahms's relationship with Robert and Clara Schumann in the autumn of 1853, Brahms's twentieth year, and the publication of Robert Schumann's article "Neue Bahnen" shortly thereafter were clearly life- and career-transforming milestones for the young composer, greatly facilitating Brahms's entry into elite musical circles and engendering extraordinarily lofty expectations for his artistic production and ultimate historical significance. In his article, Schumann hailed the relatively unknown Brahms as a musical messiah of sorts, charging him with the role of heir to and savior of the artistic principles represented by Beethoven and other great Austro-German composers of the past; these were ideals now threatened, in the minds of Schumann and Brahms, by the likes of Wagner, Liszt, and Berlioz.

Brahms's historical awareness was extraordinarily high in the mid-1850s as he struggled to compose works worthy of the attention and praise that Schumann had so publicly lavished on him. It frequently appears that narratives involving recollection, transformation, or loss that are played out over the course of a multimovement work are tied intimately to thematic allusions or structural models from works of Beethoven or other predecessors of Brahms. As we will see, this tendency is something that carries over into the middle and later stages of Brahms's career as well, evolving as Brahms himself evolves.

In the writings of Brahms and of his contemporaries, we find clear indications that instrumental music was at least sometimes conceived in narrative terms. As Leo Treitler argues, "a contemporary theoretical justification for narratological interpretations of music can be distinguished from a historical one ... through evidence that composers or critics who were their contemporaries believed their music to have a narrative character" and that, "while such evidence should not be granted unquestioned authority, it provides sufficient grounds for a narratological approach as a hypothesis."[1] Treitler cites, for example, "Robert Schumann's talk of music's successions as processions of ideas or of conditions of the soul."[2] In a letter to Adolf Schubring, Brahms himself explicitly refers to his composition of music as the building of "stories."[3] On the subject of musical meaning in nineteenth-century music more generally, I refer the reader to the work of such scholars as Robert Hatten, Leonard Ratner, Kofi Agawu, and Lawrence Kramer, among others, in addition to Treitler.[4]

Although we must exercise due caution in attributing any particular biographical or psychological meaning or significance to a work of art, it is entirely reasonable to assume that the circumstances of an artist's life are going to have some influence on the work he or she produces. As composer György Ligeti suggests, "it is a rather childish idea that a composer will write music in the minor key when he is sad, it is rather too simplistic. There is no doubt, however, that the stance of the artist, his whole approach to his art, his means of expression are all of them greatly influenced by experiences he has accumulated in the course of day-to-day living."[5] Of course, exactly what the nature of that influence is, and the degree to which the composer is aware of and deliberately reflecting that influence in his or her work is, in most cases, not something that we can (or must) definitively determine. It is my intention here to contribute to a fuller appreciation of the ways in which Brahms's historical sense may have influenced his handling of intermovement connections and to stimulate further thought and discussion on the matter.

It is not only logical, but perhaps even obvious, that the particular way in which Brahms handles a given historical reference almost necessarily reveals something of his own attitude toward the music to which he is alluding, and the idea that these works may contain biographical or expressive meaning beyond the purely abstract is very much in line with important trends in recent Brahms scholarship. One of these is a growing acceptance of the idea that Brahms's music is not nearly so devoid of extramusical meaning as it once appeared, an idea supported by a number of publications over the past several years, including the recent book *Expressive Intersections in Brahms: Essays in Analysis and Meaning*.[6] Another example is Peter Smith's 2005 book on Brahms's "Werther" Quartet, op. 60, which Smith presents as "a case study for how it might be possible to steer a middle course between the old music theory, which tends to be purely analytical and formalist, and the new musicology, which often denies itself the insights of careful musical analysis in the pursuit of critical interpretation," asserting that "the time is ripe to explore how our work can contribute still further insight into expressive content."[7] Although we will not rely here on quite the same (e.g., Schenkerian) analytical methodologies as Smith, the present study nonetheless applies these principles to works beyond his focused consideration, aiming to broaden our understanding of the types of interactions that exist between form and expressive meaning in Brahms's oeuvre.

Brahms's attitudes toward allusion and extramusical meaning were likely influenced by the attitudes of those around him. In the mid-1850s, Schumann actively encouraged the young Brahms to use models from the works of earlier composers—particularly Beethoven—suggesting that Brahms keep in mind the openings of Beethoven's symphonies and that he try to emulate certain aspects of them when composing his own works.[8] Schumann was by no means the only influential figure of the period to endorse such practices; for instance, in his *School of Practical Composition*, published in 1848, Czerny recommends that composers hone their talents by modeling their musical structures on those of masterworks.[9]

In *Palestrina and the German Romantic Imagination*, James Garratt characterizes the concept of originality in nineteenth-century German culture. He writes,

> for Schopenhauer, there is seemingly no middle ground between originality and imitation; artists lacking the inspiration and spontaneity for genius inevitably produce reflective, contrived fabrications ... [but] Schopenhauer's conception of originality, while influential ... was not shared by all his contemporaries. Goethe repeatedly dismissed the idea of originality, arguing that no artist could rely solely on instinct and inspiration ... the idea that the artist can divorce himself from other artworks and produce a work unconsciously from the gift of genius is absurd ... rather, every artist is a composite being indebted to a multiplicity of sources ... the inevitability of the author being influenced by his predecessors makes it ridiculous [in Goethe's view] for critics to attempt to discredit him by criticizing his dependence on their works....[10]

Garratt concludes that "the gulf separating Goethe and Schopenhauer, both of whom expressed these opinions at roughly the same time, is sufficient to confirm that no unified conception of originality existed in the early nineteenth century."[11]

Nonetheless, Anthony Newcomb has asserted that, in mid-nineteenth-century Germany, thematic allusions to preexisting works by other composers were on the whole something to be avoided to the extent that they tended to be viewed negatively by critics and were not generally considered to be imbued with symbolic meaning.[12] Yet these factors, along with Brahms's widely known disdain for the practice of "reminiscence hunting" on the part of critics, did not prevent him from making frequent reference, throughout his career, to works of other composers.[13] Brahms is known, on various occasions, to have openly admitted to alluding to the music of others in his own work, in some cases expecting the references to be obvious to his audience. Most infamous is his retort to one critic who had pointed out the resemblance between a theme in the finale of Brahms's First Symphony and the "Ode to Joy" melody from the finale of Beethoven's Ninth: "any ass can see that."[14] It was perhaps the very shallowness and ignorance involved in the practice of seeking superficial reminiscences without considering that they might hold any meaning (beyond, possibly, a perceived lack of originality) that Brahms found so distasteful—and in any case he may simply have resented critics for prying into his compositional processes and intentions, things about which he was extraordinarily private. Even Newcomb feels obligated to acknowledge an intended meaning behind the reference to the "Ode to Joy" in the finale of Brahms's First Symphony, a meaning that has to do with the iconic status of the referenced work itself and the relative historical position of Brahms's own music; nonetheless, Newcomb denies intended, meaningful allusion elsewhere in Brahms's oeuvre, including in the op. 8 Trio.[15]

Building on an appreciation of the importance of allusion in the music of Brahms that is reflected in the broader array of literature on this topic, with which I will be engaging deeply in the chapters to follow, I argue in this book for an alternative perspective on Brahms's approach to alluding to the music of others, both in the Trio and in general. Christopher Reynolds has already made a strong case that "for Schumann, Liszt, and others, allusive motives would have been the very essence of music: a symbolic language," claiming that "as searches for musical unity are valid for music created in a time that valorized organicism, the interpretation of textual and symbolic meaning is justified for an era that understood the potential for meaning to exist in all things."[16] All signs indicate that Brahms had a keen ear for thematic resemblances in his own music and in that of others and that, at least on many occasions, his allusions were intentional and meaningful. Kenneth Hull emphasizes that "the plausibility of Brahms's having made use of allusion in his compositions is enhanced by evidence of his keen interest in both literary and musical allusion in other contexts" and provides examples to demonstrate that Brahms was "a game-player, who enjoyed encoding musical messages for friends, who was quick to perceive the meaning of such puzzles himself, and who also used verbal allusion to test the puzzle-solving ability of his correspondents. He frequently sent cryptic messages to his friends in the form of musical quotations from vocal music which lacked ... their accompanying texts."[17] In his recent, insightful book, *Brahms among Friends: Listening, Performance, and the Rhetoric of Allusion*, Paul Berry explores in detail how some of these allusions may be understood within the contexts of Brahms's friendships, bearing special meaning for certain individuals in his life.[18]

Nonetheless, it is not necessarily the case that Brahms's handling of allusions always resulted from entirely conscious impulses, and it is certainly possible that his use of historical reference reveals things about him that he did not intend to say. As Reynolds emphasizes, the issue is not necessarily clear-cut; there is a spectrum of possibilities falling between the initial presence and the complete absence of intention. Reynolds suggests that

> the "either-or" approach to the conscious-unconscious duality, which still informs many discussions of musical creativity, overlooks the rich and complex possibility for two-way exchanges between conscious and unconscious creativity, exchanges that were already acknowledged in the nineteenth century. Composers' letters and sketches show that the path from initial

> musical inception to finished published work often progressed through many stages ... including multiple drafts, informal performances for friends, and pre-publication performances for larger audiences.... The opportunities for a composer to get to know his own work in relationship to other works were therefore numerous, extended, and varied. However the ideas for a piece came to a composer ... by the time a work was sent off for publication, the composer had had time to recognize unintended musical similarities with other works and then to enhance, obscure, ignore, or remove them. Each of these responses has implications for the issue of intentionality.[19]

Even if a composer does not initially intend to quote from the work of another composer, there are plenty of opportunities to notice resemblances between one's own compositions and other works and, if one chooses, to strengthen the parallels and take responsibility for the resemblances.[20] Furthermore, a lack of intention does not equate to a lack of meaning; indeed, the possibility that the presence and handling of a particular allusion arises from subconscious inclinations lessens neither its musical nor psychological significance.

The scope of this study is limited to Brahms's multimovement instrumental works, focusing especially, but not exclusively, on the music of Brahms's formative twenties—that is, of the period immediately following "Neue Bahnen," when Brahms had reason to be especially concerned with finding his artistic voice and comprehending his historical role. Examples from the middle and later periods of his career demonstrate that allusion continues to function similarly, even if evolving in accordance with Brahms's changing historical perspective. We will examine works in a variety of instrumental genres, including piano, chamber, and orchestral music, leaving room for further inquiry into the vocal and choral compositions.

The first chapter of this book provides some preliminary context for what follows. The chapter begins with a brief, general overview of issues surrounding historicism in Brahms's music. Examination of the interrelatedness of allusion, intermovement form, and narrative in Brahms has tended to focus on individual examples, while the fuller picture, the broader trend they represent, has not been fully appreciated. Some of the individual examples that have already been most closely examined and that are most familiar are drawn from the mature, middle-period works, whereas much more remains to be said about how this phenomenon applies to pieces from other periods, on which we must focus if we want to fill out the picture. As foundational context for this broader view, chapter 1 concisely presents three middle-period examples: the First Symphony (1862–76), the Horn Trio (1865), and the Third String Quartet (1875). Leading into the more extended analyses of other works to follow, the chapter will conclude with brief, preliminary examinations of two of Brahms's early piano sonatas.

Chapter 2 addresses the two versions of Brahms's Trio in B major, op. 8, a work composed in 1854 and then revised towards the end of Brahms's career, in 1889. Although it has long been accepted that the 1854 version contains references to songs of Beethoven and Schubert, it has escaped notice that the piece also alludes, clearly and in a structurally significant manner, to a keyboard sonata of Domenico Scarlatti. Strong musical evidence for this additional allusion is corroborated by Brahms's long-term, multifaceted engagement with Scarlatti's music as demonstrated by his correspondence, music library, performance repertory, theoretical studies, and other compositions. The chapter explores the implications of this Scarlatti allusion both for the revisions and for the issue of extramusical meaning, suggesting that the original trio represents an elegy for the musical past, whereas the revisions represent the updated historical perspective of the mature composer.

Chapter 3 is concerned with the D-Major Serenade, op. 11 (1857–58), Brahms's first completed orchestral work. Despite the fact that it represents a major milestone in his career, the Serenade has been the subject of relatively little serious analytical writing. Apart from the obvious evocation of the eighteenth century in his choice of genre, much remains to be said about the role of musical memory in this work. This chapter explores the ways in which the Serenade's initial theme is recalled and transformed over the course of the work's successive movements; examines the relationship of these thematic materials, and this process, to the finale of Haydn's last symphony; and considers the implications of such factors for Brahms's own historical self-positioning.

Chapter 4 focuses on Brahms's First Piano Concerto, op. 15 (1854–59), a work that caused its composer a great deal of trouble as it evolved from incomplete two-piano sonata to unfinished symphony before being reconceptualized, completed, and revised. Not surprisingly, scholars have cited a need for inspiration as the cause for Brahms's apparent modeling of the finale's structure on that of Beethoven's C-Minor Piano Concerto. I argue here that, even if Brahms employed this model out of necessity, the ways in which he deliberately deviates from Beethoven's template reveal something of his attitude toward that model (and perhaps toward that necessity), imbuing the connection between the concertos with a more nuanced significance. Oft-cited evidence has inspired readings of Brahms's concerto as a response to Robert Schumann's nervous breakdown or a representation of Brahms's feelings for Clara Schumann. These concerns, as well as the need to establish his artistic voice and historical position, weighed heavily on Brahms, and the chapter concludes with a consideration of how such issues may be reflected and intermingled in this work.

Chapter 5, focusing on Brahms's Fourth and final Symphony (completed in 1885), provides an example from the later repertory. A strong historicist element has always been noted in this work, particularly in the final movement, a chaconne whose main theme appears to have been drawn from Bach's Cantata 150. In this chapter, I suggest that, at a particularly striking moment in the symphony's finale, Brahms also makes reference to a Wagnerian chorus whose textual themes are closely related to those of the Bach cantata. The Symphony's finale, with its borrowed material, is shown to serve as generative material for music in previous movements. The chapter also considers what light these allusions may shed on the work's long-held associations with death and tragedy and on how these associations may relate to Brahms's underlying historicist concerns, particularly about the future of symphonic music, as well as his relationship to Wagner, who had called that future into question.

I turn now to chapter 1, which begins to explore the notion of allusion as narrative premise in Brahms's instrumental music. This and succeeding chapters will demonstrate that Brahms's references to music of other composers can in many cases be understood to hold broader structural implications and bear deeper meaning in Brahms's work than generally has been realized.

Notes

1. Leo Treitler, "Reflections on the Communication of Affect and Idea through Music," in *Psychoanalytic Explorations in Music: Second Series*, ed. Stuart Feder, Richard L. Karmel, and George H. Pollock (Madison, CT: International Universities Press, 1993), 46.

2. Treitler, "Reflections," 46.

3. In a letter to Adolf Schubring (Vienna, February 16, 1869, in Johannes Brahms, *Briefwechsel*, ed. Max Kalbeck [Berlin: Deutsche Brahms-Gesellschaft, 1915], 8, 217–218), cited in Christopher Reynolds, *Motives for Allusion: Context and Content in Nineteenth-Century Music* (Cambridge, MA: Harvard University Press, 2003), 23, 192, n. 1), Brahms states that, in sets of variations, the bass line is "the firm foundation on which I build my stories."

4. See Robert Hatten, *Musical Meaning in Beethoven: Markedness, Correlation, and Interpretation* (Bloomington: Indiana University Press, 1994) and *Interpreting Musical Gestures, Topics, and Tropes: Mozart, Beethoven, Schubert* (Bloomington: Indiana University Press, 2004); Leonard G. Ratner, *Romantic Music: Sound and Syntax* (New York: Schirmer Books, 1992); Kofi Agawu, *Music as Discourse: Semiotic Adventures in Romantic Music* (New York: Oxford University Press, 2009); Lawrence Kramer, *Musical Meaning: Toward a Critical History* (Berkeley: University of California Press, 2002); and Leo Treitler, *Reflections on Musical Meaning and Its Representations* (Bloomington: Indiana University Press, 2011).

5. György Ligeti et al., *György Ligeti in Conversation with Péter Várnai, Josef Häusler, Claude Samuel, and Himself* (London: Eulenberg Books, 1983), 20–21, quoted in Martin L. Nass, "The Composer's Experience: Variations on Several Themes," in *Psychoanalytic Explorations in Music: Second Series*, ed. Stuart Feder, Richard L. Karmel, and George H. Pollock (Madison, CT: International Universities Press, 1993), 30. Nass, a psychoanalyst, finds this sentiment consistent with those of several other composers he has interviewed.

6. Heather Platt and Peter H. Smith, eds. *Expressive Intersections in Brahms: Essays in Analysis and Meaning* (Bloomington: Indiana University Press, 2012), 3–8. Any number

of other studies may be cited here, including Dillon Parmer, "Brahms the Programmatic? A Critical Assessment" (PhD diss., University of Rochester, 1995); on the symphonies alone, Robert Fink, "Desire, Repression, and Brahms's First Symphony," *Repercussions* 2 (1993): 75–103; Reinhold Brinkmann, *Late Idyll: The Second Symphony of Johannes Brahms*, trans. Peter Palmer (Cambridge, MA: Harvard University Press, 1995); Susan McClary, "Narrative Agendas in 'Absolute' Music: Identity and Difference in Brahms's Third Symphony," in *Musicology and Difference: Gender and Sexuality in Music Scholarship*, ed. Ruth A. Solie (Berkeley: University of California Press, 1993), 326–44; and Marion Gerards, "Narrative Programme und Geschlechter-Identität in der 3. Sinfonie von Johannes Brahms: Zum Problem einer genderzentrierten Interpretation absoluter Musik," *Frankfurter Zeitschrift für Musikwissenschaft* 8 (2005): 42–57. Other examples include Kenneth Ross Hull, "Allusive Irony in Brahms's Fourth Symphony," in *Brahms Studies* 2, ed. David Brodbeck (Lincoln: University of Nebraska Press, 1998), 135–68; David Brodbeck, "Brahms, the Third Symphony, and the New German School," in *Brahms and His World*, ed. Walter Frisch (Princeton, NJ: Princeton University Press, 1990), 65–80; and "Medium and Meaning: New Aspects of the Chamber Music," in *The Cambridge Companion to Brahms*, ed. Michael Musgrave (Cambridge: Cambridge University Press, 1999), 98–132; Raymond Knapp, "Brahms and the Anxiety of Allusion" *Journal of Musicological Research* 18 (1998): 1–30; Raymond Knapp, "Utopian Agendas: Variation, Allusion, and Referential Meaning in Brahms's Symphonies," in *Brahms Studies* 3, ed. David Brodbeck (Lincoln: University of Nebraska Press, 2001), 129–89; Dillon Parmer, "Brahms, Song Quotation, and Secret Programs," *19th-Century Music* 19, no. 2 (1995): 161–90; Christopher Reynolds, "A Choral Symphony by Brahms?," *19th-Century Music* 9, no. 1 (1985): 3–25; and Reynolds, *Motives for Allusion*. See also George Bozarth, "Brahms's First Piano Concerto, op. 15: Genesis and Meaning," in *Beiträge zur Geschichte des Konzerts: Festschrift Siegfried Kross zum 60. Geburtstag*, ed. Reinmar Emans and Matthias Wendt (Bonn: G. Schroeder, 1990), 211–47.

7. Peter Howard Smith, *Expressive Forms in Brahms's Instrumental Music: Structure and Meaning in His Werther Quartet* (Bloomington: Indiana University Press, 2005), 4.

8. To Joseph Joachim (with whom Brahms was staying the time), Schumann wrote that Brahms "should always keep the beginnings of the Beethoven symphonies in mind. He should try to make something similar" (January 6, 1854, published in *Robert Schumanns Briefe. Neue Folge*, 2nd rev. ed., ed. F. Gustav Jansen (Leipzig: Breitkopf & Härtel, 1904), 390, cited and translated in Reynolds, *Motives for Allusion*, 35).

9. See Reynolds, *Motives for Allusion*, 23–25. Reynolds views the methods described by Czerny as an explanation for similarities between several of Brahms's works and their apparent models in Beethoven.

10. James Garratt, *Palestrina and the German Romantic Imagination: Interpreting Historicism in Nineteenth-Century Music* (Cambridge: Cambridge University Press, 2002), 10–11.

11. Garratt, *Palestrina and the German Romantic Imagination*, 11.

12. Anthony Newcomb, "The Hunt for Reminiscences in Nineteenth-Century Germany," in *Music and the Aesthetics of Modernity*, ed. Karol Berger and Anthony Newcomb (Cambridge, MA: Harvard University Press, 2005), 111–35.

13. On this disdain, see for example, Newcomb, "The Hunt for Reminiscences," 121, 127.

14. See, for instance, Ivor Keys, *Johannes Brahms* (Portland, OR: Amadeus Press, 1989), 168; and Mark Evan Bonds, *After Beethoven: Imperatives of Originality in the Symphony*

(Cambridge, MA: Harvard University Press, 1996), 1. For some of Brahms's somewhat less insulting admissions to other instances of allusion, see Kenneth Ross Hull, "Brahms the Allusive: Extra-compositional Reference in the Instrumental Music of Johannes Brahms" (PhD diss., Princeton University, 1989), 16–17.

15. Newcomb, "The Hunt for Reminiscences," 124–25.
16. Reynolds, *Motives for Allusion*, 181.
17. Hull, "Brahms the Allusive," 11–12.
18. Paul Berry, *Brahms among Friends: Listening, Performance, and the Rhetoric of Allusion* (Oxford, UK: Oxford University Press, 2014), 33. Berry focuses primarily on texted works—Brahms's songs—with a handful of examples from the solo piano and chamber works, but not those works examined in this book, and not focusing on intermovement issues.
19. Reynolds, *Motives for Allusion*, 103–4.
20. Reynolds, *Motives for Allusion*, 116.

1 The Notion of Allusion as Narrative Premise in Brahms's Instrumental Music

JOHANNES BRAHMS WAS possessed of an especially strong historicist sense—and lived at a time when, ironically, this made him rather modern. Up to the first half of the nineteenth century, music had a relatively short shelf life. Generally, composers wrote works for specific occasions, to fill specific practical needs, and once those needs had been met, the music had served its purpose and was put aside to make room for the new. Brahms's profound preoccupation with the music of his predecessors must be understood not only against the backdrop of the inspiring and intimidating precedent set by Beethoven, but also within the broader context of the increasing awareness of and rise of interest in preserving music history that took place during Brahms's lifetime. The latter was a phenomenon that caused Brahms great anxiety as he became one of the first of the "great composers" to self-consciously attempt to carve out a unique and lasting artistic voice for the ages. Austro-German intellectual society played a leading role in establishing the field of modern musicology in the nineteenth century, with such fundamental contributions as the pioneering historical writings of Forkel, Kiesewetter, and Ambros;[1] biographies of Bach, Mozart, Handel, and Haydn by Otto Jahn, Philipp Spitta, Friedrich Chrysander, and C. F. Pohl, respectively;[2] and the work of such influential figures as Beethoven scholar Gustav Nottebohm, theorist Hugo Riemann, and Adolf Bernhard Marx with his theory of sonata form. This was the *milieu* that produced a thriving culture of music criticism, for which the *Neue Zeitschrift für Musik*, founded by Robert Schumann, was among the most influential vehicles, as well as the first serious scholarly music journal, the *Vierteljahrschrift für Musikwissenschaft* (1885), edited by Guido Adler, along with Chrysander and Spitta. The same environment also produced such fundamental resources for music research as lexicons, bibliographies, indexes, and thematic catalogs (e.g., Ludwig von Köchel's 1862 catalog of the works of Mozart), as well as government-sponsored *Denkmäler* editions and the first critical or "collected-works" editions (*Gesamtausgaben*) for several major composers, including Bach, Handel, Palestrina, Mozart, Schubert, and Beethoven. German and Austrian universities began formally to recognize the field as a full-fledged academic pursuit by creating university faculty positions in music, beginning at Bonn in 1826; the first full professorships were awarded in Austria, at the University of Vienna in 1870, to the critic Eduard Hanslick, a great supporter of Brahms, and in Germany to Gustav Jacobsthal at Strasbourg in 1897.[3] All of this activity naturally corresponds to the laying of foundations for the development of a canon of "great works" of Western music—a canon which, in large part by consequence, prominently features the works of German and Austrian composers.

Brahms has been considered by many to be a conservative artist, particularly in comparison with the more formally and harmonically adventurous composers of the New German School, such as Wagner, Liszt, and Berlioz (Joseph Kerman, for instance, characterized Brahms as a composer "out of joint with his times")—and yet, Brahms's historical awareness as a composer actually was thus a rather modern trait.[4] In recent decades, there has been a growing realization of the ways in which Brahms's historical self-awareness links him and his music to composers and music of the modern and postmodern eras. Peter Burkholder, for example, has suggested that in fact "Brahms is the single most important influence on twentieth-century classical music—not in the way it *sounds*, but in how we think about it, how composers think about it, how music behaves, why it is written, and how composers measure their success."[5] Kenneth Hull elaborates: "modernism in music has not to do primarily with the development of new musical techniques but with aspects of the composer's preoccupation with his relationship to music of the past. In this respect, Brahms may be considered the first musical modernist."[6] Furthermore, Kevin Korsyn suggests that, "what appears modern—or rather postmodern—in Brahms is his recruitment of a plurality of modern languages. By mobilizing a number of historically differentiated discourses, Brahms becomes 'both the historian and the agent of his own language.' Thus, he knew the very modern anxiety ... of having to choose an orientation among languages."[7]

Historicism in Brahms's Music

A strong historicist tendency in Brahms's work has been noted consistently by critics and scholars from Brahms's time to the present. Brahms's interest in music of the past, a fascination encompassing repertories from folksong to sacred music to secular "art" music and spanning from the medieval Minnesänger to the nineteenth century, is reflected in a wide variety of ways to be explored in detail throughout this volume.[8] At a time when the field of musicology was just getting "off the ground," Brahms's historicist sense appears not only in his own music—through his use of passé or "archaic" genres and forms (e.g., the serenade and the chaconne) and style elements (e.g., modality) and through his employment of motivic allusions to or employment of structural models from the works of earlier composers—but also in his personal music library; in his activities as editor, compiler, and arranger of historical repertories; and in his other musicological pursuits. Brahms also played an active role in the process of canon solidification not only as a composer, but also as a musicologist engaged in editorial work on music of C. P. E. Bach, Couperin, Handel, Mozart, Schubert, Chopin, Schumann, and others.[9] Brahms's other musicological activities include, for example, his exchange of counterpoint exercises with Joseph Joachim, his collection of historical examples of parallel octaves and fifths (see chap. 3), and his examination of the Beethoven manuscripts made available to him by Gustav Nottebohm (see chap. 5).

Scholars such as Christopher Reynolds and Kenneth Hull, respectively, have dubbed Brahms "one of the most adroit fashioners of allusions," and "a master of allusion."[10] Apparent allusions in many individual works of Brahms were identified in print and by Brahms's friends even during the composer's own lifetime, with at least one instance dating from as early as 1858.[11] Not surprisingly, Brahms draws with special frequency on the works of his greatest hero, Beethoven, and it is clear that at least sometimes, as with the evocation of the "Ode to Joy" in the finale of his First Symphony, he expected his audience to recognize the references. Hull points out that, among Brahms's instrumental works, "there is scarcely an opus for which at least one quotation or allusion has not been cited somewhere in the literature"; that Brahms's friend and early biographer Max Kalbeck "alone suggests at least one instance of thematic resemblance for each of about half of the instrumental works"; and that, in several cases, multiple sources of allusion have been cited for a single work.[12] In short, as generations of critics and scholars have demonstrated, "Brahms's knowledge of the music of the past was extensive, and his use of that knowledge in his own compositional activity ... more pervasive, varied, and self-conscious than that of any previous composer."[13]

And yet despite the long-standing recognition of the role of allusion in Brahms's music on a localized level and a similarly well-established awareness of motivic connections that Brahms draws between different movements of individual instrumental works, scholars have not explored thoroughly the way in which these two phenomena interact. I will suggest ways in which Brahms's strong historicist concerns, his fascination with music of the past—which, his writings and biography would suggest, represented some combination of tendencies toward reverential homage and a "Bloomian" "anxiety of influence"—played an important and hitherto largely unappreciated role in his handling of broad formal structures and his weaving of musical narratives in multimovement instrumental works.[14] Furthermore, I will demonstrate how these works consequently may be interpreted as the composer's responses (conscious or not) to his historical orientations towards the sources on which he draws.

Historical Reference and Intermovement Narrative in the Mature Works of the 1860s–70s

This book will examine several early works, those of the 1850s, a period during which Brahms's struggles to establish and articulate himself and his own historical position were especially pressing—and, from which correspondingly, there is a particularly high density of examples of allusory narratives that appear to have a historicist significance. In his later work, I argue for the expression of similar concerns, now with regard not only to Brahms's position relative to his predecessors, but perhaps also his standing relative to contemporary trends and the significance those trends might hold for the future of music. What, then, of the works that come in between, the mature multimovement instrumental works of the 1860s and 1870s?

Brahms's historical self-image is certainly no less pertinent an issue in the 1860s and 1870s (which saw Brahms's monumental efforts at gestating a first symphony in the wake of Beethoven), but several of the most relevant examples from this central era, including some of Brahms's most iconic works, have been the subject of rigorous analytical scrutiny that has brought to light a good understanding of the relationships they embody, individually, between historical reference and intermovement narrative. What is not so well recognized and appreciated is the extent to which these instances represent a broader trend that is exemplified also by music of the earlier and later periods, about which much remains to be said. My intention in this book is to illuminate this broader perspective by demonstrating how these more familiar instances function within a larger context that is also represented by a number of examples that have not been fully appreciated. As a basis for filling out this broader perspective in subsequent chapters, I provide here a brief overview of a handful of the most relevant examples from this middle period, beginning with the most familiar: the First Symphony.

Symphony No. 1 in C Minor, op. 68 (1862–76)

The First Symphony provides some of the most famous examples of historical reference in Brahms's music. The work's allusions to the symphonic repertory of Beethoven are intimately bound up with Brahms's many years of struggle to produce a symphonic debut worthy of its Beethovenian precedents—a work that exhibited the expressive power and monumentality of a Beethoven symphony while both expressing Brahms's own voice and demonstrating the continued viability of the symphony as a genre of "absolute" music, something that had been emphatically challenged in the prose and musical writings of the New German School.[15]

The First Symphony makes reference to Beethoven's symphonic legacy in a number of important ways.[16] It is a work of massive proportions, particularly in its substantial outer movements, both of which feature extended, heavily orchestrated slow introductions of an extreme expressive intensity conveyed through the handling of dissonance, chromaticism, texture, and other elements. As a C-minor work that concludes in the parallel major, the Symphony invites comparison with Beethoven's Fifth (and to a lesser extent with the Ninth, which traces a minor-to-parallel-major trajectory in D). Like Beethoven, Brahms delays the entrance of the trombones until the arrival of C major in the final movement. In Brahms's finale, they come to the fore (mm. 47ff.) in a passage that introduces the finale's hymn-like primary expository theme in C major (beginning at m. 61)—as mentioned above, an obvious and admitted nod to the "Ode to Joy" from the parallel movement in Beethoven's Ninth. This represents a breakthrough moment in Brahms's Symphony. On a structural level, it marks the establishment of the tonic major, which appeared temporarily at the conclusion of the first movement, and which has now reemerged with difficulty from the finale's dissonant, chromatic, ponderous introduction of roughly five minutes in length. (In contrast, Beethoven's finale arrives immediately victorious in the tonic major, the culmination of a tension-filled transitional passage leading from his C-minor scherzo). In terms of personal and historical significance, this initiates the conclusion of a piece that Brahms struggled for many years to write, and it is Brahms's answer to one of the thorniest problems he needed to solve in taking up the symphonic genre after Beethoven: what to do with the finale. This point in the work represents a personal victory for Brahms that equates with the modal victory of major over minor: it is the close of his first successful, hard-won symphonic work, one that he and the critical public were ultimately to deem a worthy successor to the symphonies of Beethoven ("the Tenth," as Bülow was to call it), and in doing so without resorting to the use of vocalists, text, or explicit extramusical content in the final movement (or elsewhere), he asserts and demonstrates not only both artistic debt to and independence from Beethoven, but also the continued viability of symphonic writing that need not resort to explicit extramusical or poetic content.[17]

Another clear reference to the Fifth Symphony is Brahms's use of the rhythm and repeated notes of the so-called "Fate Motive" that pervades the Fifth's opening. Like Beethoven, Brahms invokes the motive in multiple movements; with Brahms, it in fact appears in all four.[18] As in Beethoven's Symphony, the rhythm is most prominent in the first movement, appearing with particular intensity in the development section, where it is most audible in the horn, trumpet, and timpani [e.g., ex. 1.1a (note the use of the same rhythm in the melody in the strings) and 1.1b]. The relentlessness of this insistent rhythm, which tends to appear in association with dissonance, the minor mode, and a loud dynamic level, contributes to a sense of tension and restlessness. The rhythm returns as a quiet undercurrent in overlapping statements in the horn and timpani in the coda (mm. 495ff.; ex. 1.1c), as if to caution that an underlying uneasiness remains and will need to be addressed, for the movement's C-major close in fact brings only a temporary, fundamentally incomplete resolution of modal and other tensions.

16 | *Allusion as Narrative Premise in Brahms*

Example 1.1a–c. Brahms, Symphony No. 1 in C Minor, op. 68, First Movement
(a) mm. 229–38

(b) mm. 273–81

18 | *Allusion as Narrative Premise in Brahms*

(c) mm. 492–500

Hints of the motive return in the inner movements, again as if to remind us that, despite the brighter tonalities we find here, we have not heard the last of C minor and its associated elements of disturbance. In the second movement, in E major, the rhythm can be heard in some of the melodic material (e.g., at mm. 9–11 and 90–95), but the repeated-note version appears almost immediately, recalling the first movement's close, in a single, subdued statement in the horns (ex. 1.2).

Example 1.2. Brahms, Symphony No. 1 in C Minor, op. 68, Second Movement, mm. 1–4

As if obscured by temporal and harmonic distance, the motive is recalled again more faintly at the end of the second movement by an emphasized incomplete repeated-note triplet figure (mm. 99ff.) and, just before the movement's close, in the rhythm of the timpani and the pizzicato ascending arpeggiation in the strings. Incomplete, rhythmically modified recollections of the repeated-note

Example 1.3a–b. Brahms, Symphony No. 1 in C Minor, op. 68, Third Movement
(a) mm. 87–94

motive are also heard in the middle section of the ternary-form third movement, a section contrasting sharply in key and meter with the surrounding material (see, e.g., the strings at mm. 41ff. and the winds and brass at mm. 75–76 and 83–84, intensifying in mm. 87ff., shown in ex. 1.3a). These motivic recollections spill over into the movement's closing section as well, slightly obscured by ties across the bar lines (ex. 1.3b). As in the preceding movements, the closing measures once again feature a reminiscence of the motive (incomplete as before; see mm. 154ff.), reminding us of the tensions yet to be resolved in the finale.

In the final movement, appearances of the motive are once again bound up with the ebb and flow of tension as the Symphony's minor-to-parallel-major

(b) mm. 109–20

trajectory reaches its culmination. The rhythm resurfaces as the music wanders back to the minor mode at the end of the exposition, now frequently altered so that the long note falls on a weak beat, as if, broadly speaking, the integrity and force of the motive are weakening as the establishment of C major strengthens (see mm. 156ff. (including the timpani at m. 176, shown in ex. 1.4a), recapitulated at mm. 338ff.); the motive subsides just before the recapitulation of the "Ode-to-Joy"-like theme in the tonic major (m. 186).[19] In times of transition, of heightened tension and instability, the motive tends to recur. A version resurfaces, for example, in the transition between themes in the recapitulation (starting at m. 244 and then again with greater intensity at mm. 267ff.; ex. 1.4b), now appearing as a complete lower-neighbor figure, with a melodic wobble or tremble

Example 1.4a–c. Brahms, Symphony No. 1 in C Minor, op. 68, Fourth Movement
(a) mm. 174–79

(b) mm. 273–78

expressively appropriate to the instability and tension of this passage, leading up to the return of C major. Although a triplet pulse can be heard on repeated notes at times in the accompaniment of the coda (recalling that at the work's opening), the discontinuation of clear statements of the rhythmic motive in its usual form corresponds to the ultimate resolution of modal and other tensions at the conclusion of the work. Instead Brahms devises an "ironed out," rhythmically stabilized substitute in the emphasized repeated-note quarters that usher in the *Più Allegro* (culminating in m. 391).

Significantly, Brahms marks his triumphal final statement, the C-major conclusion of his first, hard-won symphonic essay, with a gesture that seems simultaneously to represent a salute to Beethoven and a declaration of independence: in complete rhythmic unison, the orchestra gives out four bold final measures that evoke a protracted statement of the motive, augmented and punctuated dramatically with pauses. (Cf. the final measures of Beethoven's Fifth, but the rhythmic and melodic resemblance to the "Fate Motive" is closer with Brahms.) Unlike earlier statements in this work, this one evokes Beethoven's original motto not only in the rhythm and note repetition, but also in the leap downward by third to the final note (ex. 1.4c)—for Brahms, the latter part of a triadic descent from the fifth scale degree articulated over the last five measures. Although Beethoven leaps from the fifth to the third scale degree at the opening of the Fifth Symphony (as Brahms has just done in the measure before), he provides thematic resolution before the C-minor conclusion of the Fifth's opening movement by presenting the motive as a leap from the third to the first scale degree (see the first violins in the last eighteen measures). Brahms's concluding leap, however, occurs in the parallel major, actually outlining the third that distinguishes the major tonic from the minor, hammering out three strokes of the decisive third scale degree for emphasis, a celebratory confirmation of the triumph of major over minor at the Symphony's conclusion—and thus, symbolically, of Brahms's triumph over the genre that had proved such a tremendous challenge to master. (Brahms's closing gesture is obviously foreshadowed in a fifth-leap version several measures earlier, at a moment of strong harmonic resolution [mm. 444–47, also shown in ex. 1.4c].) If Beethoven's motive represented to him "Fate," then to Brahms, the motive had a similar, but more specific and ultimately ironic meaning, for the fate it represented for Brahms all the more literally was his own destiny, that of responding to and building in his own way on Beethoven's symphonic legacy.[20]

(c) mm. 434–57

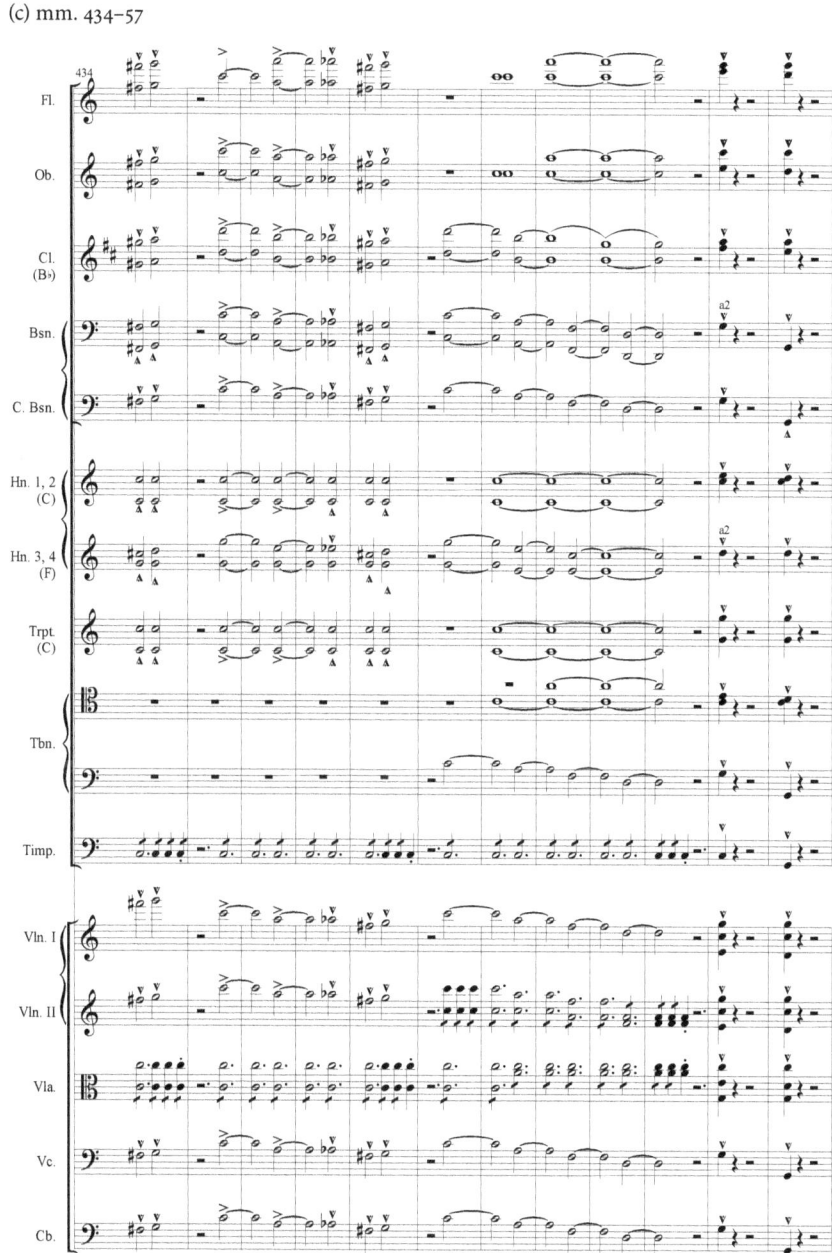

(c) mm. 434–57 (*Continued*)

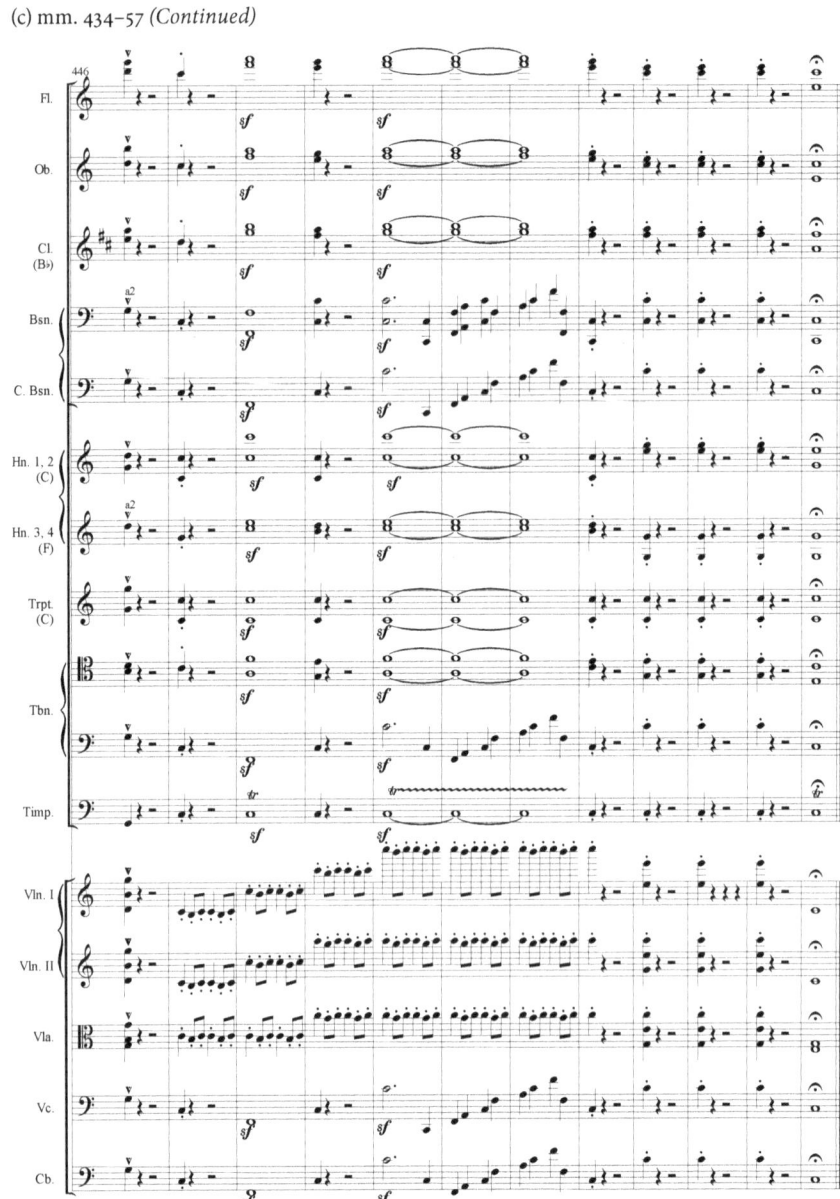

Horn Trio in E-Flat Major, op. 40 (1865)

We turn now to a work whose creation overlaps with the early stages of the First Symphony's genesis: the Horn Trio in E-Flat, op. 40, completed in May 1865. Kalbeck was correct to identify the main theme of the work's finale as a derivative of German folksong, but whereas he believed Brahms's source to be the tune "Dort in den Weiden steht ein Haus," Brahms's melody bears a closer resemblance to a different folksong: "Es soll sich der Mensch nicht mit der Liebe abgeben" (ex. 1.5a–c).[21] The text of the latter song exists in numerous versions, including an old Thüringian variant entitled "Es soll sich ja keiner mit der Liebe abgeben," which appears in *Deutsche Volkslieder mit ihrem Original-Weisen*, an anthology that Brahms is known to have owned; this is the version shown in example 1.5.[22]

This allusion is also linked with thematic materials in the Trio's earlier movements. Most often noted is the anticipation of the finale's main theme in mm. 59ff. in the third movement (ex. 1.6a).[23] However, this moment is also linked motivically to earlier passages in the third movement, as well as to the primary theme of the second movement (ex. 1.6b–d).[24] It is furthermore connected with the first movement's opening (ex. 1.6e). The resemblance to the folk tune is weaker here, as Brahms avoids the tonic pitch, leaping to the second scale degree at the outset (cf. the fifth leaps in ex. 1.6b–c) and then descends chromatically not to the tonic but to the second scale degree's lower neighbor; furthermore, it is only the second scale degree that is repeated in the melody, rather than the first and third as in the original tune. However, a comparison of the work's opening theme not to mm. 1–2 of the finale but to mm. 3–4 supports John Walter Hill's interpretation of the Trio's opening as a major-mode version of the *latter* two of the finale's initial four bars.[25] In short, Brahms's recollection of the folk tune, present to some extent in each movement, gets stronger on the whole as the work progresses, coming most clearly into focus in the final movement.

Scholars have tended to interpret the supposed allusion to "Dort in den Weiden steht ein Haus" as a nostalgic recollection of Brahms's childhood, his response to the recent death of his mother—but the issue of meaning takes on a new cast in the case of "Es soll sich der Mensch nicht mit der Liebe abgeben"/"Es soll sich ja keiner mit der Liebe abgeben."[26] The latter song, in its various versions, generally expresses what Hill refers to as a "disenchantment with love."[27] The version in Brahms's anthology, in Thüringian dialect, begins with the text:

Es soll sich ja keiner mit der Liebe abgeben	Nobody should waste his time with love.
Sie brächt ja so manche schöne Kerle um's Leben.	It's done in many a fair lad.
Heut hat mir mein Trutschel die Liebe versat,	Today my sweetheart refused me her love.
Ich hab sie verklat, ich hab sie verklat.	She did me wrong, she did me wrong.[28]

Example 1.5a–c.
(a) "Dort in den Weiden steht ein Haus" (German Folksong) From *Deutsche Volkslieder mit ihren Original-Weisen*, ed. and Eduard Baumstark, Anton Wilhelm Florentin von Zuccalmaglio, et al. (Berlin: Vereinbuchhandlung, 1840), 2:461.

Dort in den Weiden steht ein Haus,
Da schaut die Magd zum Fenster 'naus!
Sie schaut stromauf, sie schaut stromab,
Ist noch night da mein Herzensknab,
Der schönste Bursch am ganzen Rhein,
Den nenn' ich mein!

Hill proposes that the Trio's sequence of movements articulate a narrative depicting the development of a love affair, the conclusion of the romance in the somber *adagio* movement, and the protagonist's subsequent sense of liberation in the spirited finale.[29] Thus, as the folksong emerges more clearly in the Trio, so, correspondingly, do the benefits of romantic disentanglement in the protagonist's mind.

(b) "Es soll sich ja keiner mit der Liebe abgeben" (German Folksong) From *Deutsche Volkslieder mit ihren Original-Weisen*, 1:540–41.

Es soll sich ja keiner mit der Liebe abgeben,
Sie brächt ja so manche schöne Kerle um's Leben.
Heut hat mir mein Trutschel die Liebe versat,
Ich hab sie verklat, ich hab sie verklat.

Ich hat nu mein Trutschel in's Herz nei geschlaffe,
Unsü hatt gesat: sie wöll mi nit lasse,
Da reit me der teufel d'n Schulze sein Hanse
De fuht se tum Tanze.

Se getts, wenn man die Menscher zum Tanze lätt gehn,
Da mut me hald ämmer in Sorgen stehn,
Daß sie sich verliebe in annere Knachte:
Su Menscher seen schlachte.

Nu schmeckt me kä Esse, nu schmeckt me kä Trenke,
Unn bann ich söll arbet, so möcht ich versenke,
Unn bann ich söll sprech: ich hätt se nemma lieb,
So wär ich ä Dieb.

Drömen bin ich gestorbe: se latt mich begrabe
Un latt me von Schreiner vier Brette afschabe,
Un latt me zwe feurige Herzer druf male:
Ich wills bezahle.

Un latt me ach singe de Strebegesänge:
Da leit nu der Esel die Quör unn die Länge;
Im Labe, da hatt er will Liebesaffäre:
Zu Dreck muß he nun wäre.

30 | *Allusion as Narrative Premise in Brahms*

(c) Brahms, Horn Trio in E-Flat Major, op. 40, Fourth Movement, mm. 1–6

Example 1.6a–e. Brahms, Horn Trio in E-Flat Major, op. 40
(a) Third Movement, mm. 58–67

(b) Third Movement, mm. 19–22

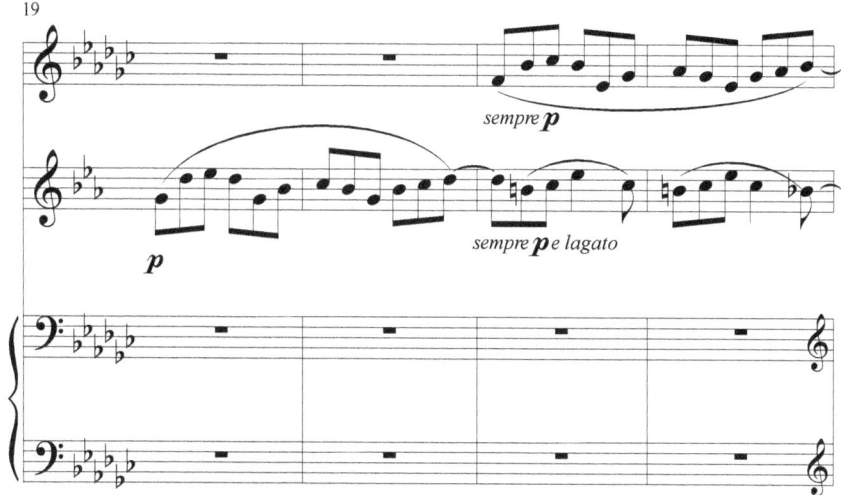

(c) Third Movement, mm. 43–44

The Trio's composition in fact coincides with a period during which Brahms was demonstrably conflicted over his continuing bachelorhood. His biggest romantic disappointment had occurred several years earlier, with Agathe von Siebold in 1859, but his correspondence indicates that, in 1864, his thoughts had

(d) Second Movement, mm. 1–20

returned to Agathe and to their broken off engagement to be married.[30] Brahms's attention may have returned to the failed love affair at this particular time for any number of good reasons, including the recent marriage of his friend Joachim and the announcement in early 1864 that Joachim was to become a father, the fact that Brahms had considered proposing marriage to Ottilie Hauer in late 1863 but had been preempted by another suitor whom she had accepted, and perhaps by his own parents' decision to separate during this same period.[31] In the summer of 1864, when his friend Julius Otto Grimm was visiting Göttingen, Brahms inquired after Agathe's home there.[32] (She herself was no longer there; she was working as a governess in Ireland.)[33] Later that summer, Brahms revisited Göttingen himself, and in September in Baden-Baden he composed his despairing songs on lost love, op. 32, and the first three movements of his String Sextet

(e) First Movement, mm. 1–8

no. 2, op. 36; as is well known, a subsidiary theme of the Sextet's first movement spells out Agathe's name. Such matters continued to haunt Brahms well into 1865. Brahms was heard to say at his mother's funeral in February that, finding himself motherless, it was time for him to marry.[34] Brahms completed his Second Sextet in May, the same month in which he finished the Horn Trio. After finishing the Sextet, Brahms reportedly told his friend Josef Gänsbacher, "Here is where I tore myself free from my last love."[35]

Brahms's sentiment that he should marry apparently did not last long, but it is evidence of an inner conflict regarding his bachelorhood during this period, a conflict whose would-be resolution is suggested by the clearest emergence of this anti-romantic song in the Trio's liberated finale. Here he solidifies his stance on the matter, as expressed in what was once thought to have been his personal motto: "*frei aber froh.*"[36] Even if the Trio's allusory narrative is not especially concerned with Brahms's biographical situation per se, it nonetheless shares with other such narratives explored in this book its status as a means through which Brahms seems to play out, as if attempting to resolve, an inner struggle.

String Quartet in B-Flat Major, op. 67 (1875)

Another example deserves at least brief mention: Brahms's third and final string quartet, written in the summer of 1875. The Quartet's allusions are neither so clear nor so pervasive as in some cases, but the work's opening is frequently likened to that of Mozart's "Hunt" Quartet, K. 458, also in B-flat major. Both works open with triadic, fanfare-like, 6/8 *vivace* themes in paired voices, doubled at the third and beginning with a descending melodic leap from the third scale degree to the first (ex. 1.7a–b).

Example 1.7a–b. Brahms and Mozart Quartets
(a) Brahms, String Quartet No. 3 in B-flat Major, op. 67, First Movement, mm. 1–23

Brahms's opening theme resurfaces later in his Quartet. Although not clearly evoked in the inner movements, it returns near the end of the theme-and-variations finale, in Variation Seven (ex. 1.8). The sense of closure this produces is not only thematic, but, on another level, tonal, for this variation corresponds to a return to the tonic following several variations in other keys. As Walter Frisch points out, the return to the work's opening theme feels natural here in the finale because the melody on which the variations are based is constructed on the "basic

(b) Mozart, String Quartet No. 17 in B-flat Major ("The Hunt"), K. 458, First Movement, mm. 1–16

Example 1.8. Brahms, String Quartet No. 3 in B-Flat Major, op. 67, Fourth Movement, mm. 94–99

Example 1.9. Brahms, String Quartet No. 3 in B-Flat Major, op. 67, Fourth Movement, mm. 1–4

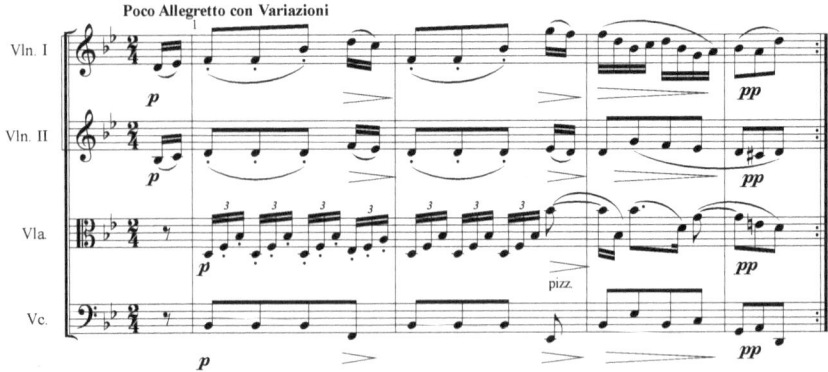

Example 1.10. Brahms, String Quartet No. 3 in B-Flat Major, op. 67, Fourth Movement, mm. 150–58

skeleton" of the work's opening signal call, emphasizing the ascending fourth from F to B-flat and outlining the vi chord; the finale theme also suggests a connection to the work's opening in its three-eighth-note groupings (ex. 1.9).[37] Also based on the work's opening is the transitional material in the first movement's exposition, which in turn resurfaces in the finale's eighth variation. The culmination of the work is the full revelation of the relationship between the primary themes of the first and last movements; this relationship is made explicit in the finale's coda, where versions of the two themes are superimposed and intertwined (ex. 1.10).

As a further preface to the analyses to come, we now turn to two preliminary case studies drawn from Brahms's earliest published multimovement instrumental works, the piano sonatas. A deeper glimpse into these less-studied examples from Brahms's formative years will hint at some of the principles that we will observe in the works to be explored at greater length in the following chapters.

Example 1.11a–c. Brahms and Beethoven Sonatas
(a) Brahms, Piano Sonata No. 1 in C Major, op. 1, First Movement, mm. 1–16

Preliminary Examples from the Early Years:
Piano Sonata in C Major, op. 1 (1852–53)

It is often remarked that the opening melody of this work both recalls the beginning of Beethoven's "Hammerklavier" Sonata and also resembles the opening of the "Waldstein" in its immediate transposition from the tonic down a whole step to B-flat (ex. 1.11a–c).[38] Furthermore, scholars have noted similarities between the Beethovenian opening theme of this Brahms Sonata and the beginning of the same work's final movement.[39] Nonetheless, closer examination reveals that the gradual evolution of this material produces a dynamic relationship between the two Brahms movements that draws Beethoven into a largely unexplored and unappreciated narrative. The finale of Brahms's Sonata not only recalls the work's opening theme, but substantially resolves certain tensions that are inherent to the initial measures of the Sonata and that remain throughout the first movement.

The opening of the Brahms Sonata is fraught with tension. The theme is stilted and choppy, comprised of irregular, short phrases separated by clear breaks. The

(b) Beethoven, Piano Sonata No. 29 in B-flat Major, op. 106 ("Hammerklavier"), First Movement, mm. 1–4

(c) Beethoven, Piano Sonata No. 21 in C Major, op. 53 ("Waldstein"), First Movement, mm. 1–7

homorhythms and octave doubling contribute to a sense of both starkness and heft. There is a general emphasis on upbeats and on jerky rhythms resulting from the alternation of eighth- and quarter-notes, and phrase-endings are placed on weak beats. Also contributing to the tension are the use of staccato, the rapid tempo, and the dramatic registral contrast in the initial gesture. Furthermore, melodic ascents are frequently impeded; the line keeps turning back on itself, and it is not until the third try that the melody finally succeeds in rising steadily. Restlessness is also indicated by the rapidity with which the music wanders from the tonic key and furthermore moves to distant tonalities. As early as m. 4, the music moves toward the subdominant and, by the downbeat of m. 6, it rests securely in the dominant, from which Brahms abruptly transposes the opening material down a step to B-flat (beginning in m. 9; ex. 1.12). This time, the octave rise (mm. 12–16) is even more tension-ridden than before, as Brahms plays with the bar line in widely-spaced, accented, dissonant chords. As the music resolves to the tonic (mm. 16–17), the melody tumbles rapidly, counteracting the efforts at ascent in the previous measures. In mm. 17–30 (ex. 1.13), the music remains harmonically restless, with the theme wandering quickly from the tonic to D minor

Example 1.12. Piano Sonata, op. 1, First Movement, mm. 9–17

Example 1.13. Brahms, Piano Sonata No. 1 in C Major, op. 1, First Movement, mm. 17–30

Example 1.14. Piano Sonata, op. 1, First Movement, mm. 172–97

(m. 21) and to E minor (m. 25), once again bringing to mind the "Waldstein," with its shift from C major to E at the parallel spot.

In the recapitulation, the tension is not only retained, but heightened.[40] The retransition is abrupt, and the return of the opening theme (m. 173; ex. 1.14) is marked by an immediate emphasis on the subdominant in place of the tonic, with the addition of the flatted seventh to the C-major triad. Further restlessness is suggested by the subsequent thematic fragmentation, as well as the more frequent changes of register and the chromatic transpositions and bass motion

Example 1.15. Brahms, Piano Sonata No. 1 in C Major, op. 1, First Movement, mm. 250–58

(mm. 181–94). Meanwhile, contributing to a feeling of urgency is the sense that some progress is being made in overcoming the initial impediment to melodic ascent: the first two phrase endings no longer turn downward, and each ascent begins a bit higher than the previous one. Nevertheless, the right hand stalls (m. 191) in its attempt to rise—and when the chromatic, rhythmically off-kilter ascent in the bass reaches its own peak (m. 194), it then descends with a degree of ease disproportionate to that expended in rising, and rather than resolving to G, Brahms turns abruptly to C minor for the second theme.

In the coda, the tension is heightened yet further. The main theme is once again heard *fortissimo*—this time beginning on a cadential 6/4 chord, with a persistent dominant pedal in the bass (ex. 1.15). The elimination of the pauses between phrases creates a greater sense of momentum and seems to push phrase-endings from the weak second beat of the measure onto the stronger third beat. However, contrary motion between the right and left hands increases the tension, and attempts at melodic ascent result in ever greater motion in the downward direction, until the line crashes down in a series of extremely dissonant chords, struggling against the natural accent patterns of the meter before coming to rest on a dominant-seventh (m. 257). The theme resurfaces in the last five measures of the movement, sounding resigned, with a written-out *ritard* and a dramatic drop in register (ex. 1.16). As the melody concludes, rather than resolving to the tonic scale degree, the line moves back down to the very same pitch from which it struggled to rise in the first measure of the piece.

Example 1.16. Brahms, Piano Sonata No. 1 in C Major, op. 1, First Movement, mm. 265–70

Example 1.17. Brahms, Piano Sonata No. 1 in C Major, op. 1, Fourth Movement, mm. 1–6

Although there is no obvious quotation of the opening motto in the work's inner movements, the melody that begins the rondo finale clearly derives from the Sonata's initial measures, and the resemblance is underscored by the shared pitch level and register (ex. 1.17). The form in which the theme appears at the beginning of the finale suggests, however, that some of the tensions originally associated with this material have now begun to resolve. The jerky, uneven alternation of eighth- and quarter-notes has now been replaced by an even patter of eighths in 9/8, creating a greater sense of fluidity and momentum. The considerably lighter texture and continuous, upward-sweeping arpeggiation in the accompaniment create a sense of buoyancy and continuity across phrase boundaries. A similar sense of momentum is conveyed by the fact that gaps between phrases no longer exceed an eighth rest in duration and are often filled with punctuating chords. A greater degree of ease with upward melodic motion is visible almost immediately, as the melody rises an entire octave on its second try (mm. 2–3), with less fragmentation than in the first movement. Unlike in earlier statements of the theme, the tonic key is now retained long enough for the ascent to be completed.

Nonetheless, although the shift from the tonic key is now delayed until after the melody succeeds in ascending the octave, it still does not take very long for

Example 1.18. Brahms, Piano Sonata No. 1 in C Major, op. 1, Fourth Movement, mm. 87–98

harmonic restlessness to set in, with the music landing on i⁶ᐟ⁴ of E minor in m. 5 and turning to E major shortly thereafter. This C-to-E trajectory is another link between the openings of the Sonata's outer movements, as it recalls the shift from C to E minor in the first movement's exposition. Furthermore, this represents another dimension of cross-movement allusory reference, as it links both movements with the "Waldstein," whose first-movement exposition also, famously, traces a shift from C to E major.[41] (C and E are also tonal focal points for the inner movements of Brahms's Sonata.)

Here in the final movement, other signs of tension do still remain. The melodic "doubling back" is still present in the theme's every attempt to rise. Failed ascents (e.g., in mm. 1 and 3) still end on weak beats, and the *sforzando* punctuating chords on both the first and last beats of the measure create a sense of instability. In the thick of the finale, when the opening theme returns after the first episode (ex. 1.18), the material appears in one of its most unsettled forms of the movement. The melody's repeated attempts to rise are once again greatly impeded. (See mm. 90, 92, and 94.) The high, rolled chords, still *sforzando* and staccato, now appear more frequently on off-beats, enhancing the feeling of tension not only through their rhythmic instability, but also through the increase in registral contrast and through the suspense created by their slow, steady ascent. Frequent key changes and striking dissonance create a sense of harmonic instability as well. The refrain theme, returning early, is stated in several keys in quick succession (starting at m. 87); finally, when the bass returns to C major (m. 95), the melody, although now more successful in its ascent, refuses to return to the tonic, creating a fleeting sense of bitonality. The melodic ascents grind to a halt; a repeated augmented sixth chord in E minor seems to force the left hand to join the right tonally on the following downbeat as the melody begins to descend, and the section draws to a close not in the tonic, but in the distant key of E. When the refrain returns (ex. 1.19), it features frequent transpositions, juxtaposition of contrasting themes, obscuring of the tonic arrival, and further fragmentation of melodic ascents, as well as the choppy phrasing that results from many of these features. As in the recapitulation of the theme in the opening movement, returns to the tonic are muddied by the incorporation of the pitch B-flat (suggesting $V^7/$IV; see mm. 187 and 189), and the music revisits predicaments already encountered earlier in the movement (cf. mm. 98ff, then cf. mm. 193–218 with 5–30), but now the melody rises steadily through an entire octave, and leading into the coda is new material with a greater emphasis on upward gestures (mm. 219ff.; ex. 1.20). Nevertheless, even in this transitional passage, all attempts at extended melodic ascent are ultimately thwarted. This, along with the off-kilter rhythms and the dominant pedal, suggests restlessness, propelling us towards the coda, where tensions associated with the work's opening will finally be resolved.

In the theme's final appearance (beginning in m. 282; ex. 1.21), there are indeed clear signs of resolution. In comparison to earlier statements of the theme, the music here is far more harmonically stable. Whereas, in the past, the return of the theme has usually coincided with a return to the tonic from some other tonality, here the tonic is established long before the theme enters (as early as m. 269), and the key is retained to the end of the work. For the first time in the theme's history, not a single attempt at ascent is interrupted by transposition or is otherwise abandoned before the octave is attained. Furthermore, the theme's octave rise is now achieved with only one attempt. It is followed by two more octave climbs, each beginning a third higher than the one before, and each concluding successfully on the first try. In the accompaniment and—at least for the first two ascents—in the melody as well, this increased fluidity of motion is emphasized by the substitution of slurs for staccato markings. Although the melody begins to descend in the final measures, the descent is slow and halting, with each step separated by pauses reminiscent of those originally associated with ascent at the opening of the work. The lack of off-beat accents in these mea-

Example 1.19. Brahms, Piano Sonata No. 1 in C Major, op. 1, Fourth Movement, mm. 173–94

Example 1.20. Brahms, Piano Sonata No. 1 in C Major, op. 1, Fourth Movement, mm. 218–21

Example 1.21. Brahms, Piano Sonata No. 1 in C Major, op. 1, Fourth Movement, mm. 280–92

sures creates a sense of stability as the left hand rises in contrary motion with the right. Ultimately, the melodic line turns upward. The right hand closes securely in the register that it struggled so hard to reach at the opening of the piece.

Other aspects of the theme's final statement also suggest the resolution of certain tensions. The high chords in the right hand are now reached solely by stepwise melodic ascent rather than by leap; they are signs of achievement, rather than symbols of an unattainable ideal. Also for the first time, each ascent concludes—and, therefore, each of the high chords appears—on a downbeat. Additionally, this is the theme's first appearance in 6/8 time (the meter of the movement's second episode). Yet the change of meter represents a restoration of sorts: the accent pattern here, more clearly than in the finale's earlier statements, mirrors that of the theme's original statement at the opening of the first movement, with the upper neighbor-notes (e.g., A in m. 283) falling once again on downbeats.

Although the tensions of the opening material have been fundamentally resolved by the end of the finale, even here, certain elements suggest lingering restlessness. Even in the triumphant ascents of mm. 282–88, the melody still doubles back momentarily after climbing the first four pitches—but due to the rhythmic momentum in this passage, the upper-neighbor figures seem to assist the ascent rather than hinder it. Additionally, the rapid upward sweep and the grace-notes immediately preceding the final chord of the piece suggest remaining instability.

Finally, rather than descending to the tonic pitch, the melody concludes by ascending *from* the tonic pitch to the third scale degree, an octave above the first melodic pitch of the piece, perhaps recalling the C-to-E tonal motions heard earlier and in so doing providing a final reminder of the work's Beethovenian heritage.

On the whole, though, it is clear that the final measures of the work conclude a process of thematic evolution that can be traced back to the very first measure of the opening movement, with its evocation of Beethoven's "Hammerklavier," and thus the work embodies a link between allusion and intermovement form and narrative.[42] In its final incarnations in the finale, the opening material of the Sonata comes to exhibit greater harmonic and rhythmic stability, and melodic ascent—formerly associated with fragmentation—becomes continuous and facile. The close association between the outer movements, which as we have seen, also invokes the distinctive tonal trajectory of the first-movement exposition of the "Waldstein," may be at least partially a result of Brahms's having been at work on the two movements at the same time.[43]

In this example, the primary thematic material returns in varied form in the final movement, whereas, in some of the previous examples, the thematic material is prefigured earlier in the work but appears fully realized only in the final movement. Examples of both types will continue to arise in the chapters to follow.

Piano Sonata in F Minor, op. 5 (1853)

The best known of Brahms's sonatas for piano, the F-Minor Sonata, op. 5, was composed primarily in October 1853, the same month in which Schumann's "*Neue Bahnen*" appeared in the *Neue Zeitschrift für Musik*.[44] Once again, signs of Brahms's engagement with specific works of Beethoven are of particular interest. Here, we focus on Brahms's use of a four-note rhythmic motive strongly evocative of the "Fate Motive"—a motive that has often been identified with later Brahms works, including not only the First Symphony, but also the German Requiem and other pieces—as well as the influence of the "Pathétique" Sonata.[45] We will observe the relevance of these sources across multiple movements of Brahms's Sonata as they inform the work on structural and narrative levels.

The rhythmic figure that evokes the "Fate Motive" is introduced early in the Sonata and in a manner that invites comparison with Beethoven's Symphony. Notated as repeated notes in triplet eighths followed by a quarter-note, the motive first appears at m. 7, coinciding with a shift to C minor, the key of Beethoven's Symphony (ex. 1.22a). Significantly, this is one of the Sonata's few passages in that key. The rhythm sounds continuously in the accompaniment for several measures—with repeated notes and an emphasis on the dominant pitch (first in C minor, then in G minor), as in the Symphony. The rhythm subsequently reappears in a variety of other keys throughout the Sonata's opening movement. [See especially mm. 55, 78–87 (ex. 1.22b), and 177.] Brahms generally begins the

Example 1.22a–b. Brahms, Piano Sonata No. 3 in F Minor, op. 5, First Movement
(a) mm. 6–16

(b) mm. 75–89

figure on a strong beat so that the long note falls on a weak part of the measure—the reverse of what occurs in the Symphony. From the first, the motive draws attention to itself by introducing not only a shift in tonal perspective, but also a metrical disturbance through its hemiolic function and the establishment of cross-rhythms between the left and right hands.

In the second movement, the rhythm begins to infiltrate the melodic line. In the first D-flat-major section, it appears several times in various forms: in diminution (mm. 67 and 91 [beginning with the decorative notes]), as triplet sixteenths followed by a dotted eighth (mm. 72–74 and 96–98), and in augmentation as three eighths and a quarter—with the long note finally appearing on the downbeat (mm. 75–76 and 99–104; ex. 1.23a–b). The motive returns in the second D-flat-major section of the movement as three eighth-notes plus a dotted quarter-note. (ex. 1.23c). Here and in all subsequent appearances for the remainder of the work, it appears with the long note still on the downbeat, perhaps suggesting an increase in stability.

In the third movement, the rhythm returns with more of a rushed, unstable quality, as triplet sixteenths plus a quarter in mm. 4–5 and 12–13, ushering in changes of key in both instances, as in its previous incarnation in the first movement (ex. 1.24a–b). It resurfaces in the trio as a somewhat-more-grounded three quarter-notes and a dotted half-note, in the bass, just as the key shifts from D-flat (beginning in m. 117; ex. 1.24c). The rhythm's three successive repeated-note accompanimental statements here are balanced by three melodic statements descending sequentially in the uppermost voice (beginning in m. 124; see also mm. 193ff. in ex. 1.24d).

In the Intermezzo, the motive appears with unprecedented intensity, pervading the accompaniment and sounding more rushed than ever in the form of triplet thirty-seconds and an eighth-note (ex. 1.25a–b). (In mm. 26–29, the motive temporarily undergoes yet greater intensification with the substitution of a sixty-fourth-note quintuplet for the usual triplet.) The figure's triplets, always articulations of a single repeated pitch, most often sound on the dominant. At moments of particular intensity, the rhythm invades the melody itself (e.g., in mm. 6–12 and 31–37). Ultimately, the accompanimental figure overtakes the melodic line; in the final measures of the movement, the motive is heard three more times in succession, now with the right hand doubling the left (ex. 1.25b). Although the movement ends *pianissimo*, lingering tension and instability are suggested by the marked accents, thickening of texture, repeated alternation between the fifth and first scale degrees, the rushed, upbeat quality of the motive, and the suspenseful pauses. Given the level of intensity with which the motive appears throughout the movement, perhaps the title "*Rückblick*" refers not merely to the fact that the intermezzo recalls material from earlier in the Sonata, but indeed to the movement's status as a glance back to Beethoven.[46]

50 | *Allusion as Narrative Premise in Brahms*

Example 1.23a–c. Brahms, Piano Sonata No. 3 in F Minor, op. 5, Second Movement
(a) mm. 65–76

(b) mm. 93–104

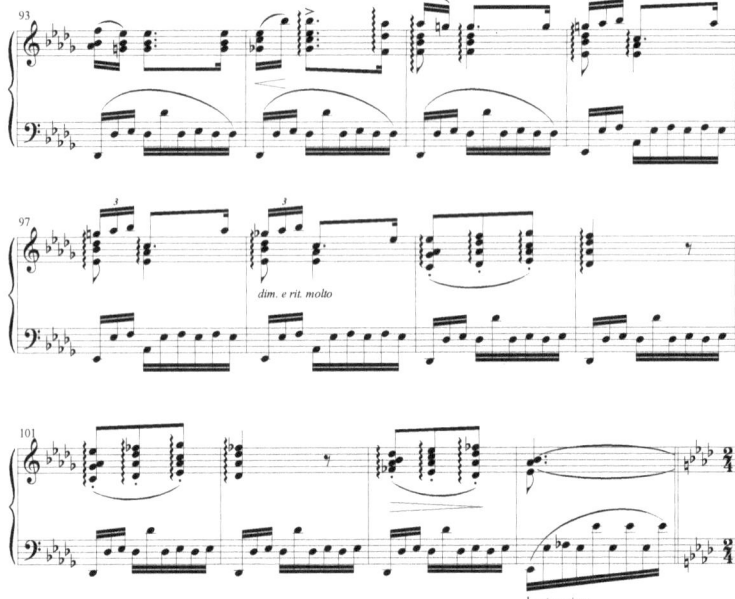

(c) mm. 144–67

The rhythmic motive, so persistent in the Intermezzo, is countered and ultimately supplanted in the finale by another four-note rhythm that embodies less tension. The "Fate" rhythm is absent from the final movement until the D-flat-major second episode. Here, after opening with off-kilter dotted and tied notes, the movement has begun to display a new emphasis on square, even

Example 1.24a–d. Brahms, Piano Sonata No. 3 in F Minor, op. 5, Third Movement
(a) mm. 4–5

(b) mm. 12–13

(c) mm. 113–32

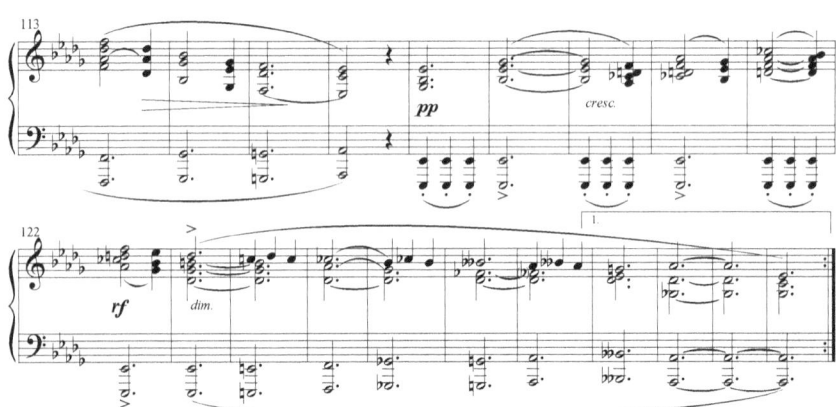

(d) mm. 188–204

Example 1.25a–b. Brahms, Piano Sonata No. 3 in F Minor, op. 5, Fourth Movement
(a) mm. 1–21

(b) mm. 36–53

rhythms—particularly on groupings of four even notes beginning on downbeats. The emphasis on these new four-even-note groupings soon grows strong enough to interfere with the 6/8 meter with the introduction of quarter-note quadruplets (mm. 157 and 159). It is almost as though Brahms has "ironed out" the "Fate" rhythm, so that all of its note values are equal, and then condensed the whole thing to fit into a single measure, smoothing over any instability or upbeat quality. The "Fate" rhythm soon begins to creep back in while disturbance is reflected in the brief emergence of D-flat's parallel minor (mm. 173–74; ex. 1.26). For several measures, the quarter-note quadruplets in the right hand are consistently countered in the left by statements of the original rhythmic motive (m. 174–85). The competition here between the two types of four-note groupings represents a sense of disruption that is reinforced harmonically by the music's movement down a half step to D major (m. 175) and then to the tritone-related key of A-flat (m. 181). The passage is fraught with tension: by m. 181, the episode's theme has disintegrated and, in its place, the right hand plays dissonant chords with nothing but reiterated E-flats in the top voice; the first and third notes of each of the right hand's quadruplet figures have been replaced with rests, creating a syncopated, stilted feel; and the left hand wavers continuously between the fourth and fifth scale degrees. The situation is defused only by the yielding of the motive to the quadruplets, which persist for some time and return to dominate the movement's

Example 1.26. Piano Sonata No. 3 in F Minor, op. 5, Fifth Movement, mm. 168–94

climax (ex. 1.27). By the time the tonic major arrives in m. 285 to lead into the coda, references to the "Fate"-like rhythmic motive (and to the unstable rhythms of the finale's refrain) have disappeared, whereas the duple quarter-notes that introduce the shift to F major recall the quadruplets of the second episode (cf. mm. 156–59), and, once F major arrives, rhythmic evenness is evident in both hands. The final measures of the piece (mm. 249ff.) are a brief summation or recapitulation of the finale's progression from the destabilized rhythm of the refrain to an emphasis on square rhythms with even, longer note values.

There can be little doubt that for Brahms and his contemporaries the rhythmic motive in Brahms's F-Minor Sonata, evoked with such deliberateness in his First Symphony, would have carried associations with Beethoven's Fifth. Beethoven's "Fate Motive" was, of course, very much in the consciousness of Brahms's contemporaries—and this was especially so for Robert Schumann, with whom Brahms was living as he composed the F-Minor Sonata. Schumann's

Example 1.27. Piano Sonata No. 3 in F Minor, op. 5, Fifth Movement, mm. 231–43

preoccupation with this rhythmic motive is also evidenced by his eagerness to find it in music he reviewed and by an anecdote he relayed to the composer and conductor Ferdinand Hiller in a letter of April 25, 1853—just months before Brahms's F-Minor Sonata was composed.[47] Here, Schumann recalls communicating with Beethoven at a séance: "yesterday for the first time we turned a table. A wonderful power! Only think! I asked it to give the rhythm of the first two bars of the C-Minor Symphony. There was a longer pause than usual, and then the answer began... very slowly at first. But, said I, the tempo is quicker, my dear table; and then he gave it right."[48]

Evidence from Brahms's scherzo for the "F-A-E" Sonata, which, like op. 5, was composed during Brahms's sojourn with the Schumanns in October 1853, as well as Brahms's "Edward" Ballade, op. 10/1, composed within months of the other two works, indicates that the rhythm of Beethoven's "Fate Motive" was "buzzing around" quite a bit in the young composer's mind during the period in which he wrote his op. 5. Brahms's "F-A-E" scherzo not only begins in the key of Beethoven's Fifth Symphony—it also concludes, like the Symphony, in the parallel major. Furthermore, as in Brahms's op. 5, the arrival of the tonic major at the conclusion of the movement (m. 238) is associated with the

Example 1.28a–b.
(a) Brahms, Piano Sonata No. 3 in F Minor, op. 5, First Movement, mm. 39–46

(b) Beethoven, Piano Sonata No. 8 in C Minor, op. 13 ("Pathétique"), Second Movement, mm. 1–4

absence (or near-absence) of the Beethoven rhythm and with the presence of even, steady dotted quarters in descending melodic lines. Thus, it is not surprising that, within a short time of having composed these works, Brahms acknowledged in a letter to Joachim that Beethoven's Fifth Symphony was among the three pieces that had made the "single most *powerful* impressions" upon him.[49]

That Brahms had Beethoven in mind while writing this sonata is suggested also by the work's relationship to two other Beethoven pieces. In his first movement, Brahms may also be drawing on the opening *Allegro* of another F-minor piano sonata (which, by the way, has a slow movement ending in D-flat major, the key in which Brahms's slow movement concludes): Beethoven's "Appassionata," op. 57.[50] James Webster suggests that the "retransition-like" recapitulation in Brahms's movement is "indebted" to that of the Beethoven movement.[51] Interestingly enough, this passage of the "Appassionata" also makes clear use of the "Fate Motive." (See mm. 129–32; the motive also permeates the end of the movement.)[52]

Note also the similarities to Beethoven's "Pathétique" Sonata. Among these are resemblances between the second theme group of Brahms's first movement and the opening of the slow movement of the "Pathétique" (ex. 1.28a–b); not only is the beginning of Brahms's melody reminiscent of Beethoven, but so is the accompaniment, and the key and dynamic level are the same. Beethoven's mm. 2–4 also compare with the same measures of Brahms's *second* movement, also in A-flat and with the same dynamic level, meter, rhythms, and textures, as well as identical melodic lines. The two slow movements correspond in later passages as well; the second portion of Brahms's "A" section (mm. 11ff.) compares with Beethoven's first episode (beginning in m. 17) in terms of rhythmic content, texture, and melodic emphasis on the large upward leap followed by stepwise third descent. Incorporated into Beethoven's melody for this episode is a rhythm not unlike the version of the "Fate" rhythm with which the melody of Brahms's second D-flat-major section begins (mm. 144ff.). In addition, in this section of the Brahms movement, we find the same sort of persistent, triplet, repeated-note accompaniment that appears in the second episode of Beethoven's slow movement (mm. 37ff.). Beethoven's slow movement is in the submediant key of his sonata and, although Brahms's movement begins in the same key as Beethoven's, it ends in the submediant key of his own piece. Beethoven's slow movement is a rondo, and we may view Brahms's *Andante* as an "ABAC" form with coda (with sections beginning at mm. 1, 37, 105, and 144, and the coda beginning at m. 179); thus, Brahms's movement may be interpreted as a rondo also, but one that lacks the final return of its refrain and, strikingly, closes in the D-flat-major tonality of its episodes rather than its A-flat-major tonic. Furthermore, the last movement of the "Pathétique," the only minor-key rondo finale in Beethoven's piano sonatas, contains episodes in VI and the major tonic, the same keys Brahms uses for the episodes in the finale of his own sonata. (Brahms reverses the order, however, placing the F-major episode first—presumably to maximize the impact of the arrival of F major at the end of the piece.)

The idea that the F-Minor Sonata draws on both Beethoven's Fifth Symphony and works from his sonata repertory is consistent with the fact that Brahms exhibits a tendency, elsewhere, to employ allusions to multiple works within a single piece of his own. This is a tendency that we will see in play in several works examined in this book.

The question of extramusical meaning in Brahms's F-Minor Sonata is raised by the work's several known and possible references to literary materials. For instance, Brahms attached to the second movement three lines from a poetic text by C. O. Sternau, suggesting to his publisher that this text "may be necessary or convenient for comprehension" of the movement."[53] The lines read as follows:

Der Abend dämmert, das Mondlicht scheint,	The evening falls, the moonlight shines,
Da sind zwei Herzen in Liebe vereint	As two hearts are joined in love
Und halten sich selig umfangen.	And hold one another in a blissful embrace.

In addition, although the theme of the second D-flat-major section of the movement (mm. 144ff., shown in ex. 1.23c) was long ago likened to the chorale "Wer nur den lieben Gott lässt walten," a resemblance has also been noted between this

Example 1.29a–b.

(a) Georg Neumark, "Wer nur den lieben Gott lässt walten," mm. 1–5: melody (with last stanza of text, as appearing in final movement of J. S. Bach's Cantata 93)

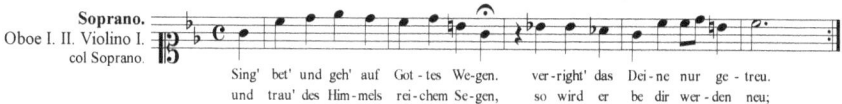

(b) Piano Arr. of Folksong: "Steh' ich in finst'rer Mitternacht" From *Unsre Lieblinge: Die schönsten Melodien für das Pianoforte*, ed. Carl Reinecke (Leipzig: Breitkopf & Härtel, [1869]), vol. 1, no. 22, mm. 1–12.

D-flat-major theme and the German folksong "Steh' ich in finst'rer Mitternacht," in which a soldier reminisces about parting from his beloved, who is now far away, a scenario that seems to correspond to that depicted in Sternau's poem (ex. 1.29).[54] However, the folksong calls to mind the refrain of the final movement of Beethoven's "Pathétique," and in light of the fact that Brahms seems clearly to refer to the slow movement of the "Pathétique" at the beginning of his second movement, it is possible that this D-flat-major material derives from Beethoven's Sonata.

On the basis of the musical similarities between the Andante and Intermezzo, particularly the clear resemblance between their arpeggiated opening themes, scholars have tended to view the Intermezzo as a reminiscence on the part of one or more of the lovers in Sternau's text—generally, as a recollection of love lost.[55] Contributing to the impression that the lovers have been separated is the suggestion, originally made by Kalbeck, that Brahms originally conceived of the Intermezzo as a depiction of "*Bitte*," another of Sternau's poems.[56] The imagery of "*Bitte*"—including a withering tree, a barren forest, and the silencing of a heartbeat—is bleak indeed. Such features as the replacement of the second movement's major keys with the

Example 1.30. Brahms, Piano Sonata No. 3 in F Minor, op. 5, Fifth Movement, mm. 36–44

relative minor of D-flat render the Intermezzo far more somber than the Sonata's first slow movement, and the funeral quality of the movement may imply that the lovers have been parted by death.[57] Bozarth seeks to explain some of the unusual formal features of the opening movement by painting the movement as a musical introduction of the protagonist of Sternau's poem, whose tale is told mainly in the slow movements, and whose personality exhibits an antithesis of flamboyance and introspection similar to that found in the character of Hoffmann's Kreisler, with whom the young Brahms strongly identified.[58] Bozarth views the scherzo, with its return to the work's opening tonality as part of the work's "series of interrelated 'character studies,'" thematically linked to the first movement.[59]

Another of Brahms's literary hints is an apparent instance of the "F-A-E" motive—as used in the "F-A-E" Sonata to represent Joachim's personal motto, "*Frei aber einsam*" (Free but lonely)—at the beginning of the F-major theme of the finale's first episode (ex. 1.30).[60] Bozarth suggests that the appearance of this motive at this particular point helps to confirm the "sense of wholeness and well-being" that comes with the arrival of F major, in contrast to the agitation of the F-minor music with which the finale begins; the protagonist of Sternau's poetry, apparently adopting Joachim's motto, is now coming to terms with the loss of his love.[61] The idea that the finale brings a sense of "wholeness" to a protagonist who was, in some sense, left incomplete at the close of the second movement corresponds to the idea that the finale brings structural closure to the earlier movement's incomplete rondo form.

If we are to accept Bozarth's interpretation of the work, then the ultimate liberation and self-discovery of Sternau's protagonist may correspond in some manner to Brahms's transformation of the "Fate" rhythm. As we have seen, in this sonata, Brahms appears to handle allusions to Beethoven's most famous rhythmic figure in such a way as to suggest his own willful transformation of that rhythm at the culmination of the work, coinciding with the resolution of other tensions. One might interpret Brahms's handling of this rhythm as a means by which he plays out, even unintentionally, his own attempts at self-liberation from the confines of Beethoven's imposing "shadow."

With Brahms's introduction to the Schumanns and the subsequent publication of Robert Schumann's *"Neue Bahnen"* in October of that year, the artistic stakes were raised dramatically for Brahms: the young composer, having been publicly touted by his prominent mentor as a musical messiah and heir to the Great Masters, was inspired, driven, and haunted more intensely than ever by thoughts of the shoes he had to fill.[62]

These examples illustrate the young Brahms's early involvement with the music of Beethoven (possessor of the largest shoes of all) as a source of material for two of his own early works. They illustrate, furthermore, the relevance of the allusory materials to the intermovement structures and narratives in those pieces. In the following chapters, as we explore in greater depth a selection of works dating from the months and years that followed, we will observe not only an ongoing engagement with the music of Beethoven and other composers, manifesting itself in other instances of allusion and modelling, but also a continuing sense of interconnectedness between these historical references and the intermovement forms and narratives in Brahms's music. My approach will frequently be more hermeneutical in an aim to bring to light the ways in which Brahms's handling of allusory references may reveal something of his intensified psychological orientation towards music history and towards securing his own place within that history relative to his musical forebears.

Notes

1. For example, Johann Nicolaus Forkel, *Allgemeine Litteratur der Musik, oder Ankleitung zur Kenntnis musikalischer Bücher, welche von den ältesten bis auf den neuen Zeiten by den Greichen, Römern und den meisten neuern europäischen Nationen sind geschrieben worden* (Leipzig: Schwickert, 1792); *Allgemeine Geschichte der Musik* (Leipzig: Schwickert, 1788–1801); and *Über J. S. Bachs Leben, Kunst und Kunstwerke* (Leipzig: Hoffmeister und Kühnel, 1802); as well as Raphael Georg Kiesewetter, *Geschichte der europäische-abendländischen Musik* (Leipzig, 1834); and August Wilhelm Abros, *Geschichte der Musik*, 5 vol. (Breslau: F. E. C. Leuckart, 1862–82).

2. These include Otto Jahn's *W. A. Mozart* (Leipzig: Breitkopf & Härtel, 1856–59), Philipp Spitta's *J. S. Bach* (Leipzig: Breitkopf & Härtel, 1873–80), Friedrich Chrysander's *G. F. Händel* (Leipzig: Breitkopf & Härtel, 1858–67), and Carl Ferdinand Pohl's *Joseph Haydn* (Berlin: A. Sacco, 1875–82).

3. Pamela M. Potter, "Musicology—Section 3: National Traditions of Musicology—Subsection 4: Germany and Austria," *Grove Music Online / Oxford Music Online*, accessed July 7, 2012. www.oxfordmusiconline.com

4. Joseph Kerman, "Counsel for the Defense," *The Hudson Review* 3 (1950): 442–43, quoted in Kevin Korsyn, "Brahms Research and Aesthetic Ideology," *Music Analysis* 12/1 (1993): 89.

5. J. Peter Burkholder, "Brahms and Twentieth-Century Classical Music," *19th-Century Music* 8/1 (1984): 75.

6. Kenneth Ross Hull, "Brahms the Allusive: Extra-Compositional Reference in the Instrumental Music of Johannes Brahms" (PhD diss., Princeton University, 1989), 25, n. 2.

7. Kevin Korsyn, "Brahms Research and Aesthetic Ideology," 90, citing Mikhail Bakhtin, *The Dialogic Imagination: Four Essays*, ed. Michael Holquist, trans. Caryl Emerson and Michael Holquist (Austin: University of Texas Press, 1981), 295. For an interesting general discussion of "historicism in nineteenth-century art, aesthetics and culture," see for instance the chapter by that title in James Garratt, *Palestrina and the German Romantic Imagination: Interpreting Historicism in Nineteenth-Century Music* (Cambridge: Cambridge University Press), 9–35.

8. On Brahms's earliest interest in and degree of influence from early music, see for example, Joachim Thalmann, "Studien zu Brahms' frühesten Kompositionen: Sein Interesse in alter Musik und dessen Niederschlag in seinem Frühwerk," in *Festschrift Arno Forchert zum 60. Geburtstag am 29. Dezember 1985*, ed. G. Allroggen and Detlef Altenburg (Kassel: Bärenreiter, 1986), 264–70.

9. See Karl Geiringer, "Brahms as Musicologist," *Musical Quarterly* 69/4 (1983): 463–70, especially 467.

10. Christopher Reynolds, *Motives for Allusion: Context and Content in Nineteenth-Century Music* (Cambridge, MA: Harvard University Press, 2003), 164; and Hull, "Brahms the Allusive," 44.

11. Hull, "Brahms the Allusive," 1–2; on the example from 1858, an observation by Julius Otto Grimm to Brahms of a similarity between one of the latter's works and passage from a Bach cantata, Hull (2) cites Virginia Hancock, *Brahms's Choral Compositions and his Library of Early Music* (Ann Arbor, MI: UMI Research Press, 1983), 114 fn. 46.

12. Hull, "Brahms the Allusive," 4.

13. Hull, "Brahms the Allusive," 1.

14. Harold Bloom's theory of "anxiety of influence" has been widely employed as a framework for understanding Brahms's psychological relationship to Beethoven, as well as comparable relationships between other artists and their imposing predecessors. For Bloom's explication of the theory, see his *The Anxiety of Influence: A Theory of Poetry*, 2nd ed. (New York: Oxford University Press, 1997).

15. For additional context regarding the challenges Brahms faced as an aspiring symphonist in this era, see for instance Raymond Knapp, *Brahms and the Challenge of the Symphony* (Stuyvesant, NY: Pendragon Press, 1997), especially 29–59, and Mark Evan Bonds, *After Beethoven: imperatives of Originality in the Symphony* (Cambridge, MA: Harvard University Press, 1996); the latter's chapter 5 is devoted to Brahms's First Symphony. On the Symphony's compositional history, see Robert Pascall, "Sinfonie Nr. 1 c-Moll op. 68," in *Brahms-Handbuch*, ed. Wolfgang Sandberger (Stuttgart: J. B. Metzler, 2009), 507–9; and Knapp, *Brahms and the Challenge*, 209–15, 321–22.

16. In his recent book *Wagner, Schumann, and the Lessons of Beethoven's Ninth* (Berkeley: University of California Press, 2015), a volume that unfortunately did not appear until the present study was essentially completed, Christopher Reynolds explores in detail the

influence of Beethoven's Ninth Symphony on Brahms's First, focusing especially on Brahms's first movement and on issues relating to counterpoint and to a technique that Reynolds calls "thematic dispersion," which he defines as "the preparation for a moment later in a work by planting varied, anticipatory forms of a musical idea earlier" (11). See Reynolds's chapter 6 for more on the relationship between these two symphonies.

17. Hans von Bülow's nickname for the work can be seen in his letter to Brahms from Hanover on October 2, 1887 in *Hans von Bülow's Letters to Johannes Brahms: A Research Edition*, ed. Hans-Joachim Hinrichsen, trans. Cynthia Klohr (Lanham, MD: Scarecrow Press, 2012); originally published as *Hans von Bülow: Die Briefe an Johannes Brahms* (Tutzing: Hans Schneider, 1994), 1.

18. Other motivic materials also appear in multiple movements of the work; among these is the chromatic gesture in contrary motion that opens the Symphony, a figure referred to by Max Kalbeck [*Johannes Brahms* (Berlin: Deutsche Brahms-Gesellschaft, 1910), 3/1: 94] as a "*Schicksalsmotiv.*" For more on motivic unity in this piece, see, for example, David Brodbeck, *Brahms: Symphony No. 1* (Cambridge: Cambridge University Press, 1997); Michael Musgrave, "Brahms's First Symphony: Thematic Coherence and Its Secret Origin," *Music Analysis* 2/2 (1983): 117–33; MacDonald, *Brahms*, 248–250; Musgrave, *The Music of Brahms*, 137–39; and Walter Frisch, *Brahms: The Four Symphonies* (New Haven, CT: Yale University Press, 2003), 57–58, 59–61, 65.

19. The form of this movement, one way in which Brahms asserts his artistic individuality in this work, can be described as a modified sonata form in which secondary development within the recapitulation serves in place of a dedicated development section. For more on this, see Frisch, *Brahms: The Four Symphonies*, 61.

20. Although I focus here on allusions to Beethoven in this work, influences of other composers, including Schubert and Schumann, may be cited as well. See Michael Musgrave, *The Music of Brahms* (London: Routledge & Kegan Paul, 1985) 134, 136, and 141 and Malcolm MacDonald, *Brahms*, ed. Stanley Sadie (Oxford: Oxford University Press, 2001; originally published in New York by Schirmer Books in 1990), 246–47.

21. The resemblance between the thematic materials of the Horn Trio and "Es soll sich der Mensch nicht mit der Liebe abgeben," identified as the variant "Es soll sich ja keiner mit der Liebe abgeben" (see below), is observed by John Walter Hill, "Thematic Transformation, Folksong, and Nostalgia in Brahms's Horn Trio, op. 40," *The Musical Times* 152/1914 (2011): 20–24. See also Max Kalbeck, *Johannes Brahms*, 3rd ed. (Berlin: Deutsche Brahms-Gesellschaft, 1921; repr. Tutzing: Hans Schneider, 1976), 2:186. ("Dort in den Weiden steht ein Haus" was also set by Brahms as his WoO 32/13 (1858); No. 3 in the *Deutsche Volkslieder*, WoO 38 (1859–62); in varied form as op. 97/4 (1884–85); and as No. 31 in his *49 Deutsche Volkslieder*, WoO 33 (1893–94), sometimes appearing under the title "Schifferlied.") Kalbeck (2: 183) also alludes to a melodic similarity with the chorale "Wer nur den lieben Gott lässt walten," although this is less convincing and has been taken less seriously; see Musgrave, *The Music of Brahms*, 110, and Hill, "Thematic Transformation, Folksong, and Nostalgia," 21.

22. On Brahms's ownership of this anthology, see Brahms to Clara Schumann, June 25, 1858, in *Johannes Brahms in seinen Schriften und Briefen*, ed. Richard Litterscheid (Berlin, 1943), 161, cited in Hill, "Thematic Transformation, Folksong, and Nostalgia," 21, fn. 3.

23. See Karl Geiringer, *Brahms: His Life and Work*, 3rd ed. (New York: Da Capo Press, 1982), 231 and Michael Musgrave, *The Music of Brahms*, 110.

24. Hill, "Thematic Transformation, Folksong, and Nostalgia," 20–21.

25. Hill, "Thematic Transformation, Folksong, and Nostalgia," 21.
26. On the more traditional interpretation, see Hill, "Thematic Transformation, Folksong, and Nostalgia," 22; Laurence Wallach, "Trio for Piano, Violin, and Horn in E-Flat, op. 40," in *The Compleat Brahms: A Guide to the Musical Works of Johannes Brahms*, ed. Leon Botstein (New York: W. W. Norton, 1999), 106–7; and MacDonald, *Brahms*, 175, 176.
27. Hill, "Thematic Transformation, Folksong, and Nostalgia," 24.
28. Original translation very kindly provided by Boston University German Studies scholar William Waters at my request.
29. See Hill, "Thematic Transformation, Folksong, and Nostalgia," 23.
30. See Johannes Brahms to Julius Otto Grimm, [July 1864] and editorial commentary in *Johannes Brahms: Life and Letters*, ed. Styra Avins (Oxford: Oxford University Press, 1997), 288–89.
31. Paul Berry, *Brahms among Friends: Listening, Performance, and the Rhetoric of Allusion* (Oxford: Oxford University Press, 2014).
32. Johannes Brahms to Julius Otto Grimm, [July 1864], in *Johannes Brahms im Briefwechsel mit J. O. Grimm*, ed. Richard Barth (Berlin: Deutsche Brahms-Gesellschaft, 1908), 111; for English translation, see *Johannes Brahms: Life and Letters*, ed. Styra Avins (Oxford: Oxford University Press, 1997), 298.
33. See Avins, *Johannes Brahms: Life and Letters*, 299.
34. See also Kalbeck, *Johannes Brahms*, 2:172 and Florence May, *The Life of Johannes Brahms* (London: Edward Arnold, 1905), 2, 35.
35. See Hans Gál, *Johannes Brahms: His Work and Personality*, translated by Joseph Stein (New York: Alfred A. Knopf, 1963), 96; originally published as *Johannes Brahms: Sein Werk und Persönlichkeit* (Frankfurt am Main: Fischer Bücherei KG, 1961).
36. See Hill, "Thematic Transformation, Folksong, and Nostalgia," 22. The existence of such a motto for Brahms was called seriously into question in Michael Musgrave, "*Frei aber froh*: A Reconsideration," *19th-Century Music* 3 (1979–80), 251–58.
37. Walter Frisch, "The Snake Bites Its Tail: Cyclic Processes in Brahms's Third String Quartet, op. 67," *Journal of Musicology* 22/1 (2005): 168.
38. See Gero Ehlert, *Architektonik der Leidenschaften: Eine Studie zu den Klaviersonaten von Johannes Brahms* (Kassel: Bärenreiter, 2005), 32ff; Dietrich Kämper, *Die Klaviersonate nach Beethoven: Von Schubert bis Skrjabin* (Darmstadt: Wissenschaftliche Buchgesellschaft, 1987), 154; and Walter Frisch, *Brahms and the Principle of Developing Variation*, California Studies in Nineteenth-Century Music 2 (Berkeley: University of California Press, 1984), 55. Brahms's op. 1 postdates most of the F-Sharp-Minor Sonata, op. 2, which was finished approximately five months earlier. (See Margit L. McCorkle, with assistance from Donald M. McCorkle, *Johannes Brahms: Thematisch-Bibliographisches Werkverzeichnis* (München: G. Henle, 1984), 1 and 4, citing Alfred Orel, "Ein Eigenhändiges Werkverzeichnis von Johannes Brahms. Ein Wichtiger Beitrag zur Brahmsfaschung." *Die Musik* 29/8 (May 1937): 530. Only the slow movement of op. 1, written in February 1852, was composed prior to this. Brahms did compose earlier works, but he suppressed them; the autograph manuscript of op. 1 (currently housed in the Österreichische Nationalbibliothek of Vienna) indicates that the C-Major Sonata was actually Brahms's *fourth* sonata for solo piano. See George S. Bozarth, "Brahms's Lieder ohne Worte: The 'Poetic' Andantes of the Piano Sonatas," in *Brahms Studies: Analytical and Historical Perspectives*, ed. George S. Bozarth (Oxford: Clarendon Press, 1990), 348.

39. See Ehlert, *Architektonik der Leidenschaften*, 175–79; F. E. Kirby, "Brahms and the Piano Sonata," in *Paul A. Pisk: Essays in His Honor*, ed. John Glowacki and Paul Amadeus Pisk (Austin, TX: College of Fine Arts, 1966): 170; and William Newman, *The Sonata Since Beethoven*, 3rd ed. (New York: W.W. Norton, 1983), 328–29.

40. Although the opening theme itself is not heard again until the recapitulation, this is, in fact, related to much of the material in the rest of the exposition and in the development. For more on the connections between the first and second themes of the movement, see, for instance, Frisch, *Brahms and the Principle of Developing Variation*, 53–54; and Newman, *The Sonata Since Beethoven*, 143.

41. My thanks to an anonymous reviewer for making this connection.

42. Whereas Brahms sustains tensions from the main thematic materials of the Sonata's first movement until he resolves them in the finale, Beethoven exhibits a tendency to resolve tensions of his opening themes in the codas of his initial movements. On Beethoven's codas, see for example Joseph Kerman, "Notes on Beethoven's Codas," *Beethoven Studies* 3 (1982): 141–60; Robert G. Hopkins, "When a Coda Is More Than a Coda: Reflections on Beethoven," in *Explorations in Music, the Arts, and Ideas: Essays in Honor of Leonard B. Meyer*, eds. Eugene Narmour and Ruth A. Solie (Stuyvesant, NY: Pendragon Press, 1988), 393–410; and Margarita Rodriguez, "Aspects of Completion in Beethoven's Middle Period Codas" (PhD diss., Michigan State University, 2012).

43. Although the Sonata's second movement was finished by April of the previous year, Brahms was working on the scherzo and the outer movements until spring 1853. See McCorkle, *Johannes Brahms: Thematisch-Bibliographisches Werkverzeichnis*, 1, citing Orel, "Ein Eigenhändiges Werkverzeichnis von Johannes Brahms," 530.

44. Movements two and four were composed some months earlier. On the compositional history of this work, see McCorkle, *Johannes Brahms: Thematisch-Bibliographisches Werkverzeichnis*, 14, citing Orel, "Ein Eigenhändiges Werkverzeichnis von Johannes Brahms," 530. See also Max Kalbeck, *Johannes Brahms*, 4th ed. (Berlin: Deutsche Brahms-Gesellschaft, 1921; repr. Tutzing: Hans Schneider, 1976), 1:120; Johannes Brahms to Robert Schumann, Hanover, November 16, 1853; and Johannes Brahms to Barthold Senff, Hamburg, December 26, 1853, in *Johannes Brahms: Life and Letters*, 25 and 31–32; and Ehlert, *Architektonik der Leidenschaften*, 314–20.

45. The relevance of this motive to various passages in the Sonata has been perceived by several scholars with varying levels of awareness; however, none acknowledges in full the extent to which the motive pervades the work, and few associate the figure explicitly with the motive from Beethoven's Fifth Symphony. See Giselher Schubert, "Themes and Double Themes: The Problem of the Symphonic in Brahms," *19th-Century Music* 18/1 (1994): 12; Ivor Keys, *Johannes Brahms* (Portland, OR: Amadeus Press, 1989), 294, n. 2; Dillon Parmer, "Brahms and the Poetic Motto: A Hermeneutic Aid?" *The Journal of Musicology* 15/3 (1997): 364, 366; Kip James Montgomery, "Cyclic Form in the Music of Brahms" (PhD diss., State University of New York at Stony Brook, 2002), 99; and Laurence Wallach, "Sonata No. 3 in F Minor, op. 5," in *The Compleat Brahms: A Guide to the Musical Works of Johannes Brahms*, ed. Leon Botstein (New York: W. W. Norton, 1999), 164. For more on thematic motivic work in the op. 5 Sonata, see for example Jürgen Schläder, "Zur Funktion der Variantentechnik in den Kalviersonaten F-Moll von Johannes Brahms und H-Moll von Franz Liszt," in *Brahms und seine Zeit: Bericht über das Symposion 1983 in Hamburg*, eds. Constantin Floros, Hans Joachim Marx, and P. Petersen (Hamburg: Laaber-Verlag, 1984), 171–97.

46. On the movement's recollection of melodies from earlier in the Sonata, see Edwin Evans, *Handbook to the Pianoforte Works of Johannes Brahms* (London: W. Reeves, 1912; repr. New York: Burt Franklin, 1970), 94. For other cross-movement thematic relationships in this work not discussed here, including relationships between the works D-flat-major themes, see also Evans's pp. 96–100 and Gerald Abraham, *A Hundred Years of Music*, 4th ed. (London: Duckworth, 1974), 164; Frisch, *Brahms and the Principle of Developing Variation*, 37 and 49–50; Kirby, "Brahms and the Piano Sonata," 175–77; and Wallach, "Sonata No. 3 in F Minor, op. 5," 164.

47. On citations of the motive in Schumann's music criticism, see Leon Plantinga, *Schumann as Critic*, Yale Studies in the History of Music 4, ed. William G. Waite, reprint ed. (New York: Da Capo Press, 1976), 163. See also Mark Evan Bonds, *After Beethoven*, 113. Bonds's fn. 13 gives thorough citations of the relevant passages of Schumann's criticism.

48. Robert Schumann, *Briefe: Neue Folge*, ed. F. Gustav Jansen, 2nd ed. (Leipzig: Breitkopf & Härtel, 1904), 370–71. The English translation given here is taken from George Grove, *Beethoven and His Nine Symphonies*, 3rd ed. (New York: Dover Publications, 1962), 180.

49. Johannes Brahms to Joseph Joachim, Düsseldorf, ca. February 22, 1855, in *Johannes Brahms: Life and Letters*, 91. The other two pieces were Beethoven's Violin Concerto, op. 61, and *Don Giovanni*.

50. Thanks to an anonymous reviewer for pointing out this tonal relationship between the slow movements of these works.

51. James Webster, "Schubert's Sonata Form and Brahms's First Maturity," Part 2, *19th-Century Music* 3 (1979): 58.

52. For more thorough comparison of these two movements, see Frisch, *Brahms and the Principle of Developing Variation*, 40–42. Frisch (42) concludes that "despite certain similarities to the 'Appassionata,' Brahms's F-Minor Sonata simply does not proceed ... according to Beethovenian classical principles." Frisch (42–49) goes on to compare Brahms's first movement with Beethoven's C-Minor Piano Concerto, op. 37, and with works of Schubert and Liszt. See also Reynolds, *Motives for Allusion*, 167–68 and Knapp, *Brahms and the Challenge*, 91. For more on what Knapp calls "allusive webs" in Brahms's music, see the rest of his chapter 4.

53. Johannes Brahms to Barthold Senff, Hamburg, December 26, 1853, in *Johannes Brahms: Life and Letters*, 31.

54. See Wilibald Nagel, *Die Klaviersonaten von Johannes Brahms: Technisch-Ästhetische Analysen* (Stuttgart: Carl Grüninger, 1915), 100. See also Bozarth, "Brahms's *Lieder ohne Worte*," 362; and Adolf Schubring, "Schumanniana," *Neue Zeitschrift für Musik*, March 28, 1862: 103; as well as Walter Frisch, "Brahms and Schubring: Musical Criticism and Politics at Mid-Century," *19th-Century Music* 7/3 (1984): 277. Bozarth gives the music and text (with English translation) of this folksong on pp. 363 and 365 of his article. Although Sternau's poem concludes with the lovers still embracing, Bozarth follows Schubring's lead in asserting that an association between this folksong and Brahms's music would help to explain the fact that this music seems to be a reminiscence of the movement's earlier D-flat-major material, and that it would also account for Brahms's ending the movement in D-flat major, "presumably the key of the soldier's memories of his beloved," instead of in A-flat, "which now appears only to have been an illusory 'home' key." See Bozarth, "Brahms's *Lieder ohne Worte*," 362, citing Schubring, "Schumanniana," 103.

55. See, for example, Parmer, "Brahms and the Poetic Motto," 367. See also Bozarth, "Brahms's *Lieder ohne Worte*," 373 and Ann Besser Scott, "Thematic Transmutation in the

Music of Brahms: A Matter of Musical Alchemy," *The Journal of Musicological Research* 15/3 (1995): 199. For more on programmatic interpretation of the andante, see also Detlef Kraus, "*Das Andante aus der Sonate op. 5 von Brahms: Versuch einer Interpretation*," *Brahms-Studien* 3 (1979): 47–51, reprinted in English in as "The *Andante* from op. 5—A Possible Interpretation" in Detlef Kraus, *Johannes Brahms, Composer for the Piano*, ed. Andrew D. McCredie in collaboration with Richard Schaal, trans. Lillian Lim (Wilhelmshaven: F. Noetzel, 1988), 29–34; Bozarth, "Brahms's *Lieder ohne Worte*," 345–78; Parmer, "Brahms and the Poetic Motto," 353–89; and Constantin Floros, *Johannes Brahms, "Free but Alone": A Life for a Poetic Music*, trans. Ernest Bernhardt-Kabisch (Frankfurt am Main: Peter Lang, 2010; originally published as *Johannes Brahms, "frei aber einsam": Ein Leben für eine poetische Musik* (Zürich: Arche Zürich, 1997), 114.

56. Kalbeck, *Johannes Brahms*, 1:121–22. See also Bozarth, "Brahms's *Lieder ohne Worte*," 364; and Parmer, "Brahms and the Poetic Motto," 366–67.

57. William David Murdoch, *Brahms, with an Analytical Study of the Complete Pianoforte Works* (London: Rich & Cowan, Limited, 1933; repr. New York: AMS Press, 1978), 220.

58. Bozarth, "Brahms's *Lieder ohne Worte*," 369–73.

59. Bozarth, "Brahms's *Lieder ohne Worte*," 373.

60. See Keys, *Johannes Brahms*, 233; Kämper, *Die Klaviersonate nach Beethoven*, 167; and Wallach, "Sonata No. 3 in F Minor, op. 5," 164; John Daverio (*Crossing Paths: Schubert, Schumann, and Brahms* (Oxford: Oxford University Press, 2002), 116–17) suggests that Brahms's handling of the "F-A-E" motive in the op. 5 finale actually reflects the influence of Schumann's Intermezzo for the "F-A-E" Sonata.

61. Bozarth, "Brahms's *Lieder ohne Worte*," 373–74.

62. For more on "*Neue Bahnen*" and on early reception of Brahms's first published works, see chapter 2, as well as Angelika Horstmann, "Die Rezeption der Werke op. 1–10 von Johannes Brahms zwischen 1853 und 1860," in *Brahms und seine Zeit*, 33–44. See also Norbert Meurs, *Neue Bahnen?: Aspekte der Brahms-Rezeption 1853–1868*, ed. Detlef Altenburg (Cologne: Studio Verlag Schewe, 1996).

2 Lovelorn Lamentation or Histrionic Historicism? Reexamining Allusion and Extramusical Meaning in the B-Major Piano Trio, op. 8

Brahms's first published chamber work, the B-major Trio, op. 8, emerged from a particularly heady period of the composer's life. In the fall of 1853, twenty-year-old Brahms appeared on the doorstep of Robert and Clara Schumann's Düsseldorf home to introduce himself to the couple. This initial meeting with the Schumanns would prove a turning point in Brahms's early career; upon playing for them several of his piano works, Brahms was immediately taken on as Robert's protégé. Within weeks, the elder composer had published what was to become perhaps his most famous piece of criticism, an article entitled *"Neue Bahnen,"* in which he characterizes Brahms as the worthiest of musical heirs, a messianic figure destined to rescue musical tradition from the dangers presented by the New German School.[1] Departing from the hospitality of the Schumanns in early November, Brahms embarked for Hanover, where he would spend several weeks visiting his good friend, the violinist Joseph Joachim. After two brief visits to Leipzig and a trip home to Hamburg for Christmas, Brahms returned to Hanover on January 3, 1854 and, prepared for an extended stay with Joachim, set to work on the B-major Trio.[2] He remained in Hanover until news of Robert Schumann's breakdown and attempted suicide sent him hurrying back to Düsseldorf at the beginning of March to care for Clara and her children. Although several months were to elapse before the work's publication, the Trio was essentially complete by this time, the end of the manuscript bearing the inscription *"Hannover. Januar 54."*[3] To several scholars, the biographical circumstances surrounding the work's creation, in combination with the Trio's incorporation of what have long been recognized as references to songs from Beethoven's *An die ferne Geliebte* and Schubert's *Schwanengesang*, have suggested a reading of the piece as a lament for Brahms's own "distant beloved," Clara Schumann.

Close analysis of the 1854 version of the Trio shows that the original version of the work contains yet a third allusory reference that has long remained unobserved. The Trio refers both clearly and in a structurally significant manner to Domenico Scarlatti's C-Major Sonata, K. 159. Along with documentary evidence from writings of Brahms and his contemporaries, other of Brahms's compositions, and his 1889 revisions to the Trio, this additional allusion is potentially supportive of the program proposed repeatedly in the existing scholarship. Nonetheless, it also compels consideration of an alternative interpretation of the Trio's allusions: as a means through which Brahms mourns the loss of the musical past and expresses perspectives on his own historical position in 1854 as well as in 1889, when he removed all three allusions.

Three Allusions in the 1854 Trio

Among the most intriguing and frequently noted features of the 1854 finale is an apparent allusion to "Nimm sie hin denn, diese Lieder," the final song of Beethoven's *An die ferne Geliebte*, in the second theme (ex. 2.1a–b).[4] Brahms may have borrowed not directly from Beethoven, but rather from Robert Schumann, as a similar variant of the theme appears in Schumann's *Fantasie*, op. 17 (ex. 2.1c).[5] Schumann's presentation of the *Fantasie* as a *"Sonate für Beethoven,"* a tribute to the master on the tenth anniversary of his death, may have provided an explanation for the work's Beethoven references for those who noticed them—the *Fantasie* also alludes to the Seventh Symphony—but Schumann admitted to Clara in the period before their marriage that the allusion to *An die ferne Geliebte* also represented a private lament of the distance imposed on them at the time by her father.[6] The text of "Nimm sie hin denn," a poem by Alois Jeitteles, represents the narrator's request that his beloved sing back to him what he has just sung to her (i.e., the preceding songs of the cycle) as a means of bridging the distance between the two lovers. It reads:

Nimm sie hin denn, diese Lieder,	Take them hence then, these songs
Die ich dir, Geliebte, sang,	that I to you, beloved, sang,
Singe sie dann abends wieder	sing them again then in the evenings
Zu der Laute süssem klang!	to the sweet sound of the lute!
Wenn das Damm'rungsrot dann ziehet	When the red of twilight then draws
Nach dem stillen blauen See,	toward the still, blue lake,
Und sein letzter Strahl verglühet	and its last rays die away
Hinter jener Bergeshöh;	behind yonder mountain heights;
Und du singst, was ich gesungen,	And you sing what I have sung,
Was mir aus der vollen Brust	what, from out of my full heart,
Ohne Kunstgepräng erklungen,	rang without artistic pageantry,
Nur der Sehnsucht sich bewusst;	conscious only of its yearning.
Dann vor diesen Liedern weichet,	Then before these songs yields
Was geschieden uns so weit,	that which separates us by such a distance,
Und ein liebend Herz erreichet,	and a loving heart reaches
Was ein liebend Herz geweiht.	that which a loving heart has sanctified.

Example 2.1a–c.
(a) Beethoven, *An die ferne Geliebte*, op. 98, No. 6: "Nimm sie hin denn, diese Lieder," mm. 9–12

(b) Brahms, Piano Trio in B Major, op. 8 (1854 Version), Fourth Movement, mm. 424–36: Beginning of Second Theme in Recapitulation

(c) Robert Schumann, *Fantasie*, op. 17, First Movement, upbeat to mm. 296–299

Example 2.2a–b.
(a) Schubert, *Schwanengesang*, D. 957, No. 12: "Am Meer," mm. 1–6

(b) Brahms, Piano Trio in B Major, op. 8 (1854 Version), Third Movement, mm. 32–36: Beginning of Second Theme

The theme of the distant or lost love is also present in the text of the other song to which Brahms alludes in the 1854 Trio. The second theme group of the Trio's penultimate movement has long been recognized as a reference to "Am Meer," the twelfth song from Schubert's *Schwanengesang*, D. 957 (ex. 2.2a–b).[7] The song's text, by Heine, recalls the reluctant final parting of the narrator from his tearful beloved. It reads:

Am Meer	At the Sea
Das Meer erglänzte weit hinaus	The sea was glittering far and wide
Im letzten Abendscheine;	in the last rays of evening;
Wir sassen am einsamen Fischerhaus,	we sat at the lonely fisherman's house,
Wir sassen stumm und alleine.	we sat silent and alone.
Der Nebel steig, das Wasser schwoll,	The mist arose, the water swelled up,
Die Möwe flog hin und wieder;	the seagulls flew back and forth;
Aus deinen Augen liebevoll	from out of your loving eyes
Fielen die Tränen nieder.	the tears flowed down.
Ich sah sie fallen auf deine Hand	I saw them fall onto your hand,
Und bin aufs Knie gesunken;	and I sank to my knees;
Ich hab' von deiner weissen Hand	from your white hand
Die Tränen fortgetrunken.	I drank up the tears.[8]

In the context of the Trio, the woman in Heine's poem is to become the "*ferne Geliebte*" of the Jeitteles text evoked in the finale.

A third clear allusive reference—to Scarlatti's Sonata (K. 159), a work that shares its key with Schumann's *Fantasie* and Schubert's "Am Meer"—altogether escaped detection until recently, when I pointed it out in an article in *19th-Century Music*.[9] Yet references to the opening of Scarlatti's Sonata (ex. 2.3) play at least as important a role in the Trio as does either of the widely recognized song references.[10] Scarlatti's theme is distinctly evocative of horn calls—perhaps even the calls of a post horn, which carry associations with distance and absence, the very themes suggested by the texts of the cited songs.[11]

The Trio's clearest reminiscence of Scarlatti is heard at one of the most intense moments of the first movement: a sequential passage at the end of the recapitulation's second theme group; the passage begins on the dominant and culminates in the grand, *fortissimo* return to B major and first-theme material (mm. 409-10). As the passage begins (m. 396; ex. 2.3), a one-measure phrase pervades the music, consisting of precisely the sequence of pitches that begins Scarlatti's Sonata (heard here on F-sharp major), except for an added leap down to the fifth scale degree. The phrase sounds first in the violin, doubled initially in parallel thirds by the cello, just as, in the Sonata, the left hand doubles the right a third below. In both works, the thirds expand to an open fifth on the fifth note of the phrase, then, on successive pitches, to a sixth—with a leap to a unison and return to the sixth—back to a fifth, and finally back to a third on the downbeat. Although the Trio movement is in 4/4, Brahms approximates Scarlatti's 6/8 meter as closely as possible, dividing the measure into twelve triplets. At the end of the measure, Brahms deviates slightly from the Sonata's

Example 2.3a–b.
(a) Domenico Scarlatti, Sonata in C Major, K. 159, mm. 1–4

(b) Brahms, Piano Trio in B Major, op. 8 (1854 Version), First Movement, mm. 396–407

rhythm, doubling the length of the notes and thereby adding a beat to the phrase. Yet, this is necessary to make the theme *more* like Scarlatti's in another respect. Had Brahms not added a beat at the end, then the note that Scarlatti had placed on the final downbeat of the opening phrase would, in the Trio, have ended end up on the relatively weak final beat of m. 396, rather than on the following downbeat. Brahms leaves off the final note of Scarlatti's phrase, giving the music an unfinished, unresolved quality appropriate to the restless nature of the passage. In mm. 398–99, the accompanimental figures in the cello and in the left hand of the piano part evoke the trill and downward step that conclude Scarlatti's phrase—and even though Brahms shifts to B minor here, the pitches in the left hand of the piano part (E–F-sharp–E–D), are remarkably similar to those found at that particular spot in Scarlatti (E–F–E–D).

The motive in m. 396 pervades the music obsessively until the triumphant return to the B-major tonic in m. 409. It appears numerous times in succession as the music modulates, and it enters in each voice, sometimes in overlapping statements. As in the Sonata, each statement of the phrase is immediately reiterated in whichever voice it has appeared, after which the music shifts to a new harmonic framework and/or that voice temporarily moves on to other material. Thus, each statement is one of an identical pair, precisely as in Scarlatti's Sonata.

Over the course of this passage in the Trio, the theme is gradually transformed. First (mm. 400–403), moving to the key of C-sharp minor via G-sharp-major harmony, the violin begins to leave out the low note that Brahms had initially added to Scarlatti's theme (it is forced to: these notes fall below the range of the instrument), and then (mm. 403–4) the upward-moving phrase-ending fails to be articulated, leaving only the repeated-note downward scalar motion, the urgency of whose successive repetitions in the piano helps to intensify the music yet further (beginning in m. 404). The repeated-note scale is eventually extended downward (starting in m. 406), finally reaching the dominant of B major, and the return to the tonic is affected by sweeping contrary-motion scales in the piano, no longer with repeated notes, but clearly the result of the evolution of Scarlatti's theme.

In the closing portion of the recapitulation and in the coda, there are further subtle references. First are the descending stepwise thirds in the piano part (mm. 412–14 and 417–19), which emulate Scarlatti's not only melodically, but rhythmically through the use of triplets, texturally through the use of harmonic thirds, and in their having been assigned to the keyboard player (ex. 2.4a). Perhaps more significant than the resemblance of these passages to the Sonata's opening is the similarity they bear to its close: in the last several measures of K. 159, the right hand continually restates, in the same rhythm, downward stepwise thirds in parallel thirds (ex. 2.4b). Furthermore, at the end of the Sonata, as in these measures of the Trio, the third descents are paired so that upward motion occurs only at the end of a six-note grouping. In this context, the content of Brahms's mm. 412–14 and

Example 2.4a–e.
(a) Brahms, Piano Trio in B Major, op. 8 (1854 Version), First Movement, mm. 412–19

(b) Domenico Scarlatti, Sonata in C Major, K. 159, mm. 60–64

417–19 may be viewed as closing gestures and as the logical outcome of the Scarlatti references in the preceding passage. The piano part in mm. 435–41, just before the coda, with its third ascents and repeated melodic notes, also resembles an inverted fragment of the Scarlatti theme. It is more easily traceable to the first measure of the movement's opening melody—although that too is arguably derived from the inversion of Scarlatti's theme (ex. 2.4c).[12] The reiteration of this fragmentary figure at increasing tempo and rising pitch level beginning in m. 435 suggests an increasing sense of futility (not found in Scarlatti's Sonata), particularly as each attempt at ascent is countered by a more rapid, fluid, and extensive descending

76 | *Allusion as Narrative Premise in Brahms*

(c) Brahms, Piano Trio in B Major, op. 8 (1854 Version), First Movement, mm. 435–41

(d) Brahms, Piano Trio in B Major, op. 8 (1854 Version), First Movement, mm. 473–78

*Die kleinen Noten können nötigenfalls wegbleiben

(e) Brahms, Piano Trio in B Major, op. 8 (1854 Version), First Movement, mm. 487–94

motion. Beneath all of this, the rolled chords of the piano and the written-out trills in the strings nod more generally to the style of Scarlatti and his contemporaries. In mm. 474–78, groups of ascending stepwise thirds appear again, each group beginning a step higher than the one before—and this time, each ascent concludes with an upward third leap and downward step similar to the stepwise third ascent and downward step concluding Scarlatti's opening phrase (ex. 2.4d). Although the plagal gesture that concludes the movement is not particularly characteristic of Scarlatti, this gesture is immediately preceded by a Baroque-sounding melodic turn (incidentally?) comprised of the all-too-familiar stepwise third descent and a counterbalancing ascent (mm. 487–90; ex. 2.4e).

Brahms and Scarlatti

As striking as any resemblances may be between the opening of Scarlatti's Sonata and these passages of the Trio, we must ask ourselves how likely a source Scarlatti would have been for Brahms. Dating from at least as early as the mid-1850s, Brahms's engagement with the music of Scarlatti was, in fact, both enduring and multifaceted, even prompting Scarlatti scholar Malcolm Boyd to comment that it was "Brahms who, of all the great nineteenth-century composers, best understood and valued Scarlatti's keyboard music."[13] Avins points out that, while staying with Clara in Düsseldorf in the spring of 1854—the very period in which Brahms was readying op. 8 for publication—he "found the opportunity to make detailed studies of early music. *He championed Scarlatti.*"[14]

Indeed, from the mid-1850s on, Brahms's continuing engagement with Scarlatti is clear from his correspondence with friends. Although much evidence of his interest in Scarlatti dates from the later years, Brahms was, in fact, involved with this repertory even in the mid-1850s. As early as 1856, he writes to Clara Schumann that, while he is "not over-fond of Scarlatti owing to the similarity of his pieces (in form and character)," he nonetheless enjoys playing individual Scarlatti works and owns "a good volume of them."[15] Brahms seems to be operating under the direct influence of Robert Schumann, who described Scarlatti's music in very similar terms in his 1839 review of Czerny's complete Scarlatti edition.[16] It appears that Brahms's attitude toward Scarlatti remained fundamentally unchanged over the decades. In 1885, he sent to his friend Theodor Billroth a book of Scarlatti sonatas along with a note saying that Billroth was sure to enjoy the pieces, as long as he didn't play too many of them at once.[17] Two days earlier, he had sent a "specimen" of Scarlatti to Elisabeth and Heinrich von Herzogenberg, recommending that the couple seek to acquire Czerny's edition of the sonatas.[18] As late as 1894, Joachim, writing to Brahms of a performance he had recently heard in Berlin, told the composer, "you would have enjoyed how splendidly he played Scarlatti on his harpsichord."[19]

Furthermore, Brahms's personal library eventually contained not only modern editions of Scarlatti's sonatas (particularly Czerny's edition of 1839), but also at least one rare first-edition and a set of handwritten manuscripts apparently copied out in large part by Santini.[20] Brahms played Scarlatti in public concerts, particularly in the 1860s and 1870s, and Florence May recalls a private performance taking place at Clara Schumann's home in 1871: "he played a wild piece by Scarlatti as I never heard anyone play before. He really did give it as though he were inspired."[21] Also beginning in the 1860s, Brahms collected and formulated written commentary on examples of parallel octaves and fifths. The examples—eventually numbering about 140—are drawn from the works of thirty-two composers dating from the sixteenth century on.[22] Of these, Scarlatti is among the five best-represented composers in the collection, his sonatas serving as source material for ten examples.[23]

The influence of Scarlatti can be found in other specific works of Brahms. Scholars have suggested the influence of Scarlatti's K. 180 in a short passage from the fugue in Brahms's Variations and Fugue on a Theme by G. F. Handel, op. 24, of 1861 and have identified "Scarlatti-esque" traits ("witty register shifts," "mischievous syncopation," "iridescent sound-effects," and the abrupt contrast of playfulness and seriousness) in the seven capriccios from Brahms's later opp. 76 and 116.[24] Of particular interest, however, is the quotation from another Scarlatti sonata (K. 223) in Brahms's song "*Unüberwindlich*," op. 72/5, of 1876. (Brahms has interpolated a staccato articulation for the Scarlatti quotation at the beginning of this song, just as in the clearest apparent references to Scarlatti in the 1854 Trio, perhaps attempting in both cases to invoke the lighter, drier touch of the keyboard instruments of Scarlatti's time.) Brahms points out the allusion in the song, labeling its initial statement "D. Scarlatti." This is the only borrowing in all of Brahms's output that the composer acknowledged in such an overt manner—yet he never elaborated upon its meaning, nor upon what reasons he may have had for directing attention to its presence.[25]

Broader Thematic-Structural Implications of the Scarlatti Reference

Not only does the influence of Scarlatti seem to be at work in the Trio's first movement, but this influence appears to extend to much of the piece. Indeed, many of the Trio's most important thematic materials exhibit strong ties to Scarlatti's Sonata. Numerous scholars have remarked upon the Trio's high degree of thematic unity, highlighting motivic connections within the first movement in particular.[26] Antonio Baldassarre suggests that Brahms distributes the distinctive motives of the first movement's main theme among two "partial subjects" that comprise the movement's second theme group: "Partial Subject 1" (mm. 84–98), which resembles the opening theme both rhythmically and in its stepwise motion from B, now *down* a third (cf. m. 1 and m. 85), and "Partial Subject 2" (mm. 98–103), which again presents the rhythm of m. 1 (m. 98), followed by a retrograde of that rhythm (m. 99), also in ascending stepwise thirds—D-sharp to F-double sharp, G-sharp to B. The descending-sixth leap in m. 100 inverts the prominent third motive. Baldassare posits that "the division of the second subject into two partial subjects is primarily justified through the division of the motives which constitute the main theme."[27] A number of important cross-movement relationships have long been recognized as well. Max Kalbeck was among the first of many to assert that several of the work's primary melodic materials derive from one fundamental thematic motive. He presents this motive as the series of pitches that opens the scherzo (shown in ex. 2.8a), but without the note repetitions and in half-notes in 4/4 time.[28]

The existence of a Scarlatti reference suggests a somewhat different reason from the one Baldassarre has proposed for the division of the first movement's second theme group, and it also provides a new context in which to view most of the thematic correspondences that have been identified in past scholarship. Scarlatti's melody is never evoked with such clarity as in the opening movement, but it may well be this theme itself that resurfaces, in various guises, throughout the work, helping to unify the piece and to generate the sense of an ongoing story.

Although clear reference to Scarlatti's theme occurs relatively late in the first movement, the relationship between the Trio's opening melody and that theme suggests that Brahms had Scarlatti in mind from the very beginning. In other words, he may have worked backward in order to create new thematic material that would logically culminate in the near-quotation of the Sonata.[29] At first glance, any resemblance between the Scarlatti theme and the descending portion of the main theme (mm. 2–3)—in particular, the fact that both involve stepwise descent from the fifth scale degree to the tonic pitch—may appear innocuous enough. Yet, the resemblance between the themes becomes stronger when the opening melody enters in the violin (starting in m. 20; ex. 2.5). Here, the strings move in parallel sixths suggestive of, but not yet fully realizing, the "parallel-thirds" texture of the Sonata. More importantly, most of the half-notes in the melodic descent have been broken into quarters so that, as in the Sonata, the descent now begins in even note values and involves a repetition of the third pitch (e.g., in mm. 22 and 26). Furthermore, the phrase ending has been modified so that, immediately following the descent of a fifth, there is only an upward leap of a third plus a downward step to the second scale degree—just as in Scarlatti's opening phrase. The meter and some of the note values are different, and some of the note repetitions are missing from the melody; still, the basic shape of Scarlatti's phrase is unmistakably present. Beginning in m. 37, the first three notes (F-sharp–E–D-sharp) of the stepwise descent from the Trio's opening theme are, as a group, isolated and repeated

Example 2.5. Piano Trio in B Major, op. 8 (1854 Version), First Movement, mm. 20–28

several times in succession, generally in parallel thirds, sounding simultaneously in all three instruments. Eventually (from m. 52), this provokes isolated shifts to triple meter, with each third descent articulated in successive eighth notes, as in Scarlatti's Sonata. (This material is clearly related to that found in mm. 412–14 and 417–19, already discussed above [ex. 2.4a]. Evidence for an evolutionary relationship between this passage and the one beginning at m. 412 includes the fact that the third descents here appear first singly and then [starting in m. 64] are paired to form gestures that descend further, more closely resembling those in the later passage.) Fragments of the Scarlatti theme (filtered through Brahms's opening melody) continue to resonate at the close of the first theme group and in the transition (beginning at m. 63) to the second theme group of the exposition.

The second theme group of the exposition (beginning at the upbeat to m. 84) in turn derives from materials noted in both the first theme group and transition. An audible augmentation connects the second theme's opening stepwise third descent to the gestures in the transition (mm. 63 and 67–68), whose derivation from Scarlatti I have just suggested. Note also the placement of the bar line between the second and third notes (ex. 2.6) and the slurs in both forms of

Example 2.6. Piano Trio in B Major, op. 8 (1854 Version), First Movement, mm. 83–86

Example 2.7. Piano Trio, op. 8 (1854 Version), First Movement, mm. 98–103, Piano Part, Left Hand: Fugato Subject

the motive. Following the second theme's initial downward third, a scalar ascent concludes with an upward third leap and stepwise descent (mm. 85–86), recalling the contour of Scarlatti's phrase. The Trio's second theme does not return in this form in the recapitulation; it is replaced by the tumultuous passage containing the Scarlatti reference. For this reason, and because of the theme's spare texture and stilted nature, the exposition's second theme looms as a precursor to, or even a germinal form of, the allusion to Scarlatti that is to come.

In the development section (beginning in m. 163), relevant aspects of the first and second themes naturally resurface and continue to evolve, but more remarkable is the relevance of the unrealized fugato in the exposition and its counterpart in the recapitulation.[30] The fugato subject (ex. 2.7) is first introduced within the second theme group of the exposition (mm. 98–103). It is highly chromatic and has a distinctly "Bachian" sound, complete with trills and turns.[31] It is introduced in a single unaccompanied voice, sounding thoroughly like a fugue subject, but it appears only once before yielding to a strikingly different folksong-like third theme (beginning in m. 124). Like the second theme proper (mm. 84–98), the fugato is in a germinal state in the exposition. At the beginning of the recapitulation's second theme group (m. 354), the subject sounds in place of the second theme proper, blossoming into a full fugato in four parts, with an abundance of trills. (Brahms does not include the trills when he cites Scarlatti's theme in the first movement of the Trio. The citation goes by so rapidly there, and in a context so busy, that such ornamentation would have been cumbersome if retained.) With the subject's potential fulfilled, the fugato culminates not in a return of the folk-like third theme, but in the arrival of the intense passage in which Scarlatti's influence is fully revealed (beginning in m. 396). Even though it follows rather than precedes the fugato in the recapitulation, this passage substitutes for what may be considered its own germinal material, the exposition's second theme proper. Much as the rapid tempo, pervasive repetition, and frequent modulation and mode shift associated with the revelation of Scarlatti's phrase may betray an underlying anxiety, there is also something victorious and celebratory about this passage. With its relatively clear harmonic content, it brings a sense of relief and clarity after a highly chromatic, dissonant passage of four-part polyphony.

It is surely significant that the Scarlatti theme is ushered in by material so explicitly evocative of Baroque musical idioms, and that it is not until the fugato is fully realized that the Scarlatti theme is able to enter in its purest form. By leading up to this theme's unveiling with material that so clearly brings to mind the period in which Scarlatti worked, Brahms seems to be leaving us an important clue to the theme's origin. This provides an explanation for the bizarre bipartite structure of the exposition's second theme group: the second theme proper and the fugue subject are grouped together because both are germinal entities whose eventual flowering in the recapitulation results in the exposition of the Scarlatti theme in its full glory. (In the revised version, the second theme and the fugue subject are removed together as well.)

The opening of the scherzo, the Trio's second movement (ex. 2.8a), like that of Scarlatti's Sonata, consists primarily of triple-meter scalar motion in even note values at the rate of one note per beat, with every other scale degree repeated and the first statement of each repeated note appearing on the downbeat. The staccato markings may also link this material to the Trio's earlier Scarlatti reference: although Scarlatti does not employ such markings, Brahms has used them more frequently in the tumultuous sequential passage in the first movement—that is in association with Scarlatti's theme—than anywhere else in that movement. The resemblance between the scherzo and Sonata melodies is even more apparent when the scherzo theme is inverted so that, as in the Sonata, the stepwise motion begins in the downward direction, and the line eventually ascends

Example 2.8a–d. Piano Trio in B Major, op. 8 (1854 Version), Second Movement
(a) mm. 1–9

(b) mm. 52–56

a third. Interestingly, the scherzo theme's initial statement in this form is the movement's only phrase in C major, the key of Scarlatti's Sonata (cf. Scarlatti's opening—minus the upbeat—with Brahms's mm. 52–56; ex. 2.8b). As in the first movement, the main thematic material is most closely linked to Scarlatti's theme in precisely the passage where the movement reaches the peak of its excitement, achieving its loudest dynamic level, most intense use of *sforzando*, thickest texture, and all-around most rollicking character (ex. 2.8c).

Even the theme of the Trio section (ex. 2.8d) may have its origins in Scarlatti. Its reiterated stepwise ascents from B to D-sharp, mimicking those of the scherzo's opening, appear to be an outgrowth of the failed ascent of the repeated-note scale apparently derived from Scarlatti's theme. The Trio theme's evolution from this scale, accomplished via inversion and fragmentation, occurs right before our eyes at the end of the scherzo (ex. 2.8c), Like Scarlatti's melody, this theme (as well as

(c) mm. 69–119

the scherzo theme and its inversion, for that matter) is treated with heavy emphasis on parallel thirds and sixths.

In the coda of the second movement, the scherzo theme is fragmented to the point of nonexistence, and the music fades out, with a chromatic descent that begins at m. 431 and leads to the arrival of the tonic major at m. 451. The fading

of the theme, the change to major and to the tonic, the chromatic descent leading to this shift, as well as the harp-like string plucking at the movement's close all suggest a sort of transfiguration or transcendence. Judging by the song reference in the third movement, this may represent the protagonist's last blissful moment with his beloved—a moment recalled with sadness in the *Adagio non troppo*, which continues in the key of B major.

(d) mm. 165–71

Example 2.9. Piano Trio in B Major, op. 8 (1854 Version), Third Movement, mm. 1–12

The opening theme of the third movement seems also to derive from Scarlatti's Sonata. With regard to pitch sequence, the opening of the *Adagio* (ex. 2.9) is all but identical to a B-major transposition of Scarlatti's melody (divested of its trills). The sole discrepancy appears in m. 3, where Brahms omits Scarlatti's second scale degree and leaps instead to scale degree four before descending. Furthermore, the dominant pitch added to the theme in the Trio's first movement is now removed, and the final note of Scarlatti's phrase (the second scale degree), absent from the first two movements, finally reappears. The allusory phrase is now complete, even if the half-cadence with which it ends suggests a need for further resolution, just as, in "Am Meer," the protagonist's relationship with his beloved has come to an end, except perhaps in his thoughts.

Yet the work is becoming increasingly distant from its source, just as the protagonist suggested by the song references is becoming increasingly distant from his beloved. The opening of the *Adagio* may resemble that of Scarlatti's Sonata in some respects, but the character of the Sonata melody is thoroughly transformed here. The once-sprightly triple-meter theme has slowed dramatically and appears in quadruple meter, soft and *sempre legato* rather than loud and staccato, and in unequal note values. The new rhythm seems, in fact, to derive by diminution from that of the "Am Meer" reference, with which it also shares some melodic characteristics; compare mm. 1–3 and mm. 33 (third beat) –34 of Brahms's *Adagio*. The *Adagio*'s opening phrase, however, does not appear to be simply derivative of "Am Meer" and unrelated to Scarlatti's melody, but rather to meld aspects of both sources. The Adagio's opening theme, it is true, shares with the Schubert reference a certain rhythmic quality, a stepwise fourth descent followed by motion up a third, and a texture strikingly similar to that in Schubert's piano part. Still, the melody more closely parallels the theme from Scarlatti's Sonata due to the initial stepwise descent from the dominant to the tonic pitch and its concluding motion from the third to the second scale degree.)

In keeping with the sense of loss and despair conveyed by the text of the Schubert song about to be cited, the melody is now somber and solemn—perhaps even prayerful (note the chorale-like texture). It has also strayed about as far as possible from Scarlatti's theme without being totally unrecognizable as its derivative. Indeed, it is only in light of what we have observed in the first two movements that it might occur to us to consider a connection. The *Adagio*'s opening theme is a quiet reminiscence of what has come before, complete with the distortions and inaccuracies inherent to such recollections.

Further distortion occurs later in the movement. When the theme returns at m. 58, it is harmonized in unexpected ways. The left hand's contrary-motion ascent, which initially extended to only the first four melodic notes, now continues to the end of the phrase in direct contrast with the parallel-motion accompaniment Scarlatti assigned to his theme. In the next statement (mm. 58-68), Brahms effects both chromatic and modal shifts over the course of the phrase. When the theme returns at the close of the movement (m. 149), it remains in B major, but appears only in fragmented form—in the end, no longer departing from the fifth scale degree, but from the first (m. 151) and sixth (m. 152). Ultimately, what has been lost cannot be recaptured and is, in fact, becoming more and more difficult to recollect.

88 | *Allusion as Narrative Premise in Brahms*

Example 2.10. Piano Trio in B Major, op. 8 (1854 Version), Fourth Movement, mm. 1–17

Scarlatti's theme is relatively absent from the finale. If the finale's opening is in any way derivative of the Scarlatti theme, then it is certainly the least recognizable and most fragmented, frustrated rendition of that theme in the Trio. It contains Scarlatti's note repetition, but in a context so unstable that his scalar motion is impossible to achieve; instead, stepwise advancement occurs only chromatically, and by no more than one or two notes in either direction (ex. 2.10).

Later in the movement, as we know, Brahms alludes to "Nimm sie hin denn diese Lieder," an entreaty to the listener to recall and sing back earlier melodic material. Within the context of the Trio as a whole, the triple-meter, repeated-note scalar descents of Beethoven's theme—departing from the fifth scale degree as in Scarlatti's Sonata—perhaps hint at the melody we are to recall first and foremost, the one that seems to have served as the basis for so many themes in the piece. Yet the connection of these descents to Scarlatti's theme is again far more tenuous than are the resemblances cited in the first three movements. They never quite attain the melodic shape of Scarlatti's phrase as a whole, only hinting at it at best—and they evoke Scarlatti neither texturally, nor rhythmically, nor harmonically. (The closest resemblance is achieved at the end of the theme group [mm. 124–28], where—unlike before—only the third scale degree is repeated and the melodic descent reaches the first scale degree.) What most weakens the likelihood of their derivation from Scarlatti's Sonata, of course, is that they appear within the context of a clear allusion to an entirely different work. As if to depict the protagonist's distance from his beloved, Brahms has allowed the Scarlatti theme, once transfigured, to fade—mostly or entirely—out of the picture.[32] The loss of the beloved, as described in the texts of the cited songs and as represented by the loss of Scarlatti's phrase, seems to correspond to the sense of tragedy implied by the finale's unprecedented agitation and remarkable minor-mode ending.

A Secret Program?: The Trio as Lament

It has been proposed numerous times that the song references in the Trio represent Brahms's means of encoding the work with a covert expression of his own insatiable romantic longing for Clara Schumann—in other words, that Brahms, in conceiving his finale as a lament for Clara, not only borrows the musical content of the Beethoven reference in Schumann's op. 17 *Fantasie*, but also confers upon it essentially the same extramusical significance as that intended by Schumann. A secret meaning of this sort in op. 8, scholars have suggested, could have been intended for Clara herself or—more plausibly—allowed Brahms an outlet for "autobiographical fantasy" and was never intended to be fully understood by others.[33]

The Trio's broad progression of moods and characters—from the passion of the glorious opening theme to the more tentative character of the scherzo, the somberness of the slow movement, and the agitation of the finale—certainly does nothing to dispel the impression that the work is concerned with the ever-increasing distance between some protagonist and his beloved. And the story, it would appear, does not end happily. The Trio's restless, angst-filled finale is certainly appropriate in character for the portrayal of a love that is ultimately not to be fulfilled. The movement features choppy phrasing and several interruptions in momentum, a restricted melodic range (particularly in the refrain), chromaticism, uneven rhythms, dissonance, harmonic instability, and minor modality. Remarkably, the finale closes, as it began, in B minor, rather than reverting to the B-major tonality of the Trio's first movement, ostensibly the main key of the work. Walter Niemann proposes that "those who know how to read between the lines and notes might already find, hidden in this seething, simmering finale ... the whole story of Brahms's love and suffering. In it he has not surmounted his hopeless love: the end—the great coda—is all furious rage and despair."[34] For Malcolm MacDonald, the "soaring" reference to Beethoven's song in the exposition of the finale, "burgeoning soon into a love-duet for violin and cello, is incontrovertible evidence that the Trio contains intimate messages readable (at that time) only within the immediate Schumann circle."[35] Parmer is even more explicit, suggesting that the allusion to "Am Meer" presents "an equation of the 'lonely fisherman's house' [in the song text] with the Schumann household, the absent fisherman with Robert himself, the tearful woman with Clara, and the sympathetic listener with the young Brahms."[36] This particular parallel is problematic, as all evidence indicates that the Trio was essentially complete by the end of January 1854, and Robert Schumann's absence after being taken to Endenich did not occur until after his suicide attempt at the end of the following month.[37]

Nevertheless, the prominence of the Schumanns in Brahms's mind in January 1854 is unquestionable. Only the previous autumn, Brahms had had the life-altering experiences of making the Schumanns' acquaintance, being taken into their home and under Robert's wing, introduced by them to a number of prominent musical figures, and lauded by Robert in the *Neue Zeitschrift für Musik* as a savior of music, sprung forth "like Minerva fully armed from the head of Jove"—in short, as a musical god.[38] Even in January, the young composer's head must still have been swimming. Almost immediately upon departing from Düsseldorf, Brahms expressed his tremendous gratitude for Schumann's support—and indicated the considerable anxiety Schumann's praise had provoked: "You have made me so extremely happy that I cannot attempt to express my thanks in words. ... The public praise that you have deigned to bestow upon me will have so greatly increased the expectations of the musical world regarding my work that I do not know how I shall manage to do even approximate justice to it."[39] Brahms would struggle with this anxiety for many years to come, perhaps never entirely surmounting it. Although he had left Düsseldorf in November, Brahms was still in frequent contact with the Schumanns in the months following, and his correspondence from this period mentions, on multiple occasions, his intention to dedicate to Clara his F-sharp-Minor Piano Sonata (published as op. 2).[40] In mid-January, while Brahms was hard at work on the Trio, he and Joachim received a visit from the Schumanns, who had just returned from a trip to Holland.[41]

It is worth noting, as well, that the Trio is the only opus among Brahms's first ten not to bear a dedication. It is conceivable that Brahms avoided dedicating the work because he had Clara in mind while writing it and did not want to make this too explicit. Song references aside, following so quickly on the heels of op. 2, a second dedication to Clara may have aroused unwanted attention.[42] Dedicating the work to someone else, on the other hand, could have conflicted with his conception of the piece as some sort of statement for or about Clara.

The Trio's Scarlatti reference may, in fact, lend support to the idea that the work expresses Brahms's longing for Clara, as Brahms would have had good reason to associate her with Scarlatti's music. Clara incorporated Scarlatti sonatas into her concert repertory for many decades, from as early as the 1830s. All evidence indicates that she was both highly unusual and well-known for choosing to perform these pieces so consistently—to the extent that, in the introduction to his Scarlatti edition of 1839, Czerny singled her out for mention in this regard, writing, "in most recent times, Liszt and Clara Wieck have demonstrated, through public performance of [Scarlatti's] fugues and sonatas, how indestructible his values and brilliant impact remain."[43] (Based on what is known of the two performers' repertories, one can assume that Czerny is referring to Liszt when he mentions the fugues and to Clara when he mentions the sonatas.) The generally innovative nature of Clara's concert repertory is emphasized by, for instance, David Ferris and Nancy Reich, both of whom specifically characterize the programming of Scarlatti works as a notable departure from precedent and from the prevailing practice of Clara's time.[44] Although Moscheles played Scarlatti sonatas in a series of three soirées in 1837, and Liszt is known to have performed the "Cat's Fugue" (K. 30) the following year, these appear to be relatively isolated instances for each, and certainly exceptions to the usual tendencies in concert programming of the era.[45] Indeed, as Malcolm Boyd relates, pianists of the time "seem to have regarded Scarlatti's keyboard works mainly as pupil-fodder, or to have ignored them altogether. Those who could appreciate their musical qualities were often reluctant to include them in their recitals, and Chopin is even reported to have aroused censure when he gave his pupils the sonatas to work on. It seems that Scarlatti's music was seldom played in public during the nineteenth century."[46] The *Statistik der Concerte im Saale des Gewandhauses zu Leipzig*, for instance, lists no more than four such performances in the entire period between November 1781 and March 1881—and on two of these occasions, Clara herself was the one at the keyboard.[47] It is certainly possible that Clara and Brahms played or discussed Scarlatti's music together—perhaps even K. 159 in particular—during Brahms's stay with the Schumanns in the fall of 1853. And, as all evidence of Brahms's specific interest in Scarlatti seems to postdate the fall of 1853, it is also plausible that it was Clara herself who encouraged Brahms's enthusiasm for Scarlatti's music in the first place.[48]

A New Interpretation

Despite Clara's close relationship to the music of Scarlatti, however, the reference in Brahms's Trio strongly suggests another context for interpretation. Regarding the allusion to *An die ferne Geliebte* in Schumann's *Fantasie*, Christopher Reynolds asserts that perhaps modern-day interpreters, "informed by letters and diaries that Schumann's contemporaries could not have known, have been blinded by the resonances of the private message (i.e., Schumann's longing for Clara in the period before their marriage) to what Schumann's musically literate contemporaries might have read into this allusion."[49] In Beethoven's song cycle, "Nimm sie hin denn, diese Lieder" invites the listener not only to reconsider the happier times depicted in previous songs, but to recall the songs themselves and sing them back. Reynolds suggests that, by referencing Beethoven's song in the *Fantasie*, a work presented publicly as a tribute to that composer, Schumann "may have fulfilled the instruction to sing the poet's own song back to him as a way of achieving a musical—if not spiritual—union with Beethoven. In this public sense the allusion contains a message of lovers surmounting separation rather than longing."[50] If, as of early 1854, Brahms were unaware of the *Fantasie*'s secret program, this may well describe how he would have interpreted Schumann's allusion to *An die ferne Geliebte* in 1853–54.

Whether this was the case, and Brahms followed Schumann's example, or whether the idea occurred to Brahms even without this stimulus, Reynolds's interpretation of the *Fantasie* seems a particularly apt framework in which to view the surfacing of the same theme in Brahms's Trio. What if the beloved, distant entity lamented in the Trio is not Clara—represented by references to the Scarlatti repertory she loved and may have shared with Brahms—but instead Scarlatti himself, or perhaps, more broadly, what Scarlatti (and the fugato and, for that matter, Beethoven and Schubert) would have represented to Brahms: the musical past? Within the context of Brahms's Trio, by the time this material surfaces, the melodies or "songs" we have heard are none other than Scarlatti's K. 159 and related material, Schubert's "Am Meer," and "Nimm sie hin denn diese Lieder" itself—and Brahms, having inherited them, has just sung them back, just as the text of the last allusion commands. As we have seen, Brahms's handling of the Trio indeed suggests a scenario in which Scarlatti seems to recede irretrievably into the past. The near-exact quotation in the first movement—whose minor deviations from the original (including perhaps its initial placement a tritone away from Scarlatti's C major) still suggest Brahms's removal, in time and space, from his source—gives way to less similar, usually inverted statements in the scherzo. In the third movement, the allusion becomes a slow, nostalgic, and mournful quadruple-meter reminiscence without note repetition. Successive statements of the slow movement's opening phrase distort the material even further until, if present at all, it is reduced to nothing more than the agitated repeated neighbor-note figures at the opening of the finale. It is perhaps finally subsumed into the reference to *An die ferne Geliebte*, almost seeming to demonstrate Beethoven's absorption of the influences of his own predecessors. Is this Brahms singing Scarlatti's song back to him through the music of Beethoven, as paraphrased by Schumann? Brahms seems to acknowledge and accept his musical legacy, even while mourning its representative sources. His ultimate inability to satisfactorily bridge the distance between himself and the past may provide an explanation for the tragic nature of the work's conclusion.

Why would Brahms allude to Beethoven through music of Schumann? Perhaps this was simply his way of acknowledging the earlier allusion—possibly made with similar intent—in Schumann's *Fantasie*. Beyond that, though, by accepting the material from Schumann's hands, Brahms demonstrates, in music, the role Schumann played not only as a successor to Beethoven, but as a mentor, as a conduit, through which Brahms was delivered his musical legacy. In January 1854, still reeling from "*Neue Bahnen*" and all its implications, Brahms indeed had more reason than ever before to be thinking seriously of his relationship to the musical past, and of Schumann's role in clarifying and shaping this relationship.

Why might Brahms have chosen Scarlatti in particular as representative of the musical past? While Brahms had taken a particular interest in Scarlatti by early 1854, his interest in Bach and in Renaissance music, although surely present around the time of the Trio's composition, seems to have intensified slightly later, especially around 1856, during the period of his counterpoint exchange with Joachim.[51] Furthermore, as noted earlier, the resemblance of Scarlatti's theme to the calls of a post horn may suggest associations with distance and absence, themes suggested by the Schubert and Beethoven songs to which the 1854 version of the Trio also alludes.

The 1889 Revisions Revisited

This new interpretation receives further support from the circumstances surrounding the revisions Brahms made to the Trio decades after its composition. Brahms's correspondence with Joachim indicates that, even before the Trio was published in November 1854, the young composer was not entirely comfortable with the result of his efforts and would have liked to revise the piece.[52] He seems not to have indicated as much to his publisher, possibly because the revisions he had in mind would have been too time-consuming or because he did not have a clear sense of how he wanted to revise the piece. In 1888, however, when Simrock purchased the publication rights to the works—by then out of print—that Brahms had originally published with Breitkopf & Härtel, he offered Brahms the opportunity to revise any of these pieces, as he wished.[53] Brahms made substantial modifications to the B-major Trio alone.[54]

Brahms drastically revised the Trio in 1889, making three major alterations: he substituted entirely new second theme groups for those of the first, third, and fourth movements. The material he replaced, then, encompasses the two song references, as well as the Scarlatti allusion and its associated fugato. Identification of the Scarlatti reference thus seems to reveal for the first time that the portions Brahms replaced are *precisely* those containing the clearest allusions to the music of others—not just in the third and fourth movements, as has been recognized, but in the first movement as well. This strengthens the notion that Brahms's main objective in revising the work was to expunge borrowed material.[55]

To a point, motivation for the revisions should be considered in purely musical terms. If, in 1854, Brahms harbored insecurities about the work's musical integrity, then these doubts remained and, in fact, intensified in his mind over thirty-five years. After having revised the piece, Brahms expressed to Simrock his disdain for the original, stating simply that "the old one is bad" and adding that the work would "continue to sell poorly not because so much of it is ugly, but because so much of it is unnecessarily difficult."[56] In keeping with Brahms's own statement about the unnecessary difficulty of the original, many have cited the greater simplicity and tightness of structure as a benefit of the revisions.[57] Other stylistic benefits have been cited as well; Gardenal da Silva, for example, recognizing the interconnectedness of the various thematic materials in the original, emphasizes that the revised second theme groups afford greater variety and contrast than do the originals, and Margaret Notley observes that Brahms's revisions transform the "small, static gestures" of the original first movement into gestures that are "larger and more intense, more in keeping with the sweep of the opening theme."[58]

Despite any purely musical improvements the revisions may represent, when reworking the Trio, Brahms pointedly removed both of the song references, replacing them with entirely new themes; if the allusions did have some extramusical meaning, then, presumably, removal of the references would have some corresponding significance. Several scholars have suggested that the excision of the song references may signify Brahms's attempt to expunge his youthful characterization of Clara as "*ferne Geliebte*"—particularly as these allusions had recently been identified by critics and might seem suggestive. Ivor Keys conjectures that the allusions represented not only "a formal misfit," but also "an unbearable reminder" of Schumann's breakdown and of Brahms's unfulfilled relationship with Clara—while MacDonald suggests that, at the age of fifty-six, Brahms was embarrassed by the youthful confession of his feelings for Clara, and that this may explain why the material that replaces the allusion to "Nimm sie hin denn, diese Lieder" seems to "stamp out all memory" of the song.[59] Noting that by the time of the revision, both Schumann's and Brahms's references to "Nimm sie hin denn diese Lieder" had been observed in print, Hull suggests that Brahms may have feared it was only a matter of time before it occurred to some of his contemporaries that both allusions to the song "might be related, and connected to the most obvious link between the two men: their attachment to Clara."[60] Yet among those familiar with the version that had already circulated for decades, Brahms would only have drawn greater attention to the references by excising them. Furthermore, we must consider the attitude Brahms expressed about the original upon publication of the revisions.

Uncharacteristically, Brahms did not rescind the earlier version, writing to Simrock, with striking offhandedness: "What about the old edition? It really is unnecessary to discuss it or make a decision about it—I just think that it should not be advertised along with the new edition. If it is requested, send it, and if you find it necessary and advisable to reprint it one of these days, then go ahead (possibly allowing it to replace the new edition as well!). But this would be redundant."[61] If the revisions were motivated by fear that something hidden in the original would come to light, then why would Brahms have allowed it to be reissued, perhaps even in place of the new version? Brahms may also have felt that Simrock would not have kept the first version out of print even if Brahms had expressed a wish that he do so. Upon sending the revised version to the publisher, he writes "What you now do with the old one, whether you melt it down or print it anew is quite seriously all the same to me. Incidentally, it would also be useless to have a particular wish in that regard."[62]

Yet, if Brahms's attitude suggests he was not trying to *hide* the allusions or downplay their real or perceived meaning, then why would he remove the borrowings? At fifty-six, Brahms had ostensibly made some progress in coming to terms with his position in music history. Although he alluded to earlier composers even in late works, perhaps by 1889, he no longer felt a need to make so explicit his efforts to sing back to his predecessors the melodies they had left him—nor to make these the central concern of a multimovement work. In retrospect, his use of Beethoven's song to suggest that this is what he was doing may have struck him as immature in its lack of subtlety. In 1889, Brahms was certainly not about to revise all of his earlier works simply to infuse them with the spirit of his current self, but what better piece to rework than one conceived as an emerging composer's self-conscious representation of his relationship to his predecessors? Furthermore, the revisions coincide precisely with a point in his career at which critics had begun to suggest that Brahms's creative powers were ebbing.[63] It is even possible that, in supplanting the work's allusory materials with new, more thoroughly original themes, the aging Brahms hoped on some level to demonstrate (whether to critics who had become aware of the allusions, or simply to himself) that he was capable of even greater artistic independence and original inspiration than that which he exhibited at the age of twenty—and thus to counter what Notley refers to as "the notion that the composer had entered a final period of creative decline."[64]

Even in 1854, Brahms's reservations about the Trio, while surely stemming at least in part from purely structural considerations, may have had something to do with his mixed feelings about the allusions the work contained and, perhaps, a fear that their message was too pronounced; even in the original version of the Trio, he seems somewhat secretive about the source of his inspiration. As we have seen, clear statements of the Scarlatti phrase occur only in one short passage of one movement, and each individual statement in that passage is quite rapid. Brahms lifts the veil on the source of his inspiration for only a fleeting moment, much as the borrowed theme seems to pervade the rest of the work in more subtle ways. Perhaps, during the 1850s, his ambivalence over the influence of past masters even had something to do with the fact that essentially all of the explicitly Baroque-style works he composed during the 1850s—including gavottes, gigues, and sarabandes—remained unpublished for many years (in quite a few cases, until after his death).[65] The young Brahms's mixed feelings about his debts to pre-existing works seem also to be indicated by such things as his infamously suspicious denial, in 1853, that his Scherzo, op. 4, was inspired by music of Chopin.[66]

Although Brahms removed the allusions themselves in revising the Trio, he did leave traces of the Scarlatti theme embedded in the final version. The basic melodic materials of the various first theme groups and refrains, most of which are related to the borrowing, all remain in place. Yet, with the removal of the first movement's more explicit evocation of K. 159, it would never reasonably occur to anyone to connect this material to the source from which it seems actually to have derived. Even in 1889, then, Scarlatti's influence may be felt, but by then so subtly as to remain nearly undetectable even to one who subjects the piece to intense study.

Perhaps the Trio really is a young man's expression of love for an unattainable woman. But perhaps it is his mournful acknowledgement of the distance between himself and the ultimately unresurrectable past, an outgrowth of his youthful struggle to reconcile his own position in history during a time when that issue had become especially pressing. The situation may represent some intermingling of the two that was not clear to Brahms himself. Although, in the end, we can never be sure precisely what Brahms had in mind—nor on what level of consciousness—while composing the Trio, the work's allusions certainly remain suggestive given the circumstances in which the young composer found himself at the dawn of 1854.

Notes

1. Schumann's article appeared in the *Neue Zeitschrift für Musik* on October 28, 1853.
2. According to Max Kalbeck [*Johannes Brahms*, 4th ed. (Berlin: Deutsche Brahms-Gesellschaft, 1921; repr. Tutzing: Hans Schneider, 1976), 1:149], Brahms began work on the Trio in the summer of 1853 while visiting the Rhineland, "sketches for his four movements

were already underway in Mehlem and Düsseldorf," and January 1854 was merely the month of the work's completion. We have no way of knowing what form the piece might have taken in its earliest stages, however, as there are no surviving sketches [Walter Frisch, *Brahms and the Principle of Developing Variation* (Berkeley: University of California Press, 1984), 56].

3. Hans Gál, editor's commentary in Johannes Brahms, *Complete Piano Trios* (1926; repr., Mineola, NY: Dover Publications, Inc., 1988), v. For corroboration of the work's completion (or near-completion) by this time—an issue the significance of which will become apparent later—see also Styra Avins's editorial note in *Johannes Brahms: Life and Letters*, ed. Styra Avins, trans. Josef Eisinger and Styra Avins (New York: Oxford University Press, 1997), 37. We know that Brahms first performed the work at the piano for Clara and others in March 1854 and that the following month, she participated in what appears to have been the Trio's first performance, albeit a private one. See Berthold Litzmann, *Clara Schumann: An Artist's Life, Based on Material found in Diaries and Letters*, trans. and abridged from the 4th ed. by Grace E. Hadow, with a preface by W. H. Hadow (1913; repr., New York: Vienna House, 1972), 2:67–69. By mid-June, Brahms had made arrangements with Breitkopf & Härtel for the Trio's publication. See *Johannes Brahms: Life and Letters*, 46–47: letter from Brahms to Joseph Joachim, Düsseldorf, June 19, 1854.

4. Hermann Kretzschmar first remarked upon this allusion in print during Brahms's lifetime. See Kenneth Ross Hull, "Brahms the Allusive: Extra Compositional Reference in the Instrumental Music of Johannes Brahms" (Ph.D. diss., Princeton University, 1989), 25, n. 3. Kalbeck also acknowledged this song reference, now generally accepted, in *Johannes Brahms*, 1:155.

5. See, for instance, Malcolm MacDonald, *Brahms*, Master Musicians Series, ed. Stanley Sadie (Oxford: Oxford University Press, 2001; originally published in 1990 by Schirmer Books), 78–79.

6. See Christopher Alan Reynolds, *Motives for Allusion: Context and Content in Nineteenth-Century Music* (Cambridge, MA: Harvard University Press, 2003), 126; Hull, "Brahms the Allusive," 89; and Ivor Keys, *Brahms Chamber Music* (Seattle, WA: University of Washington Press, 1974), 45.

7. This thematic reminiscence was remarked upon in print by Mandyczewski as early as 1890. See Roger Moseley, "Brief Immortality: Recasting History in the Music of Brahms" (PhD diss., University of California, Berkeley, 2004), 49. This allusion, too, was recognized by Kalbeck, *Johannes Brahms*, 1:152.

8. Translation adapted from that given in Dillon Parmer, "Brahms, Song Quotation, and Secret Programs," *19th-Century Music* 19/2 (1995): 183. Brahms's treatment of "*Am Meer*" may evoke some of the specific images conjured up by the text, particularly the flowing of water (see, e.g., mm. 101–14) and crying (e.g., the cello writing in the passage beginning at m. 115). In passages such as the one beginning in m. 42, the texture is evocative of a love duet. See also Eric Sams, "Brahms and His Clara Themes," *The Musical Times* 112/1539 (1971): 433.

9. This chapter is based on that article: Jacquelyn Sholes, "Lovelorn Lamentation or Histrionic Historicism? Reconsidering Allusion and Extra-Musical meaning in the 1954 Version of Brahms's B-Major Trio," *19th-Century Music* 34/1 (2010), 61–86.

10. The material in the Trio that I identify as allusive to Scarlatti also bears some resemblance to the opening of Paganini's Caprice in E Major, op. 1/9. Although it certainly possible that Brahms had Paganini in mind as well, this passage of the Trio resembles Scarlatti's theme much more closely than it does Paganini's with respect to meter and rhythm. As

we shall see, the likelihood of a direct connection to Scarlatti is further strengthened by Brahms's pairing of the apparent allusion with music that is distinctly evocative of the Baroque Era and by what is otherwise known of Brahms's close involvement with the music of Scarlatti.

11. Thanks to Eric Chafe and Bruce Brown for their suggestions to this effect in personal communications with the author.

12. The relationship between the Trio's opening and the theme of Scarlatti's Sonata is addressed in greater detail below.

13. Malcolm Boyd, *Domenico Scarlatti—Master of Music* (New York: Schirmer Books, 1986), 219.

14. Avins, editorial note in *Johannes Brahms: Life and Letters*, 38. The italicization is my own.

15. See *Letters of Clara Schumann and Johannes Brahms, 1853–1896*, ed. Berthold Litzmann (1927; repr., New York: Vienna House, 1973) 2:75: letter to Clara Schumann, December 4 [i.e., 5], 1856.

16. See Robert Schumann, *On Music and Musicians*, trans. Paul Rosenfeld, ed. Konrad Wolff (New York: Pantheon, 1946; repr. W. W. Norton, 1969), 87–88.

17. See *Johannes Brahms and Theodor Billroth: Letters from a Musical Friendship*, ed. and trans. Hans Barkan (Norman, OK: University of Oklahoma Press, 1957), 153: letter from Brahms to Theodor Billroth, May 8, 1885.

18. See *Johannes Brahms: The Herzogenberg Correspondence* ed. Max Kalbeck, trans. Hannah Bryant (London: John Murray, 1909; repr., New York: Vienna House, 1971), 225: letter from Brahms to Heinrich and Elisabeth von Herzogenberg, Vienna, May 6, 1885.

19. See Johannes Brahms et al., *Briefwechsel*, ed. Max Kalbeck, 4th ed. 16 vols. (Berlin: Deutsche Brahms-Gesellschaft, 1921; repr. Tutzing: Hans Schneider, 1974), 6:289: letter from Joseph Joachim to Brahms, Berlin, April 12, [1894].

20. See Franzpeter Goebels, "Scarlattiana: Bemerkungen zur Scarlatti-Rezeption von Johannes Brahms," *Musica* 40/4 (1986), 322; and Florence May, *The Life of Johannes Brahms*, 2nd ed., enlarged and illustrated (1905; repr., Neptune City, NJ: Paganiniana Publications, Inc., 1981), 1:39.

21. See Goebels, "Scarlattiana," 320–22. Interestingly, on April 7, 1867, in Vienna, Brahms performed a program that featured Schumann's C-Major *Fantasie*, op. 17, alongside works by Beethoven and Schubert, a Scarlatti fugue, a Bach toccata, and Brahms's own Variations and Fugue on a Theme by G. F. Handel, op. 24 (Goebels, 320–22 and May, *The Life of Johannes Brahms*, 2:388). This combination indicates especially clearly his lingering preoccupation with the same group of sources—in one case, precisely the same work—upon which he appeared to have drawn thirteen years earlier while composing op. 8. It also pairs these sources with as explicit a demonstration as possible of his interest in modeling original material upon specific works of earlier—and particularly Baroque—composers. See also May, *The Life of Johannes Brahms*, 1:5–6 and Renate and Kurt Hofmann, *Johannes Brahms als Pianist und Dirigent: Chronologie seines Wirkens als Interpret* (Tutzing: Hans Schneider, 2006), 368.

22. See Goebels, "Scarlattiana," 326; and Paul Mast, "Brahms's Study, *Oktaven und Quinten u.a.*: With Schenker's Commentary Translated," *Music Forum* 5 (1980), 2–196. Margaret Notley provides a detailed discussion of Brahms's "Oktaven und Quinten" in "Music Pedagogy, Musicology, and Brahms's Collection of Octaves and Fifths: Historical Decline, Personal Renewal," chapter 4 of her book, *Lateness and Brahms: Music and Culture in the Twilight of Viennese Liberalism* (New York: Oxford University Press, 107–43.

23. The Scarlatti examples are Nos. 37–39 and 101–7. See Mast, "Brahms's Study," 55, 117, 118, and 121). Brahms refers to each sonata in Examples 101–5 by its number in the Czerny edition. See Mast, "Brahms's Study," 117, n. 114. The other four composers represented in Brahms's study by at least ten examples each are J. S. Bach (from whose works well over twenty examples are drawn), Mozart (thirteen examples), Marenzio (twelve), and Beethoven (eleven). Of the remaining twenty-seven composers, none is represented in more than four examples.

24. See Boyd, *Domenico Scarlatti*, 221 and Goebels, "Scarlattiana," 327, respectively.

25. Predictably, this has led to speculation, none of which is particularly relevant to the meaning of the allusion in the Trio. The most pertinent interpretation is that of Paul Berry (*Brahms among Friends: Listening, Performance, and the Rhetoric of Allusion* [Oxford: Oxford University Press, 2014], 221–24), who reads the allusion as one intended for Clara Schumann. See also Hull, "Brahms the Allusive," 21; and Eric Sams, *The Songs of Johannes Brahms* (New Haven, CT: Yale University Press, 2000), 245.

26. See Frisch, *Brahms and the Principle of Developing Variation*, 57–60; Fabio Roberto Gardenal da Silva, "Brahms' [sic] Piano Trio op. 8, in B Major: A Comparison between the Early (1854) and Late (1860) [sic] Versions," (PhD diss., New York University, 1993)," 52–53; and Antonio Baldassarre, "Johannes Brahms and Johannes Kreisler: Creativity and Aesthetics of the Young Brahms Illustrated by the Piano Trio in B Major, op. 8," *Acta Musicologica* 72/2 (2000): 159–60.

27. Baldassarre, "Johannes Brahms and Johannes Kreisler," 160.

28. Kalbeck, *Johannes Brahms*, 1:153. (Furthermore, Kalbeck identifies, here, basic correspondences between the Trio's fundamental motive and motives from the finale of Brahms's Horn Trio, op. 40 (composed 1865), the death march from the German Requiem, op. 45 (composed 1865-68), Brahms's two-voice setting of the "Edward" Ballade, op. 75, no. 1 (composed 1877), and "Dort in den Weiden," a traditional Lower-Rhenish folksong arranged by Brahms sometime before 1886, when it was published as his op. 97, no. 4.) Although Kalbeck does not elaborate much on his general statement, he does observe an apparent derivation of the slow movement's opening theme from the second and third complete measures of the first movement (1:154). The idea that multiple movements of the Trio are subtly derived from one basic thematic idea has been echoed in, for instance, Gerald Abraham, *A Hundred Years of Music*, 4th ed. (London: Duckworth, 1974), 165; Sams, "Brahms and His Clara Themes," 433; Frisch, *Brahms and the Principle*, 51; Baldassarre, "Johannes Brahms and Johannes Kreisler," 150, 164–65; and Peter H. Smith, *Expressive Forms in Brahms's Instrumental Music: Structure and Meaning in His Werther Quartet* (Bloomington: Indiana University Press, 2005), 27. Sams actually suggests that the Trio may be "the first monothematic chamber work." Da Silva has identified the Trio's thematic connections somewhat more thoroughly than most in "Brahms' [sic] Piano Trio op. 8, in B Major," 52, 53–54 (his Examples 2 and 3), 69.

29. Not surprisingly, those who have noticed the connections between the movement's various themes usually view the situation from the opposite perspective—as the derivation of all secondary themes from the opening subject of the movement. See da Silva, "Brahms' [sic] Piano Trio op. 8, in B Major," 52 and 113–14. Donald Francis Tovey views the sequential passage beginning in m. 396 not as the revelation of a source for earlier thematic material, but rather as nothing more than ostentatious development of the movement's opening theme, the result of an inexperienced composer's attempt to create a climax on that theme. See his "Brahms's Chamber Music," in *The Main Stream of Music and Other Essays*, ed. Hubert J. Foss (New York: Oxford University Press, 1949), 227.

30. For more on the development, see Sholes, "Lovelorn Lamentation or Histrionic Historicism?," 73–74.

31. In a paper entitled "Brahms and the 'Angel of History': A Critical Reading of the Revision of the Trio, op. 8," delivered in New York City on March 23, 2012 at the *Brahms in the New Century* conference sponsored by the American Brahms Society, Benjamin Korstvedt pointed out the similarity between this fugue theme and the fourth of Schumann's op. 60 fugues on the name "BACH" (which can be spelled musically with the notes B-flat [i.e., B in German]—A–C–B [i.e., H in German]).

32. Although he does not identify a Scarlatti quotation in the piece, da Silva ("Brahms' [*sic*] Piano Trio op. 8, in B Major," 79) does comment generally that in the finale, "no [intra-movement] thematic derivation or integration exists in the sense encountered in the previous movements. Also, there is no integration in the broader realm of intermovement thematic relationship. The key relationships between the themes (B minor, F-sharp major, E-flat major) also [do] not correspond to anything found before in the piece. In other words, this movement … is the least integrated in the overall form of the Trio."

33. The term "autobiographical fantasy" has been applied in this context by Sams in "Brahms and His Clara Themes," 434. On the practice of "private" allusion in nineteenth-century music, see Hull, "Brahms the Allusive," 239–40.

34. Walter Niemann, *Brahms*, trans. Catherine Alison Phillips, 4th printing (New York: Alfred A. Knopf, 1941; originally published in 1920 in Berlin by Schuster & Loeffler), 267.

35. MacDonald, *Brahms*, 79.

36. Parmer, "Brahms, Song Quotation, and Secret Programs," 184. Parmer admits that there is no clear evidence to support this interpretation.

37. Similarly problematic in this regard (and in terms of musical evidence) is Eric Sams's suggestion ("Brahms and His Clara Themes," 433) that Brahms deliberately depicts parallels between his own biographical circumstances and the plot of Schumann's opera *Genoveva* by referencing specific passages from the opera in the Trio.

38. Schumann, "*Neue Bahnen*," as translated in Florence May, *The Life of Johannes Brahms*, 1:132.

39. See *Letters of Clara Schumann and Johannes Brahms*, 1:1: letter to Robert Schumann, Hanover, November 16, 1853.

40. From Leipzig in the mid-to-late November 1853, Brahms writes to Albert Dietrich, "Would Frau Schumann take it unkindly if I dedicated the F-sharp-minor sonata to her? Do write to me about it" (*Johannes Brahms: Life and Letters*, 25). On the twenty-ninth of that month, now in Hanover, Brahms writes to Robert Schumann, "May I set your wife's name at the head of my second work? I hardly dare, and yet I should like so much to give you a small token of my reverence and gratitude" (*Johannes Brahms: Life and Letters*, 27–28). Clearly, she had already won a special place in his heart, whether or not the feelings he had for her were consciously amorous at this time.

41. Avins, editorial note in *Johannes Brahms: Life and Letters*, 36. See also Litzmann, *Clara Schumann: An Artist's Life*, 2:50–51 and May, *The Life of Johannes Brahms*, 1:161.

42. He would also dedicate to Clara his op. 9, a set of variations on a theme by her husband, written in the summer of 1854.

43. Cited in Goebels, "Scarlattiana," 320.

44. See David Ferris, "Public Performance and Private Understanding," *Journal of the American Musicological Society* 56/2 (2003): 351–52, 377, 384–85; and Nancy B. Reich, *Clara Schumann: The Artist and the Woman* (Ithaca, NY: Cornell University Press, 2001), 253.

45. See Emil Smidak, *Isaak-Ignaz Moscheles: The Life of the Composer and His Encounters with Beethoven, Liszt, Chopin, and Mendelssohn* (Aldershot, Hampshire: Scolar Press, 1989), 115; and Alan Walker, *Franz Liszt* (New York: Alfred A. Knopf, 1983), 1:256.

46. Boyd, *Domenico Scarlatti*, 219.

47. *Statistik der Concerte im Saale des Gewandhauses zu Leipzig* (published, separately paginated, as the final 104 pages of Alfred Dörffel, *Geschichte der Gewandhausconcerte zu Leipzig vom 25. November 1781 bis 25. November 1881, im Auftrage der Concert-Direction verfasst von Alfred Dörffel* (Leipzig: [Breitkopf & Härtel], 1884), 62 and 91.

48. Goebels suggests this as well in "Scarlattiana," 320.

49. Reynolds, *Motives for Allusion*, 126.

50. Reynolds, *Motives for Allusion*, 127. Reynolds asserts here that this is precisely the message behind Schumann's allusion to the same song in "Singet nicht in Trauertönen," op. 98a/7 (written in 1849 and published in 1851). (See *Motives for Allusion*, 143–44.) Brahms's own quotation is usually likened to the allusion in the *Fantasie*, op. 17. Quotations of the same melody are in fact generally acknowledged in several other Schumann works, including "Süsser Freund," op. 42/6 (1840); the string quartet, op. 41/2 (1842); and the Second Symphony, op. 61 (1845–46). See Hull, "Brahms the Allusive," 63.

51. Thanks to Daniel Beller-McKenna for pointing this out to me. See David Brodbeck, "The Brahms-Joachim Counterpoint Exchange, or, Robert, Clara, and 'the Best Harmony between Jos. and Joh.," in *Brahms Studies. I.*, ed. David Lee Brodbeck (Lincoln: University of Nebraska, 1994), 30–80. See also Virginia Hancock, *Brahms's Choral Compositions and His Library of Early Music* (Ann Arbor, MI: UMI Research Press, 1983).

52. On one occasion, Brahms mentions his desire to change "a few things" in the work. See *Johannes Brahms: Life and Letters*, 44: letter to Joachim, Düsseldorf, April 1, 1854. After submitting it to his publisher, he notes that he would have liked to hold on to the manuscript a bit longer as he "would certainly have made changes in it later." See *Johannes Brahms: Life and Letters*, 47: letter to Joachim, Düsseldorf, June 19, 1854.

53. Gardenal da Silva, "Brahms' Piano Trio op. 8, in B Major," 87.

54. At first, Brahms had considered reworking the F-Minor Sonata, op. 5, as well, but he did not follow through on this (MacDonald, *Brahms*, 338).

55. See Sams, "Brahms and his Clara Themes," 434; Hull, "Brahms the Allusive," 237; and Moseley, "Brief Immortality," 50.

56. *Johannes Brahms: Life and Letters*, 678: letter to Fritz Simrock, Vienna, December 13, 1890.

57. For detailed comparisons of the two versions, which are largely beyond the scope of this discussion, see for instance Edwin Evans, *Handbook to the Chamber and Orchestral Music of Johannes Brahms* (London: W. Reeves, 1912; repr. New York: Burt Franklin, 1970), 1:14–15; Niemann, *Brahms*, 266; Tovey, "Brahms's Chamber Music," 220–30; Ivor Keys, *Johannes Brahms* (Portland, OR: Amadeus Press, 1989), 195; *Brahms Chamber Music*, 48–49; Gero Ehlert, liner notes for Johannes Brahms, *Complete Piano Trios*, vol. 3, Trio Parnassus, Musikproduktion Dabringhaus und Grimm MDG 303 0657-2, trans. Susan Marie Praeder, 10; da Silva, "Brahms' [sic] Piano Trio op. 8, in B Major," especially 112, 113, 115–18, 141–42; MacDonald, *Brahms*, 79–80; Baldassarre, "Johannes Brahms and Johannes Kreisler," 163, 166; and Margaret Notley, "Discourse and Allusion: The Chamber Music of Brahms," in *Nineteenth-Century Chamber Music*, ed. Stephen E. Hefling (New York: Schirmer, 1998), 244–46, 271–72. See also Ernst Herttrich, "Johannes Brahms—Klaviertrio H-Dur Opus 8: Frühfassung und Spätfassung: Ein Analytischer Vergleich," in *Musik, Edition, Interpretation: Gedenkschrift Günter Henle*, ed. Martin Bente (München: G. Henle Verlag, 1980), 218–36;

Robert Mayerovitch, "Brahms's Stylistic Evolution: A Comparison of the 1854 and 1891 Versions of the B-Major Piano Trio, op. 8" (DM diss., Indiana University, 1986); and Franz Zaunschirm, *Der Frühe und der Späte Brahms: Eine Fallstudie anhand der Autographen Korrekturen und Gedruckten Fassungen zum Trio Nr. 1 für Klavier, Violine und Violoncello Opus 8*, Schiftenreihe zur Musik, 26 (Hamburg: Wagner, 1988). See also Adolf Schubring's critique of the 1854 version, originally published in the *Neue Zeitschrift für Musik* 56 (1862), appearing in English translation by Walter Frisch in "Five Early Works by Brahms," in *Brahms and His World*, 116–18, as well as Christopher Kent Thompson, "Brahms and the Problematizing of Traditional Sonata Form" (PhD diss., University of Wisconsin, Madison, 1996), 152–91.

58. da Silva, "Brahms' [sic] Piano Trio op. 8, in B Major," for example 112 and 118, and Notley, "Discourse and Allusion," 271–72.

59. Keys, "Brahms Chamber Music," 45; and MacDonald, *Brahms*, 341.

60. Hull, "Brahms the Allusive," 237–38. See also Moseley, "Brief Immortality," 48–50.

61. Brahms to Fritz Simrock, Vienna, December 29, 1890, in Brahms, *Briefwechsel*, ed. Max Kalbeck (originally published in 1919 by the Deutsche Brahms-Gesellschaft; repr. Tutzing: Hans Schneider, 1974), 12:38–39. The translation given here is based on those presented in Parmer, "Brahms, Song Quotation, and Secret Programs," 182–83 and Baldassarre, "Johannes Brahms and Johannes Kreisler," 166.

62. Brahms to Fritz Simrock, Vienna, December 13, 1890, in *Johannes Brahms: Life and Letters*, 678.

63. Notley, *Lateness and Brahms*, 48–49. Citing, for instance, August Göllerich's 1889 appraisal of Brahms as an "undoubtedly a gifted, only all too brooding talent who has left behind him the period of his best inspirations," she observes that "a perception that Brahms's creativity was waning must have become widespread, since Schenker felt moved to counter it in an 1891 review." Göllerich's review, translated here by Notley, originally appeared in the *Deutsches Volksblatt* on February 9, 1889. Heinrich Schenker's review, entitled "Johannes Brahms: Fünf Lieder für eine Singstimme mit Pianoforte, op. 107," appeared in *Musikalisches Wochenblatt* 22 (1891), 514.

64. Notley, *Lateness and Brahms*, 49.

65. These pieces are catalogued as WoO 3-5 (1854–55). Additional Baroque-style organ works were composed slightly later and cataloged as WoO 7–10. On these pieces, and on the influence of earlier historical periods on Brahms's writing during this time, see Robert Pascall, *Brahms Beyond Mastery: His Saraband and Gavotte, and Its Recompositions* (Burlington, VT: Ashgate, 2013) and Brodbeck, "The Brahms-Joachim Counterpoint Exchange," especially 49–54.

66. See Hull, "Brahms the Allusive," 27, n. 13.

3 Musical Memory and the D-Major Serenade, op. 11

THE D-MAJOR SERENADE, op. 11 (1857–58), is the first orchestral work that Brahms was to complete. Despite the fact that it represents a major milestone in his career, the Serenade has been the subject of relatively little serious analytical writing, and much remains to be said about the relationship between historical reference and intermovement connections in this work. As we will see, the last main theme to be introduced in the piece recalls the Serenade's initial melody, but with smoother rhythms, streamlined melodic motion, and clarified harmonic content; the recapitulatory statement of this finale theme in some ways represents a more satisfying recapitulation of the work's opening than we find in the first movement itself; and this recollection in the finale is, in fact, the culmination of a gradual process involving the inner movements as well. This chapter aims to demonstrate that not only does the Serenade carry historicist associations simply by virtue of its genre and general style, but the relationship between the thematic materials involved in this particular work and those in the final movement of Haydn's last symphony, especially when considered in light of the fact that Brahms once intended op. 11 to be his own first symphony, may furthermore suggest a parallel between the work's ongoing concern with recalling its initial theme and Brahms's own preoccupation with the past.

The Serenade as Historicist Work

Scholars and critics from Brahms's own time to the present have frequently taken the opportunity to observe that his op. 11, in its genre and with its prominent pastoral winds and rustic drones, makes deliberate reference to the eighteenth century, evoking the folk-tinged, witty spirit of Haydn in particular.[1] Indeed, the nineteenth century itself saw the composition of relatively few orchestral serenades; Brahms's are among the best known of these.[2] The strong Classicist influences in the D-Major Serenade may reflect Brahms's study of the orchestral music of Haydn and of Mozart's wind serenades, as well as the fine wind playing of the court orchestra at Detmold, where Brahms was employed as pianist, teacher, and conductor during the time of the work's composition.[3] Particularly

104 | *Allusion as Narrative Premise in Brahms*

in light of the fact that, at one point during the work's composition, Brahms clearly conceived of the Serenade as a "symphony-serenade" or simply as a symphony, it would not be surprising if he had had one or more specific symphonic models in mind.[4] Although passages of the Serenade have frequently been identified as reminiscent of specific works of Beethoven (especially Symphonies One, Two, and Six; the Septet; and the "Spring" Sonata) and of Schubert and Schumann, the piece has been associated more consistently and more frequently with Haydn than with any of these nineteenth-century composers—not only in terms of general style, but with regard to one symphonic work in particular.[5] As early as 1863, Theodor Billroth wrote, after hearing the work at its Zurich premiere, that the Serenade's "main theme is indeed quite good, but little new, and it is, to us, as if we had heard in any one of the symphonies of Haydn something entirely similar."[6] Indeed, in the years that have followed, most have come to agree that Brahms's Serenade evokes the final movement of another D-major work, Haydn's Symphony No. 104 (the "London" Symphony).[7] We will explore this issue more thoroughly later in the chapter. Meanwhile, let us turn to some aspects of the Serenade's intermovement motivic construction that will prove important in this regard.

The Finale's Second Theme as Recollection of the First Theme of the Serenade

For reference, I present an outline of the finale's basic structure (table 3.1). The movement takes the form of a rondo (Brahms's designation) with a single episodic theme to contrast with the refrain, but it can also be viewed as a sonata-rondo in which the second theme group is recapitulated before the first. Although "rondo" and "sonata-rondo" are both valid designations for the movement's structure, the sonata-oriented framework will be most useful for our purposes in this chapter. This is due to the ways in which the recapitulatory function of the latter part of the movement operates with respect to the rest of the final movement and resonates with the work's sonata-form first movement and with the work as a whole.

The recapitulation of the finale's second theme recalls the Serenade's opening in terms of texture and orchestration. At the recapitulation the horn returns, for the first time in the finale, to its original role as lone melodic instrument and, in the viola and cello, the melody is supported by the same open-fifth drone heard at the beginning of the work. The finale's recapitulatory statement also brings a return of the sustained trill heard on the same pitch in the opening theme's exposition but absent from its recapitulation.

Yet, although it has gone largely, if not entirely, unremarked, the resemblance between the work's opening and the second theme of the finale (i.e., the first and last substantial melodies introduced in the work) is not limited

Table 3.1. Brahms, Serenade No. 1 in D Major, op. 11 (1857–58), Sixth Movement: Basic Structure

Exposition:	A (mm. 1-71; D major)
	B (mm. 71-110; A major)
Development:	A' (mm. 110-41; begins in D major, ends in C major)
	Developmental episode (mm. 142-88; begins in C major, ends in D minor; comprised of material derived from sections A and B)
Recapitulation:	B' (mm. 189-238; D major)
	A" (mm. 238-328; moves from D minor to B-flat major before arriving in D major)
Coda: (mm. 328-53; D major)	

merely to tonality, texture, and orchestration: there is also a strong *thematic* correspondence (ex. 3.1). When stated in D major in the finale's recapitulation, the pitch sequence that begins the finale's second theme is nearly identical to that heard in the opening melody of the Serenade. In both cases, in the same register, the line descends from the fifth to the first scale degree, primarily by stepwise motion, but with a skip between the fourth and second degrees (mm. 6–7 of the first movement and 190–91 of the sixth). In both movements, this is followed by a downward leap to the fifth scale degree, upward motion to D and E, a leap back down to A, and then continuation of the upward motion, from E to F-sharp.

The finale's second theme is recapitulated before its first, and even when the movement's initial theme does return subsequently, Brahms seems to underplay the significance of that event as a factor in the resolution of tensions, a circumstance that contributes to our sense that it is, indeed, the recapitulation of the finale's second theme that brings the most satisfying sense of return. Although the movement's second theme is recapitulated in the tonic, that key is deliberately withheld from the beginning of the first theme's return: just as the refrain theme arrives, the music shifts to the parallel minor (m. 238) and then to B-flat major (mm. 241–42) before finally arriving back at D major. Arrival on the tonic harmony itself is delayed until eleven measures into the refrain. Furthermore, as the refrain progresses, the subdominant becomes increasingly prominent, ultimately supplanting D major as the key of the refrain's final thematic material (mm. 298–317). D returns only for the final cadential measures preceding the coda.

Recognizing the second theme of the finale as a version of the Serenade's opening melody may help us to explain the reversal of the first and second themes in the finale's recapitulation. The finale's second theme seems to usurp the role of its first not only in the recapitulation, but also in the closing section of the work,

106 | *Allusion as Narrative Premise in Brahms*

Example 3.1a–b. Serenade No. 1 in D Major, op. 11
(a) First movement, mm. 1–16

(b) Sixth Movement, mm. 189–98

where the second theme is reinvoked, while the first, a more traditional source for coda material, is not. By placing the movement's second theme at the head of the recapitulation, Brahms perhaps acknowledges that the theme is, in some sense, a *first* theme—that of the work as a whole.

Nevertheless, the finale's second theme is in some ways significantly distinct from the melody that opens the work. The two themes differ in rhythmic content, for example. In contrast with the more unsettled dotted quarters and syncopated upbeats of the original theme, the finale adopts a stable quarter-eighth-eighth rhythm, while the occasional melodic triplet helps to smooth transitions between subphrases. Furthermore, in the finale, the melody begins with a triumphant octave leap upward, and the third scale degree is eliminated from the head motive so that the line moves directly downward: $\hat{5}$-$\hat{3}$-$\hat{5}$-$\hat{4}$-$\hat{2}$-$\hat{3}$-$\hat{1}$ becomes $\hat{5}$-$\hat{4}$-$\hat{2}$-$\hat{1}$. In removing the third scale degree from the span between the fifth and first, the finale's version not only simplifies and streamlines the gesture, but also removes ambiguities, present at the outset of the work, as to which notes of the melody are principal ones, and which are merely decorative—that is, as to where the governing harmony is dominant and where it is tonic. The finale's recapitulation thus not only recalls the opening of the work, but also brings a smoothing of rhythmic tensions, facilitation of melodic motion, and clarification of harmonic content.

The Finale as Resolving Tensions Left Unresolved in the First-Movement Recapitulation

The melody's long-awaited return, in the original key and near-original texture and orchestration, represents a recapitulation on a grand scale. Indeed, the finale's recapitulation of its version of the Serenade's opening in some respects compensates for the shortcomings of the first movement's own recapitulation of the original theme and for the disintegration of that theme at the first movement's close.

The initial movement, in fact, scarcely contains a proper, tonic-key recapitulation of the Serenade's opening. Although the harmony leading into the recapitulation (mm. 357ff. in ex. 3.2) is the dominant-seventh of D, the thematic return does not coincide with resolution to the tonic. The avoidance of D major at this juncture is all the more striking in light of the fact that the development ends in the parallel minor—so the tonic key is not merely evaded here, but is actually a point of departure. Instead, at the expected moment of resolution, the seventh is added to the D major harmony, rendering the prolonged chord a dominant-seventh in G; thus, Brahms elides the tonic and subdominant keys at the point of recapitulation. The incongruousness of the original melodic pitch sequence and the new harmonic context here gives us the feeling that things are not as they should be. The theme is then restated in the clarinet, but the

Musical Memory and the D-Major Serenade, op. 11 | 109

restatement corrects the wrong problem, shifting the melody down a fifth to fit within the G-major context, rather than adjusting the harmonic context to fit the D-major melody. When D major does, in fact, return (mm. 377ff.), the melody breaks down before reaching its natural conclusion (mm. 381–82), and the music immediately moves to B minor (m. 383). This incomplete, rhythmically

Example 3.2. Serenade No. 1 in D Major, op. 11, First Movement, mm. 351–83

110 | *Allusion as Narrative Premise in Brahms*

Example 3.2. *(Continued)*

restless phrase, no longer featuring the horn as sole melodic instrument as in the exposition, is the closest thing in the movement to a tonic-key recapitulation of the opening theme.

Even when the theme resurfaces at the end of the first movement, intact, tonic-key statements are thwarted. At the end of the recapitulation, the theme

Example 3.2. *(Continued)*

reappears for an apotheosis-like statement in the tonic, *fortissimo*, in full orchestra (mm. 501ff.), but it gets caught almost immediately in circular repetition and then slips away; the jubilant, would-be summative statement has disintegrated. Falling melodic lines, the dropping out of the upper winds and trombone, and the rapid decline to *pianissimo* convey a sense of deflation as the recapitulation draws to a close. With the onset of the coda (m. 524), the music immediately moves away from the tonic, and the theme once again sounds in the "wrong" key (ex. 3.3); as in the recapitulation, the melody is supported by a harmonic context a fifth too low. Furthermore, although the arrival of the recapitulation brought a statement above a dominant-seventh prolongation a fourth too high (i.e., in G major rather than in D), the beginning of the coda brings a statement over a similar prolongation yet a fourth higher: the melody suggests a G major context, but is heard within the key of C major. Thus the harmonic trajectory has continued yet further along its incorrect path down the circle of fifths. The music slows to a halt, pausing for several beats of silence (mm. 541–42), and in the final measures (ex. 3.4), the work's opening theme fades into non-existence. That this theme is never fully recapitulated in the tonic in the first movement makes all the more significant the similarities between this theme and the final new theme of the work, for it appears that it is left to the finale to recapitulate the work's opening material—or something clearly reminiscent of that material—in its original key and instrumentation.

Example 3.3. Serenade No. 1 in D Major, op. 11, First Movement, mm. 525–39

Musical Memory and the D-Major Serenade, op. 11 | 113

Example 3.4. Serenade No. 1 in D Major, op. 11, First Movement, mm. 550–74

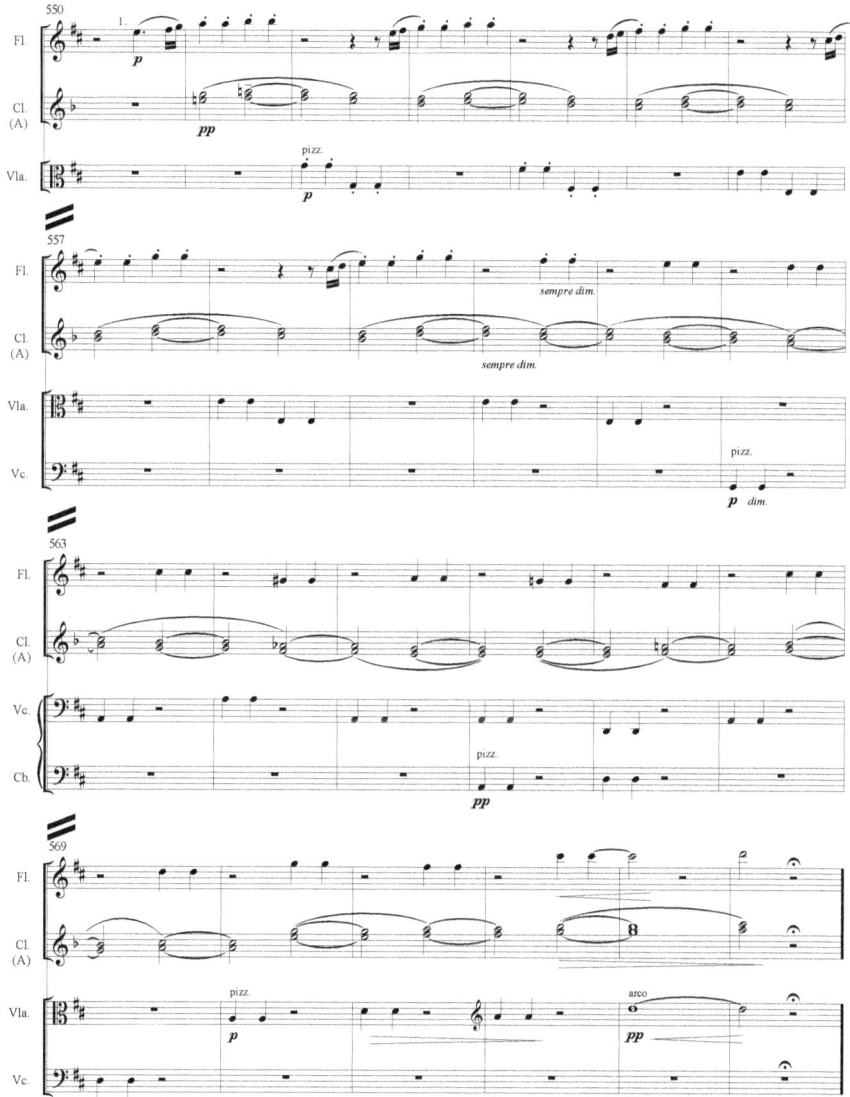

The Finale's Recollection as Culmination of an Extended Cross-Movement Process

Although the finale evokes the work's initial theme much more clearly than do any of the intervening movements, its recollection of the opening melody does not arise "out of the blue." Rather, this recollection represents the culmination of a process, played out in the inner movements, whereby the theme's head motive gradually begins to be reconstituted and streamlined. In the second movement, there is little, if any, recollection of the motive. The movement's uniquely dark and disturbed character—conveyed by such elements as the minor mode, registral depth, melodic angularity and complexity, dissonance, and syncopation—may even reflect an initial sense of loss or disorientation created by the disintegration of the Serenade's opening theme at the end of the first movement.

The third movement not only brings a return to the major mode and duple meter, as well as a calm pace and gentle, lilting character, but also initiates the recollection of the Serenade's opening motive, at first with the concluding first scale degree withheld, and then, as the movement progresses, in more complete forms. The opening of the third movement in fact seems to foreshadow that of the finale: the first theme groups of the two movements are extremely similar in terms of instrumentation and texture and resemble one-another in rhythmic and melodic character as well (ex. 3.5).[8] With respect to recalling the first-movement theme, the openings of the third and sixth movements represent analogous moments—and, furthermore, the parallel in function between these moments within the context of this narrative corresponds to other musical similarities between the two passages. The third movement initiates the process of thematic "recovery," and the finale's opening group leads directly to the unveiling of the theme in its recollected version. In the transition between the theme groups of the third movement's exposition, $\hat{5}$-$\hat{4}$-$\hat{3}$-$\hat{4}$-$\hat{2}$ (arguably, an elaboration on $\hat{5}$-$\hat{4}$-$\hat{2}$) appears several times, starting in B-flat major in the violin, doubled in the upper voice of the second violin and, at the octave, by the viola, with some rhythmic similarity to the parallel spot in the head motive of the opening movement (ex. 3.6). The change from dotted, uneven rhythms to even ones, the longer, more lyrical phrasing, and the legato articulation all help to make the melodic material in this passage stand out from what has come before, associating it with a local sense of relaxation. Nonetheless, the passage culminates in an upward-drifting melodic line that frustrates our desire for resolution down to the tonic pitch. The $\hat{5}$-$\hat{7}$-$\hat{1}$ fragment in the viola (in B-flat) in mm. 89–91 may be derived by inversion from the last three notes of the $\hat{5}$-$\hat{4}$-$\hat{2}$-$\hat{1}$ motive, and, as the exposition draws to a close, a fleeting $\hat{4}$-$\hat{2}$-$\hat{1}$ is heard in F in the flutes, doubled in the clarinet and violin parts (mm. 94–95) (ex. 3.7). Although the note of resolution—the first scale degree—is now provided, the fifth is not, and thus the motive remains incomplete, even

Example 3.5a–b. Serenade No. 1 in D Major, op. 11
(a) Third Movement, mm. 1–6

(b) Sixth Movement, mm. 1–4

Example 3.6. Serenade No. 1 in D Major, op. 11, Third Movement, mm. 39–45

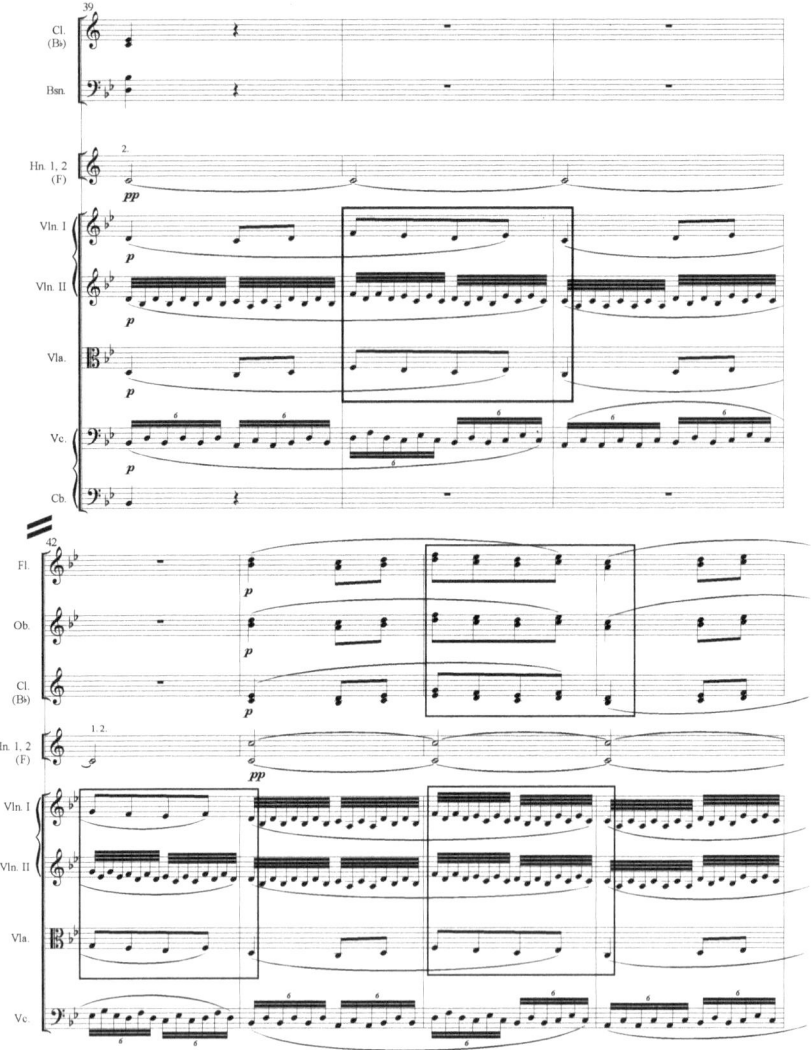

if less egregiously so than before. Also, the figure appears now in a key more distant from both the tonic of the movement (B-flat) and that of the piece (D), so the attainment of the first scale degree provides less resolution than it would have in mm. 40ff. The figure is stated clearly now, without elaboration, but it passes quickly and is also de-emphasized by its positioning at the *beginning* of a cadential gesture; our attention is drawn more forcefully to the notes that follow

Example 3.7. Serenade No. 1 in D Major, op. 11, Third Movement, mm. 89–95

and complete the phrase. The concluding gesture of the phrase is not unrelated, however; it is a simple inversion of the motive's last three notes.

In the development, additional fragments appear in the violins in D-flat ($\hat{4}$-$\hat{2}$-$\hat{1}$ and $\hat{5}$-$\hat{4}$-$\hat{2}$; ex. 3.8a)—and then the first complete $\hat{5}$-$\hat{4}$-$\hat{2}$-$\hat{1}$ (ex. 3.8b) is heard, although with chromatic decoration and still in a distant key. As material from the second theme begins to emerge in the clarinets, Brahms interpolates in sixteenths a lingering memory of the figure, hearkening back more directly in its incorporation of the third scale degree as penultimate pitch, as well as in its placement of the melody in the clarinets, with accompaniment in the lower strings (ex. 3.8c).

At the beginning of the coda (ex. 3.9), the figure resurfaces in B-flat (closer to D major), gradually evolving, in successive statements, from $\hat{3}$-$\hat{2}$-$\hat{3}$-$\hat{2}$-$\hat{1}$ (mm. 231–32) to $\hat{4}$-$\hat{2}$-$\hat{3}$-$\hat{2}$-$\hat{1}$ (mm. 232–33) to $\hat{5}$-$\hat{4}$-$\hat{2}$-$\hat{4}$-$\hat{3}$-$\hat{1}$ (mm. 234–35), with the second theme's characteristic off-kilter rhythm giving way to flowing sixteenths only as the evolution reaches its final stage, as though some difficulty has been overcome. Now, with the melody left to a single wind instrument, and with the thinning of the string parts, the orchestration even more closely approximates that of the Serenade's beginning—although the horn, so conspicuous at the opening of the piece, remains silent. As the third movement concludes, Brahms abandons the motto, and the music gradually dies away.

118 | *Allusion as Narrative Premise in Brahms*

Example 3.8a–c. Serenade No. 1 in D Major, op. 11, Third Movement
(a) mm. 115–16, First and Second Violin Parts

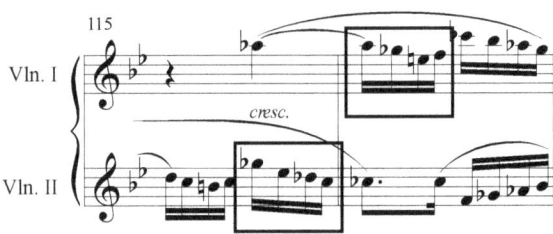

(b) mm. 118–19, String Parts

(c) mm. 120–23, Wind Parts

Example 3.9. Serenade No. 1 in D Major, op. 11, Third Movement, mm. 231–35

Although connections to the Serenade's opening motto are tenuous, in the G-major minuet that comprises the first half of the fourth movement, reminiscences of the opening motive nevertheless continue to emerge in the minor-mode minuet that constitutes the latter half of the movement.[9] Here, the figure undergoes additional transformation, with the removal of the third scale degree from the motive and the establishment of a pure version of the $\hat{5}$-$\hat{4}$-$\hat{2}$-$\hat{1}$ motto with which the finale is eventually to begin its more thorough recollection of the Serenade's opening. Although fragmentary derivatives of this motive appear throughout the G-minor minuet (ex. 3.10), the establishment of the complete figure coincides precisely with the single melodic gesture that brings the minuet to conclusion (before the coda; also shown in ex. 3.10) and is thus clearly associated with a sense of resolution, representing the culmination of the movement. Brahms states this concluding figure in slow, even quarter-notes, with slurred-pizzicato articulation, factors that set the gesture apart from what precedes it and lend it a particular sense of deliberateness. Nonetheless, in the fleeting echo of this gesture in the coda, the motto appears at the wrong pitch level and turns upward at the end instead of down (G–F–D–E-flat in m. 25 of the G-minor minuet).

The fifth movement ushers in not only the return of other key elements of the work's opening—including the D-major tonality and the placement of the opening melody in the horn, with light accompaniment in the low strings—but it also brings an increase in the prominence of references to the work's opening theme.

Example 3.10. Serenade No. 1 in D Major, op. 11, Fourth Movement (Menuetto II), mm. 1–28

Example 3.10. *(Continued)*

In the cello line that accompanies the melody at the beginning of the movement, we hear not the more streamlined version of the motto, but the version, heard in the development and coda of the *Adagio*, that complicates the original theme by adding an extra leap up from the second scale degree: 5̂-4̂-2̂-4̂-3̂-1̂ (mm. 1–2 and 9–10 of the fifth movement, shown in ex. 3.11). Emerging in the melody in its simpler form at the movement's first conclusive moment of rest (5̂-4̂-2̂-1̂ in mm. 15–16, also shown in ex. 3.11), this first D-major appearance of the streamlined motive, like the statement at the end of the G-minor minuet, brings a localized sense of resolution. Not only is the melodic gesture simplified here, but the attainment of the tonic scale degree now coincides with the downbeat and is thus more stable on a metrical level than in its appearance in the cello. Any resolution this provides is temporary, however, for the movement's other references to the motto generally occur in more unsettled or complicated forms. (See, e.g., mm. 21ff. and 35ff.)

As the scherzo draws to a close, references to the motive proliferate, and the figure's successful completion, which seems increasingly difficult, becomes a matter of primary concern. In mm. 51–54, the more complicated version (5̂-4̂-2̂-4̂-3̂-1̂) surfaces for the first time in the solo horn, the work's original

Example 3.11. Serenade No. 1 in D Major, op. 11, Fifth Movement, mm. 1–16

melodic instrument in both the movement and, more importantly, the work (ex. 3.12). The first note is tied over the bar line, creating a sense of hesitance or difficulty, as if particular effort is required to recall the motive, and the scherzo's usually clear phrasing gives way to a chaotic series of overlapping statements. As this comes to a culmination, the horn becomes stuck on the motto's initial note, oscillating between registers and leaving subsequent statements to other instruments. Having reached a dramatic apex, after nearly ten measures in which the $\hat{5}$-$\hat{4}$-$\hat{2}$-$\hat{4}$-$\hat{3}$-$\hat{1}$ figure has sounded *continuously*, the movement ends with the only pure statement of the simplified $\hat{5}$-$\hat{4}$-$\hat{2}$-$\hat{1}$ since mm. 15–16, sounding simultaneously in several voices. Now that the simplified motive is finally established in D major, the stage is set for the finale's more complete recollection of the work's opening.[10]

The finale's recollection of the opening theme is, then, the culmination of a gradual process that has already been underway for some time before the final movement begins. In its appearances in the previous two movements, the streamlined figure has served as a concluding gesture (marking the ends of the second minuet and of the fifth movement's first period and closing out the latter movement altogether), yet the role of the motive in the Serenade's opening is not that of concluding gesture, of course, but of head motive, a role it resumes in the finale's second theme. The figure's recurrent use as a concluding gesture actually reflects its broader role within the work as a whole, for the establishment of $\hat{5}$-$\hat{4}$-$\hat{2}$-$\hat{1}$ in D major—a resolution-bringing figure in and of itself, as it represents prolongation of the dominant, concluding with motion to the tonic—and the finale's ensuing use of this figure within the context of a recollection of the Serenade's opening theme are what ultimately provide resolution of much of the work's ongoing tension and help to bring the piece to conclusion.

The introduction of the finale's first theme brings a temporary increase in tension, rendering the ultimate resolution associated with the second theme that much more significant by contrast. As the finale begins (ex. 3.5b above), the streamlined $\hat{5}$-$\hat{4}$-$\hat{2}$-$\hat{1}$ motive, established so decisively at the end of the scherzo, is temporarily abandoned. The finale's initial theme has an almost anticipatory sound, an anxious sense of forward motion and momentum unparalleled in earlier movements. The characteristic rhythm of this theme, in stark contrast to the scherzo's even quarters, is a jerky, stilted, off-kilter, eighth-sixteenth rest-sixteenth rhythm that repeats over and over, homorhythmically in all sounding voices, making the music seem almost as though it is galloping along *towards* something—as if driven on towards the more lyrical, rhythmically stable, and harmonically clear second theme group, where many of the work's lingering tensions are to be resolved.

When the finale's second theme is recapitulated (ex. 3.1b), the material brings even more stability and resolution than in its expository statement. In

Example 3.12. Serenade No. 1 in D Major, op. 11, Fifth Movement, mm. 50–64

the recapitulation, the second theme not only arrives in the tonic key, but it stays there for all complete subsequent statements, whereas in virtually none of its earlier appearances, whether in this movement or in its original version in the first movement, is the motto articulated twice consecutively in any one key, let alone in D major.[11] Also, the triplet accompaniment heard in the expository statement is replaced, in the recapitulation, with sixteenths, eradicating the "three-against-four" cross-rhythm. Finally, this is the first time since the initial movement in which a reminiscence of the work's opening horn melody is heard in the original instrument.

Ultimately, the past can never quite be recaptured; reestablishment of the work's opening theme in the finale is not only inexact, but, inevitably, temporary. In the coda, reminiscences of the Serenade's opening become wispy and evanescent, the memory ultimately dissolving as the work closes. However, the work does not end tragically; in fact, its conclusion is decidedly triumphant, dominated by clear, consonant, major harmonies and even rhythms, and in the final measures, a prominent melodic ascent in an extremely high register in the first violin. Even the circular horn and trumpet calls in mm. 346–53, although never evolving into a full thematic statement, sound like victory cries, blaring out at the apex of excitement; with their controlled rhythm and sustained, high As on the downbeats, the horn and trumpet appear, here, to be reveling in their own sounds, as if proud of the horn's accomplishment in having, at last, properly recapitulated the work's opening theme in some form. That feat is not reiterated as the Serenade concludes, but perhaps its repetition is unnecessary. Recollecting the work's opening theme is an important goal of the piece, but the triumphant ending suggests that, once that recollection has been accomplished in the proper key and instrumentation, the apparently inevitable re-fragmentation of the thematic material is of relatively little consequence.

Relationship to Haydn's Symphony No. 104

The relationship of the Serenade to the last movement of Haydn's final symphony is of particular interest here—because the resemblance between the two works involves precisely the thematic material with which we have been primarily concerned in this chapter. As has been pointed out on several occasions, the main theme of the Haydn movement begins with a two-measure figure that is of remarkable similarity to the one in Brahms's D-major scherzo (ex. 3.13).[12] Like Haydn, Brahms introduces the figure at the outset of the movement and in a solo string part, with the winds silent except for a pair of horns. Also commonly recognized is the pertinence of this Haydn material to the opening theme of Brahms's Serenade; the first phrase of the Serenade not only begins similarly, with an elaborated version of $\hat{5}$-$\hat{4}$-$\hat{2}$, but, also like Haydn's opening phrase, concludes

Example 3.13. Haydn, Symphony No. 104 in D Major, Fourth Movement, mm. 1–10

with a gesture leading from the fifth scale degree up by leap to an E–F-sharp neighbor figure immediately preceding the final note (cf. mm. 9–11 of Brahms with mm. 5–6 of Haydn). Brahms's version is more unsettled, however; Haydn ends his phrase by resolving to the tonic, whereas Brahms sustains the tension by returning to E in the melody and shifting to the dominant key. Moreover, Haydn divides his theme into balanced, eight-measure antecedent-consequent pairs, whereas Brahms's phrasing is aperiodic and less evenly balanced.[13]

Yet, oddly, the relationship of Haydn's melody to the second theme of Brahms's finale appears to have gone unnoticed in the literature thus far. The elements that Brahms's last theme most clearly shares with his opening melody are precisely those that both movements have in common with Haydn's theme: not only the initial $\hat{5}$-$\hat{4}$-$\hat{2}$, but also the phrase-ending melodic gesture (A–E–F-sharp). In fact, although any possible reference to Haydn's theme may be less "on the surface" in Brahms's finale than in the scherzo, since the theme has been simplified, Brahms nevertheless seems, in some ways, to emulate Haydn's opening even more closely in the finale. (Additionally, in the finale, the reference is heard in the melody, whereas, in the scherzo, it appears primarily as accompanimental or counter-subject figure.) For instance, although the Haydn reference is introduced *forte* in the scherzo, both the opening theme of the Serenade and the last-movement reincarnation tend to appear mostly at low dynamic levels, especially *piano*, the dynamic at the beginning of Haydn's own finale. The drone-like accompaniment at the opening of the Serenade, recalled in the finale but not in the scherzo, is reminiscent of that at the beginning of Haydn's finale. Furthermore, unlike the drone at the Serenade's opening, the one in the finale (at mm. 71ff.) is similar to Haydn's in that it accompanies the violin melody as a sustained tonic pitch in the cello beneath octaves on the dominant in the horn. In the finale, Brahms returns from a triple to a duple meter more closely resembling not only the one Brahms employed in his own first movement, but also Haydn's own meter. Even rhythmically, Brahms's second finale theme itself is not so different from the melody of Haydn's last movement; Brahms's quarter-eighth-eighth pattern is essentially Haydn's quarter-quarter-half rhythm in reverse and diminution, and Haydn employs a quarter-eighth-eighth figure in the third measure of his own theme.

Additional similarities between the Brahms and Haydn works help to support the idea that, while composing his Serenade, Brahms had Haydn's Symphony in mind. Not only are the works scored for ensembles almost identical in composition, but both works employ precisely the same collection of primary key areas for movements and large sections; apart from the shared tonic, these include D minor, B-flat major, and G major, which—in both works—shifts briefly to its parallel minor and then back. (See Haydn's slow movement and Brahms's pair of minuets.) Also, even apart from the apparent references to the opening of Haydn's finale, there are specific moments when Brahms appears almost to recall a parallel point in Haydn's Symphony; compare, for instance, the triplet-eighth gesture in Haydn's final measures (m. 330 of the finale) with the triplet sixteenths at the end of Brahms's slow movement (m. 249). The opening of Brahms's slow movement, already compared to the first theme of the Serenade's finale, is also in some ways similar to Haydn's own slow movement. Brahms's slow movement, which appears originally to have been marked "*Andante*" like Haydn's (see n. 4), shares with Haydn's slow movement its time signature and dynamic marking, a largely homorhythmic texture involving simultaneous pauses in all parts, the double-dotted-eighth-sixteenth rhythm, and an opening gesture consisting of upward stepwise motion and an upward fourth leap. Although Haydn's movement starts with strings only, the addition of the bassoon in m. 17 produces an orchestral texture much like that at the beginning of Brahms's *Adagio*. The double-dotted-eight-sixteenth figure and predominantly homorhythmic bassoon-plus-strings texture of both movements seem to derive, in turn, from the Symphony's slow introduction. Additionally, like Haydn, Brahms returns to D major at the beginning of his penultimate movement.

Even more relevant, the head motive of the main theme from Haydn's opening movement, a likely source for Haydn's finale theme, includes the $\hat{4}$-$\hat{2}$-$\hat{1}$ figure (mm. 17–18, shown in ex. 3.14). Furthermore, the figure is articulated here not in the quarter-quarter-half rhythm of Haydn's finale, but in the exact reverse: half-quarter-quarter, of which the quarter-eighth-eighth rhythm of Brahms's finale theme (where, likewise, the fourth and second scale degrees fall on the two shorter notes) is a diminution. Thus, if Brahms is attempting, in his D-Major Serenade, to evoke Haydn by referring to the theme from the last movement of Symphony No. 104, then he also emulates the eighteenth-century master by presenting the allusive material, in one form or another, in both of his outer movements—for Haydn originally presented the relevant material, in one form or another, in both of his.

The effort to recall the first theme of the Serenade later in the work is perhaps more fundamentally an attempt to recapture the music of Haydn's finale, which threatens to fade into the musical past—and which, indeed, is merely *evoked* at best and never fully reconstructed in its original form. This particular movement of Haydn is an especially apt choice for a young composer seeking to depict his taking up of the reigns from the earlier master(s): it is the last movement of Haydn's final symphonic work. Brahms, thinking, at one point, that the Serenade might be his own first symphony (and knowing that it was to be his first orchestral piece), chose Haydn's last symphonic movement as a literal starting point for his work, and ultimately granted his work a generic classification and orchestration that hint at its eighteenth-century origins.[14]

Whether deliberately or not, the young composer situates himself with respect to the musical past not only by emulating it, but also by providing a tangible demonstration of how he can build upon the musical legacy he has inherited, thereby bringing it, in one sense or another, to a logical next stage. Consider, for a moment, the pair of D-major movements that conclude the Serenade. The fact that Brahms's penultimate movement is in D major helps to highlight the

Example 3.14. Haydn, Symphony No. 104 in D Major, First Movement, mm. 17–20

similarity of its material to the main theme of Haydn's finale (which, of course, is also situated in that key). Haydn's $\hat{5}$-$\hat{4}$-$\hat{2}$-$\hat{4}$-$\hat{3}$-$\hat{1}$ figure remains fundamentally unmodified over the course of the Symphony's final movement. Brahms, however, employs this figure not in his last but in his second-to-last movement; what was the end of the story with Haydn is not so with Brahms. As we have seen, Brahms eventually allows the figure to evolve into the more streamlined version heard in the Serenade's finale. In this sense, Brahms helps to resolve melodic tension or complication that Haydn leaves unresolved at the end of his Symphony; Brahms brings things "full circle" by returning to a simplified figure more closely resembling that heard at the beginning of the first theme of Haydn's opening movement.

For all of these reasons, the Serenade's final movement bears greater significance, both within the context of the work itself and with respect to its source material in Haydn, than has been previously appreciated. As do other works examined in this study, the D-Major Serenade manifests a strong sense of historical self-consciousness in a movement-spanning narrative that depicts its composer's attempts to cope with or reconcile a distortion or "loss" of allusory material drawn from a canonic work by a revered master. Through such narratives, Brahms reveals his struggle to simultaneously acknowledge, connect with, and even recapture the music of the past while still building upon it in a meaningful, original manner. Seen within this context, the triumphant nature of the Serenade's closing measures appears to suggest that, by the late 1850s, the young composer was optimistic and perhaps even genuinely confidant about his abilities to carry on successfully despite the fading of things past. In so doing, he would fulfill the role prescribed for him in Schumann's *"Neue Bahnen"*: the role of heir to the great Classical masters.

Notes

1. See Hermann Deiters, *Johannes Brahms*, Sammlung Musikalischer Vorträge 23–24, ed. Paul Graf Waldersee (Leipzig: Breitkopf und Härtel, 1880), 8, cited in Thomas Schipperges (*Serenaden zwischen Beethoven und Reger: Beiträge zur Geschichte der Gattung*, Europäische Hochschulschriften, 36 (Frankfurt am Main: Lang, 1989), 178; Malcolm MacDonald, *Brahms, Master Musicians Series*, ed. Stanley Sadie (Oxford: Oxford University Press, 2001), 106; Michael Musgrave, "Serenade No. 1 in D Major, op. 11," in *The Compleat Brahms: A Guide to the Musical Works of Johannes Brahms*, ed. Leon Botstein (New York: W.W. Norton, 1999), 40; Walter Niemann, *Brahms*, 4th printing, trans. Catherine Alison Phillips (New York: Alfred A. Knopf, 1941; originally published in Berlin: Schuster & Loeffler, 1920), 272, 304–5; Jan Swafford, *Johannes Brahms: A Biography* (New York: Alfred A. Knopf, 1997), 204–5; and Ivor Keys, *Johannes Brahms* (Portland, OR: Amadeus Press, 1989), 163–64. Viktor Urbantschitsch ["Die Entwicklung der Sonatenform bei Brahms," *Studien zur Musikwissenschaft* 14 (1927): 273]

identifies as a further "conscious archaism" Brahms's use of sonata-allegro form for a slow middle movement, for although such a formal structure was "characteristic" of Mozart's andantes, the sonata-form slow movement had "already disappeared" with Beethoven. In fact, it had not quite done so—the slow movements of Symphonies One, Two, and Four, for example, as well as some of the sonatas and chamber works, contain slow movements in this form—but it is indeed an extreme rarity in Brahms's oeuvre.

2. On the serenade in the nineteenth century, see Hubert Unverricht and Cliff Eisen, "Serenade," *Grove Music Online*. Accessed April 12, 2006. www.grovemusic.com; Schipperges, *Serenaden zwischen Beethoven und Reger*; and Niemann, *Brahms*, 303.

3. Musgrave, "Serenade No. 1 in D major, op. 11," 40. See Max Kalbeck, *Johannes Brahms*, 4th ed. (Berlin: Deutsche Brahms-Gesellschaft, 1921; repr. Tutzing: Hans Schneider, 1976), 1:318.

4. The work existed in a number of incarnations, including versions (not surviving) for chamber ensemble and for small orchestra. For more on the Serenade's genesis and sources, see Margit L. and Donald McCorkle, *Johannes Brahms: Thematisch-Bibliographisches Werkverzeichnis* (München: G. Henle, 1984), 32–36; Johannes Brahms, *Serenaden: Nr. 1 D-dur für grosses Orchester Opus 11, Nr. 2 A-dur für kleines Orchester Opus 16*, ed. Michael Musgrave, Neue Ausgabe sämtlicher Werke, ser. I: Orchesterwerke, vol. 5 (München: G. Henle Verlag, 2006), xiff.; and Robert Pascall, "Serenade Nr. 1 für grosses Orchester D-Dur op. 11," in *Brahms-Handbuch*, ed. Wolfgang Sandberger (Kassel: Bärenreiter, 2009), 497–98.

5. On the Serenade's associations with Beethoven, Schubert, and Schumann works, see Kalbeck, *Johannes Brahms*, 1:319–20; Schipperges, *Serenaden zwischen Beethoven und Reger*, 181, 183, 188 fn. 96, 192, 193 and 198; Michael Vaillancourt, "Brahms's 'Sinfonie-Serenade' and the Politics of Genre," *Journal of Musicology* 26/3 (2009): 398–402; Constantin Floros, *Johannes Brahms, "Free but Alone": A Life for a Poetic Music*, trans. Ernest Bernhardt-Kabisch (Frankfurt am Main: Peter Lang, 2010); originally published as *Johannes Brahms, "frei aber einsam": Ein Leben für eine poetische Musik* (Zürich: Arche Züich, 1997), 84–85; Walter Frisch, "Brahms, Johannes"; John Horton, *Brahms Orchestral Music*, BBC Music Guides, 2nd printing (Seattle, WA: University of Washington Press, 1978), 24; Michael Musgrave, *The Music of Brahms*, Companions to the Great Composers (London: Routledge & Kegan Paul, 1985), 42, 126; and MacDonald, *Brahms*, 106.

6. Schipperges, *Serenaden zwischen Beethoven und Reger*, 178, citing a review written by Billroth and published in a Zurich newspaper on November 10, 1863, as republished in *Billroth und Brahms im Briefwechsel, mit Einleitung, Anmerkungen und 4 Bildtafeln*, ed. Otto Gottlieb (Berlin: Urgan & Schwarzenberg, 1935), 498.

7. Although, in the minds of Brahms and his contemporaries, this theme would have been associated undeniably and inextricably with Haydn's well-known symphony, Haydn himself may well have borrowed the melodic material from preexisting folk repertory. On the melody's relationship to "Hot Cross Buns," Smetana's Czech Dances, and a Croatian folk melody, see H. C. Robbins Landon, *Haydn Symphonies*, BBC Music Guides (London: British Broadcasting Corporation, 1968), 64; and Antony Hodgson, *The Music of Joseph Haydn: The Symphonies* (London: Tantivy Press, 1976), 148.

8. On the motivic similarities between the opening passages of these two movements, see also Schipperges, *Serenaden zwischen Beethoven und Reger*, 202.

9. As to the G-major minuet, see the $\hat{4}$-$\hat{2}$-$\hat{1}$ in the flute at mm. 17-18; the $\hat{6}$-$\hat{4}$-$\hat{3}$ in mm. 22–23—equivalent to $\hat{4}$-$\hat{2}$-$\hat{1}$ in the key of the previous movement—and its transposition

up by third immediately following; as well as the $\hat{8}$-$\hat{7}$-$\hat{5}$ (retrograde inversion of $\hat{4}$-$\hat{2}$-$\hat{1}$) at m. 26. The last three of these are each extracted from broader contexts in which the notes of the motto are not necessarily the most important ones (e.g., the $\hat{8}$-$\hat{7}$-$\hat{5}$ in the coda is part of a $\hat{8}$-$\hat{7}$-$\hat{5}$-$\hat{6}$ gesture that reduces to $\hat{8}$-$\hat{7}$-$\hat{6}$).

10. The melody of the trio section, featuring the horn in the work's tonic key and descending from the fifth scale degree to the first by way of the second, could also be considered a recollection of the work's opening motive, but here Brahms skips the fourth scale degree instead of the second.

11. Technically, the one exception occurs at the beginning of the first movement's recapitulation, where the theme sounds twice in G major—but only in the second of these statements does it sound at the appropriate pitch level for that harmonic context; in the first statement, as we have seen, the melody begins on A, as if in D major.

12. See Musgrave, *The Music of Brahms*, 126 and "Serenade No. 1 in D Major, op. 11," 42; and Schipperges, *Serenaden zwischen Beethoven und Reger*, 192–95. Even Kalbeck (*Johannes Brahms*, 1:319) remarks upon the resemblance between Brahms's fifth movement and the then-popular "*Dreschthema aus dem Finalsaze der Haydnschen D-dur-Symphonie, das damals von den Spatzen auf dem Dach gepfiffene.*"

13. For additional comparative analysis of the two movements, see Schipperges, *Serenaden zwischen Beethoven und Reger*, 181–88, as well as Vaillancourt, "Brahms's 'Sinfonie-Serenade' and the Politics of Genre," 398. Vaillancourt suggests here that Brahms's alteration of this material represents an expansion in accord with the greater scale of the Serenade's first movement in comparison to that of Haydn's finale. "Thus," he suggests, "transformative allusion serves not so much to conceal [the motive's] source as to suggest a course for the entire movement, expanding the motive to almost three times its original length and generating a movement more than twice the size of the original. Furthermore, it supports the notion that allusion was more for Brahms than a matter of mere melodic *Anklänge*; rather, it was a generative element intended to have an impact on large-scale structure." Vaillancourt's conclusion here is in accordance with my own, although I extend this further to encompass not only the "large-scale structure" of the individual movement, but to the broader, multimovement structure of the entire Serenade.

14. Similar historicist concerns may once have prompted Brahms's mentor, Robert Schumann, to allude to the same Haydn symphony. There is a rather striking resemblance between the opening of Haydn's Symphony No. 104 and the initial measures of Schumann's Symphony No. 2 in C Major, op. 61 (1845–46). Anthony Newcomb suggests that Schumann's apparent allusion "proclaims as effectively as a poetic preamble ... Schumann's courageous and ambitious decision to measure for the first time his particular methods and abilities against the overwhelmingly, even terrifyingly prestigious tradition of the Viennese Classical symphony" ["Once More 'between Absolute and Program Music': Schumann's Second Symphony," *19th-Century Music* 7 (1983–84), 240]. Christopher Reynolds also discusses Schumann's allusion to Haydn here, as well as an allusion to the same Haydn opening at the beginning of Mendelssohn's "Reformation" Symphony; see Christopher Alan Reynolds, *Motives for Allusion: Context and Content in Nineteenth-Century Music* (Cambridge, MA: Harvard University Press, 2003), 37.

4 A Historical Model, an Emerging Soloist, a Young Composer in Turmoil: The Piano Concerto in D Minor, op. 15

Brahms's D-Minor Piano Concerto, op. 15, involved the longest, most complicated, and most difficult gestation of any of Brahms's compositions of the period, occupying the composer from 1854 to 1859 as it evolved from unfinished two-piano sonata to incomplete symphony before being reconceptualized, completed, and revised as a concerto. The first two movements of the Concerto have often been read, respectively, as a direct response to Robert Schumann's suicide attempt in early 1854 and as a reflection of Brahms's feelings for Clara Schumann, who had come to rely on Brahms for emotional and practical support during the period of her husband's subsequent decline and death at the asylum at Endenich. By looking more carefully at the work's *final* movement and at the relationship of that movement to the piece as a whole, we come to a fuller understanding of how the work may also reflect the other main category of stressor on Brahms during this time: his struggles to produce a large-scale work for orchestra and to establish his own artistic voice and historical position.

A Brief Compositional History

To more fully illustrate the degree of Brahms's difficulties in producing this concerto, I begin with a brief review of what is known of the work's compositional history. As no sketches or drafts survive, some of the details have remained unclear—but it appears that three movements of the original two-piano-sonata version, which did not include a finale, were drafted by the spring of 1854.[1] By the following summer, Brahms had decided that the piece required more substantial instrumentation and began converting it into a symphony, possibly in capitulation to pressure from Robert Schumann to write an orchestral work.[2] Brahms orchestrated the first movement and composed two inner ones—but in early February, before composing a finale, he envisioned himself, in a dream, performing the work as a piano concerto.[3] Inspired by this vision, the inexperienced symphonist set about recasting the piece as a concerto, thereby easing the difficulties he had experienced in attempting to complete the work as a symphony. Brahms replaced the inner movements with an *adagio* comprised of at least partially new material, and he finally composed a finale.[4] Drafts of the first, second, and third movements of the Concerto were completed by mid-October 1856, early January 1857, and mid-December 1856 respectively.[5] Brahms remained generally frustrated with the work and continued revising for over a year longer.[6] As Malcolm MacDonald recounts, "the Concerto was essentially complete by March 1858, when Brahms first played it in a private rehearsal under Joachim; but he continued tinkering with it right up to the first public performance in January 1859, and was hardly satisfied even then."[7]

A Beethovenian Model

The final movement of the Concerto is long thought to have been modeled on that of Beethoven's Piano Concerto No. 3 in C Minor, op. 37, and, particularly given the strain involved in the composition of Brahms's Concerto, it is not surprising that scholars have tended to interpret the primary significance of this modeling as evidence of Brahms's need for artistic inspiration.[8] I argue here that, even if Brahms did employ his model out of a perceived necessity, the ways in which he deliberately *deviates* from Beethoven's template reveal something of his attitude toward that model (and perhaps toward that perception of necessity), imbuing the connection between the two concertos with a more nuanced, and ultimately greater, significance than has previously been realized.

Although there is no clear thematic borrowing on Brahms's part, the confluence of several features strongly implies a relationship between the Brahms and Beethoven finales.[9] Both movements are 2/4-time sonata-rondos that begin in the minor mode and end in the parallel major; both have first episodes in the relative major and lyrical second episodes in the submediant; and, up to the coda, the proportions of the two movements are remarkably similar (table 4.1). Even within individual sections, the movements often resemble one another closely in terms of phrase structure, texture, and instrumentation—as, for instance, at their openings (cf. ex. 4.1 and ex. 4.2).

Among the most distinctive elements shared by the two finales is the short fugato following the second episode. The fugatos are located at nearly identical places within their respective movements, and both develop the refrain theme in a largely staccato manner and without the soloist. Furthermore, in each finale, the fugato is followed by the refrain's initial appearance in the major mode (Beethoven places it in the key of the lowered mediant; with Brahms, it is in the mediant key), with the theme in the piano, lightly accompanied by the strings, and both higher in pitch and lower in dynamic level than in earlier refrain statements. In both cases, as Rosen observes, this initial major-mode statement of the refrain theme leads, via "extensive arpeggios on a dominant pedal followed

Table 4.1 The Finales of Brahms's Piano Concerto No. 1 in D Minor, op. 15, and Beethoven's Piano Concerto No. 3 in C Minor, op. 37: Basic Structural Outlines

Brahms, op. 15 (D Minor): Finale	Beethoven, op. 37 (C Minor): Finale
[Exposition:]	[Exposition:]
A (mm. 1–41; D minor); transition (mm. 42–65)	A (mm. 1–55; C minor); transition (mm. 56–67)
B (mm. 66–117; F major); transition (mm. 118–43)	B (mm. 68–103; E-flat major); transition (mm. 103–26)
[Development:]	[Development:]
A′ (mm. 144–80; D minor)	A′ (mm. 127–81, including cadenza (m. 152); C minor)
C (mm. 181–237; B-flat major)	C (mm. 182–229; A-flat major)
Extended transition (mm. 238–96):	Transition (mm. 230–97):
• fugato based on C and A themes (mm. 238–74)	• fugato based on A theme, followed by free development (mm. 230–53)
• further development of refrain material (mm. 275–96)	• further development of refrain material (mm. 264–97)
[Recapitulation:]	[Recapitulation:]
A″ (mm. 297–328; D minor); transition (mm. 328–47)	A″ (mm. 298–318; C minor); transition (mm. 319–30)
B′ (mm. 348–68; D minor); transition (mm. 369–75)	B′ (mm. 331–64; C major); transition (includes brief recollection of refrain; mm. 364–407)
Cadenza (mm. 376–409; D minor to D major to D minor)	Cadenza (m. 407; dominant prolongation in C major)
Coda (mm. 410–536)	Coda (alludes briefly to refrain, but consists primarily of free material for soloist and orchestra together; mm. 408–64; C major)
• material based on C theme (mm. 410–41; D major)	
• material based on refrain (mm. 442–98; D major)	
• second cadenza (mm. 499–517; D major)	
• conclusion (mm. 518–36; D major)	

by brilliant passagework," to a proper recapitulation of the refrain in the tonic minor.[10]

However, there is no slavish imitation on Brahms's part; he distinguishes his finale from its model in select but significant ways. The most dramatic of these coincides with a moment in the work at which we find the culmination of several intermovement processes. These include (1) the evolution of the soloist (a persona metaphorical for the composer himself) from hesitant and troubled to assertive and liberated, (2) the definitive establishment of the tonic major, and (3) the gradual transformation of melodic material originally suggestive of tension and struggle into triumphant victory calls. These processes provide an important

Example 4.1. Beethoven, Piano Concerto No. 3 in C Minor, op. 37, Third Movement, mm. 1–13

Example 4.1. *(Continued)*

138 | *Allusion as Narrative Premise in Brahms*

framework for interpreting possible motives and meanings behind Brahms's adoption and handling of the Beethoven model. To that end, we will now examine how each of these three processes plays out in Brahms's Concerto, and this will ultimately provide a context for the subsequent examination and interpretation of the differences between Brahms's finale and its model.

Example 4.2. Brahms, Piano Concerto No. 1 in D Minor, op. 15, Third Movement, mm. 1–14

Example 4.2. *(Continued)*

The Evolving Role of the Soloist

In the opening movement, the solo part is relatively unassertive. The initial entry of the soloist appears quite late, following a full ninety measures of orchestral exposition. The orchestral opening makes quite an impression. The work begins rife with tension, *fortissimo* and heavily accented, with persistent, unresolving dominant prolongation, rumbling timpani, and what Swafford calls "snarling horns" (ex. 4.3).[11] Although there is an immediate emphasis on B-flat harmony, the work begins in the "daemonic" key of D

Example 4.3. Brahms, Piano Concerto No. 1 in D Minor, op. 15, First Movement, mm. 1–11

minor, and the music is inflected with chromaticism and repeated trills that clash at the tritone with the ominous, low tonic pedal.[12] The opening melody, with its initial off-kilter rhythm, is jerky, angular, and disjoint. However, when the piano does enter, rather than re-stating the opening material, it articulates something far less formidable. Rather than "bursting onto the scene" with a restatement of the striking opening passage, the piano enters with new, decidedly less dynamic material (ex. 4.4). Entering *piano espressivo*, the

A Historical Model, an Emerging Soloist, a Young Composer | 141

Example 4.4. Brahms, Piano Concerto No. 1 in D Minor, op. 15, First Movement, mm. 89–97

soloist proceeds at a relatively slow pace, employing a persistent "stutter"-like off-then-on-the-beat note-repetition pattern that lends the music a hesitant quality.[13] Furthermore, the autonomy of the soloist at the outset is compromised by the fact that he plays only with orchestral accompaniment until the arrival of the second theme group. Even there (mm. 157ff.), although the soloist takes the initiative in introducing the new F-major melody, the piano part remains reserved and unvirtuosic. As before, the arrival of new thematic material in the piano coincides with a lessening of tension, an increased quietude and solemnity; for the first several measures, the soloist moves in generally even, steady note values, producing a simple, almost chorale-like chordal texture.

Throughout the movement, not only are the themes that are introduced in the piano relatively unassertive, but the soloist struggles unsuccessfully to state the more powerful material played by the orchestra at the opening. In the exposition, the closest the soloist comes to stating the first theme is in one brief, interrupted, accompanied phrase taken from the *end* of the theme—and even this occurs surprisingly late (m. 110). Here, the piano allows the orchestra to interject after only three measures and then to reappropriate the theme entirely. He tries several times in the development to recapture the assertive first-theme material, but does so only once (mm. 252–55), and even here, as in the exposition, manages to articulate only the fourth and final phrase (in transposition). As before, when the orchestra takes over, it develops the very motive that has eluded the soloist's grasp.[14]

Among the soloist's boldest moments in the first movement is when, bringing the development section to a close, he attempts, with tremendous effort, to counterbalance the united forces of the ensemble and then takes the initiative to bring about the recapitulation by finally appropriating the movement's opening material—and yet the results are calamitous. At mm. 306ff. (ex. 4.5), the development has built to a climax. The orchestra moves homorhythmically, pulsating in a percussive, rapid-fire repeated-note pattern suggestive of a fearful trembling (and, perhaps, of the "Fate Motive" from Beethoven's Fifth Symphony). Against the massive force of the orchestra is pitted the soloist, who, entirely alone, interjects thick, widely spaced chords into the breaks in the orchestral part. In a texture that spans from low to extremely high registers, the dominant is repeatedly hammered out by both soloist and orchestra. The culmination of the suspense is the soloist's attempt to initiate the recapitulation by finally appropriating the main theme of the movement. Even here, the soloist remains incapable of stating the theme without committing a striking *faux pas*: over the orchestra's D pedal, he begins not with the B-flat-major chord heard at the Concerto's opening, but with an *E-major* chord a tritone away! The piano thus transforms the D pedal into a grating dissonance, the seventh of the harmony, rather than a grounding

Example 4.5. Brahms, Piano Concerto No. 1 in D Minor, op. 15, First Movement, mm. 306–28

Example 4.5. *(Continued)*

pitch. Whether we interpret this as a disastrous "mistake" on the soloist's part or as willful defiance of the orchestra's D pedal (and the listener's expectation), the piano has once again failed to state the powerful opening theme in its "correct" form.

Before the soloist is able to try again, the orchestra not only reclaims the first theme of the movement, so hard won by the soloist, but then proceeds to

A Historical Model, an Emerging Soloist, a Young Composer | 145

Example 4.5. *(Continued)*

lay claim on the soloist's own material. When the theme of the piano's original entrance returns in D minor (m. 341), it is heard in the strings and winds, while the piano is entirely silent. In the exposition, the piano had introduced this theme quietly, whereas the orchestra brings it in more forcefully, *fortissimo*.

In the recapitulation, the soloist finally regains control of his own theme (at m. 355), but his statement here is less assertive and more troubled than the orchestra's. The music has grown very quiet and has departed from the tonic key to the fairly distant F-sharp minor, in which it seems restless; the first measure of the melody repeats itself, and the phrase overflows beyond the original, neat four-bar structure as Brahms touches on other key areas.

The soloist is ineffective in stating other thematic material throughout the movement as well, becoming frantic and frustrated, breaking down, and finally ceding to the orchestra. For instance, cf. the orchestral material in mm. 46ff. with the soloist's attempted restatements in mm. 278ff. and 444ff. At mm. 461ff., as well, the soloist wrests melodic control from the orchestra at least temporarily, but continues to struggle, with choppy phrases, chromaticism, false starts, and repeated-note wavering between pitches, before finally relinquishing the melody to the orchestra (m. 474); by contrast, the orchestra manages to state the material without these signs of instability and to do so, furthermore, in coincidence with the conclusive return of the music to the tonic key.

In addition, the first movement is not only lacking a cadenza (missing, as well, from the entire Second Piano Concerto, in which the soloist asserts himself forcefully from the start), but, despite being quite technically demanding, is generally lacking in solo virtuosic display or filigree, a factor that helps to account for the Concerto's infamous failure with its initial audience in Leipzig.[15] Although this is, in all likelihood, partly the result of the work's previous conception as a symphony, the finished product should stand on its own terms. Having decided to convert the work into a concerto, Brahms did, in fact, make revisions to the first movement (perhaps even replacing the entire second theme group) and could have added more opportunities for virtuosic display had he wished to do so.[16] That he ultimately assigned the more assertive themes to the orchestra and less assertive ones to the soloist (particularly when simple adjustments to the dynamic level, thickness of texture, etc. could have made that contrast less clear), and that the piano comes more to the fore later in the work, were matters of choice.

In the soloist's quest for autonomy, the Concerto's second movement represents an intermediary stage; even if the piano maintains some restraint, it is on more equal footing with the orchestra, no longer being continually thwarted, interrupted, preempted, overwhelmed, suppressed, and frustrated by the ensemble. As in the first movement, the piano enters with its own theme, but with some hesitancy, quietly and with its characteristic "stutter" pattern of off-then-on-the-beat note repetition (ex. 4.6). Here, however, the soloist enters after only thirteen measures, and his reserve contrasts far less markedly with the character of the orchestral entrance, which is also quiet. Unlike in the previous movement, the soloist is entirely unaccompanied in his first several measures and in much subsequent material. Furthermore, it is the soloist who succeeds in bringing the movement to its first satisfying full cadence in the tonic (mm. 21–27)

Example 4.6. Brahms, Piano Concerto No. 1 in D Minor, op. 15, Second Movement, mm. 14–18

and who, unaccompanied, summons the strength to launch the central portion of the movement *poco forte* (m. 37). When the orchestra reenters (m. 44), it does so softly and tenderly, but even when a loud, staccato arpeggio rises in the strings (mm. 46–47), the piano is not fazed, simply mimicking the ascent on the relative major and tacking on two extra notes in a triumphant, martial rhythm (m. 47–48). The orchestra responds by backing down, employing the hesitant "stutter" pattern initially associated with (but now entirely absent from) the piano part (mm. 48–49). When the gentle orchestral material enters once again (at m. 52), and the winds and strings falter in their successive attempts to close their phrase, the piano steps in and is able to do so effortlessly (even if not on the tonic), accomplishing what the orchestra could not. The soloist simultaneously smooths out the dotted rhythm (mm. 57–58). In the recapitulation (m. 71), the piano retains the melody, with little or no accompaniment, for a full nine measures. The soloist neatly side-steps some of his previous note repetition (cf., e.g., mm. 14 and 71) and embarks, slowly but steadily, on a treacherous chromatic passage harmonized with a series of suspensions. Although the path may be strenuous, the soloist is no longer timid and moves with determination, eventually trading his syncopated rhythms for deliberate emphasis on each beat and gradually building to a passionate, powerful *fortissimo*. By contrast, when the winds enter at mm. 79–80, reduced to only one or two players per part, they hesitate. With their ascending fourth leaps and descending scalar motion, they aim at recapturing the movement's opening—but it now proves elusive. Here in the *Adagio*, the soloist finally launches the Concerto's first proper cadenza (m. 95; ex. 4.7); this remains extremely modest in its level of virtuosity, length, and dynamic level, but does represent an opportunity for display, to which the orchestra responds only briefly and quietly to close the movement.

In the finale, the soloist emerges as a more truly confident, assertive character—and ultimately transcends his struggles for autonomy. He no longer waits to be introduced by the orchestra, instead plunging headlong into solo exposition, stating the entire, spirited main phrase of the rondo refrain with neither interference nor support from the ensemble. Whereas, in the first movement, the soloist must struggle throughout to state the initial theme, and whereas the opening phrase of the slow movement is never repeated by the soloist, the first theme of the finale is his own from the start. Furthermore, the material with which the soloist initiates the finale is substantially bolder and more determined in character than that with which he made his first entrance in either of the preceding movements, even exhibiting more momentum and unimpeded drive than did the prior movements' orchestral openings. In the first and second movements, the soloist's initial entries were quiet, but here, the piano begins *forte*, which is especially striking in contrast with the low dynamic level of the second movement's orchestral conclusion. Furthermore, the finale, with its more forward-moving 2/4 meter, begins with the fastest tempo and rhythms of all three movements' openings, exhibiting neither the laboriousness of the first movement nor the dreamy, almost trance-like quality of the second. Contributing to the sense of drive and urgent momentum is an undercurrent of sixteenth-notes clacking away steadily in the accompaniment, and there is an unmistakable sense of defiance in the immediate and prominent use of syncopation—particularly in the way the refrain begins with a displaced anacrusis-like figure. There is also a certain confident efficiency in the clean, even parsing of phrases into four- and eight-bar units, something not found in the main themes of the earlier movements, with their uneven, extended phrasing. The initial gesture of the finale's crisply articulated refrain melody is a confident series of upward leaps and steps traversing an eleventh

Example 4.7. Brahms, Piano Concerto No. 1 in D Minor, op. 15, Second Movement, mm. 92–95

without hesitation or impediment, with a triumphant trill thrown in along the way. The final movement is the only one to begin with, or in which the piano is first introduced with, such an emphasis on triumphal ascent, or with an initial gesture so determinedly prolonged and uni-directional.

Yet, as Niemann remarks, although the finale begins with "joyous impetus, virile and full of rugged character," it nonetheless still exhibits a fundamental "element of strife"; the soloist's struggle is not yet complete.[17] The same rhythmic qualities (e.g., syncopation) that give the refrain its drive also lend the theme a certain underlying anxiety. Despite the lack of impediment to the finale's opening ascent, the melody subsequently exhibits circularity, immediate repetitions of short units of material, and unsteady dotted rhythms. Furthermore, resolution to the tonic is withheld until after the orchestra appropriates the melody (mm. 9–10).

Nevertheless, as the movement continues, so does our sense that the soloist now possesses a greater degree of control and boldness than does the ensemble. Whereas, in earlier movements, the orchestra and piano each entered with their own themes, at its initial entry in the finale (m. 9), the orchestra follows the piano's lead, restating the soloist's refrain melody. At m. 35, when the strings and winds attempt to steal the theme away from the piano, interrupting the soloist to begin again louder and higher, they falter, unable to finish the four measures that the soloist has just completed without incident; just as the strings seem to give up, the piano returns (m. 46), providing a measure of stability and a melodic line to be shadowed by the strings and winds. In the first episode (mm. 66ff.), the soloist maintains the "upper hand," carrying the melody for a full thirty-two measures to completion, rather than relinquishing it to the orchestra as it did the less directed, assured second themes of the previous movements. Loud, thick, defiantly syncopated, ascending chords in the soloist's right hand help to convey a sense of forcefulness. The orchestra, by contrast, follows the piano softly and *dolce*, with a hesitant, chromatic melodic line in the strings, each attempt at ascent thwarted by a downward turn. Introduced by a brief introductory fanfare in the brass (mm. 119–22), the soloist returns, almost as if to rescue the passage from the orchestra's ineptitude. *Fortissimo*, with thick, rolled chords, rapidly descending scales in octaves, and other rapid figuration, the soloist reclaims control, guiding the music back to the tonic.

In the central portion of the movement, there is an important step toward the reconciliation of soloist with orchestra. As the refrain returns (m. 144), it is once again the soloist who takes the initiative, but he leaves the final statement of the theme to the orchestra. Although it takes the ensemble three attempts to complete its final phrase (mm. 173–79), it eventually succeeds, concluding the refrain with a full cadence in the tonic. This newfound sense of resolution and finality seems to be the impetus behind the flowering of the idyllic B-flat-major episode (beginning in m. 181), with the only prominent melody in the finale not to be introduced by the soloist. That the calm idyllicism of the second episode can be the outcome of an orchestral conclusion that accomplishes a level of resolution not yet attained by the soloist himself—that the adoption of the piano's thematic material by the orchestra no longer represents a tragic, threatening, or otherwise stress-inducing circumstance to be met with a defensive response—suggests a new stage in the development of the soloist's sense of self.

Indeed, in subsequent passages of the movement, the soloist continues to resurface in a self-assured manner. At the recapitulation of the second theme (beginning in m. 348), the piano is restored to the role of primary melodic instrument, and then it launches directly into the longest and most elaborate cadenza of the work thus far.

Transcendence of the Minor Mode

The protagonist's transcendence of difficulty, the birth of his assertiveness, is paralleled, here, by an important development in the modal trajectory of the Concerto. In particular, at the conclusion of the cadenza, D minor is transcended as the music shifts to the parallel major. The establishment of the tonic major at the end of the Brahms's Concerto is itself the culmination of another ongoing, intermovement process.

Although D major surfaces several times in the Concerto's opening movement, the tonic major is not permanently established there. The music reverts from D major to the parallel minor immediately preceding the piano's initial entrance and at the conclusion of the recapitulation's second theme group, and the movement ends firmly in the minor mode. The movement sometimes exhibits a tendency to avoid even the tonic minor, displaying tonal ambiguity or conflict at structurally significant points where the tonic is expected—most notably, at the opening and at the beginning of the cataclysmic recapitulation. Even in the movement's coda, there remains a tendency to avoid local resolutions to the tonic minor (e.g., at mm. 464 and 470).

The second movement begins and ends in D major, but it too fails to establish the key permanently. The music never remains in D major for long; the mode reverts to minor for the movement's central section; and arrival in the tonic major is delayed in both the recapitulation and coda, occurring in the latter only at the very last moment. At its close, the movement has lulled us into a false sense of security in the major mode. The arrival of the finale, hurtling into its initial refrain with brusque tempo and duple meter, syncopation, and high dynamic level, uproots things, breaking the spell that has just been cast and returning us to the minor tonic. It is as if the gentle, more lightly scored slow movement is nothing more than an idyll in which the angst-filled striving heard elsewhere is only temporarily suspended.

In the final movement, Brahms heightens the drama by delaying the arrival and establishment of D major until quite late, conspicuously withholding it from certain key passages. For instance, the first major-mode transformation of the finale's refrain (starting at mm. 274–75), although immediately preceded by rhythmically augmented references to the "fate"-like motive that heralded the *first* movement's initial shift into D major, appears in *F* major, not in the tonic; when the theme does next return to the tonic (m. 297), it has reverted to the minor mode. Even more significantly, although the first episode originally appears in F major, its recapitulation is heard in the *minor* tonic. Unlike in the previous movements, it is the soloist himself who, in the initial cadenza (mm. 398–403), ushers in the first brief glimmer of D major and who, unaided, sets up the more definitive arrival of the major tonic at the cadenza's elision with the beginning of the coda (m. 410; ex. 4.8) This, in combination with the fact that the arrival and permanent establishment of D major coincide with the point at which the soloist has finally broken into unaccompanied, improvisational figuration, as if liberated from constraint, suggests that the work's transcendence of the minor mode is not unrelated to the change that takes place for the soloist in the finale.

Although D major has been a long time coming in the finale, its arrival signals a noticeable reduction in harmonic variety, and other signs also indicate that a sense of dramatic resolution has been reached. Interestingly, the first thematic

Example 4.8. Brahms, Piano Concerto No. 1 in D Minor, op. 15, Third Movement, mm. 392–419

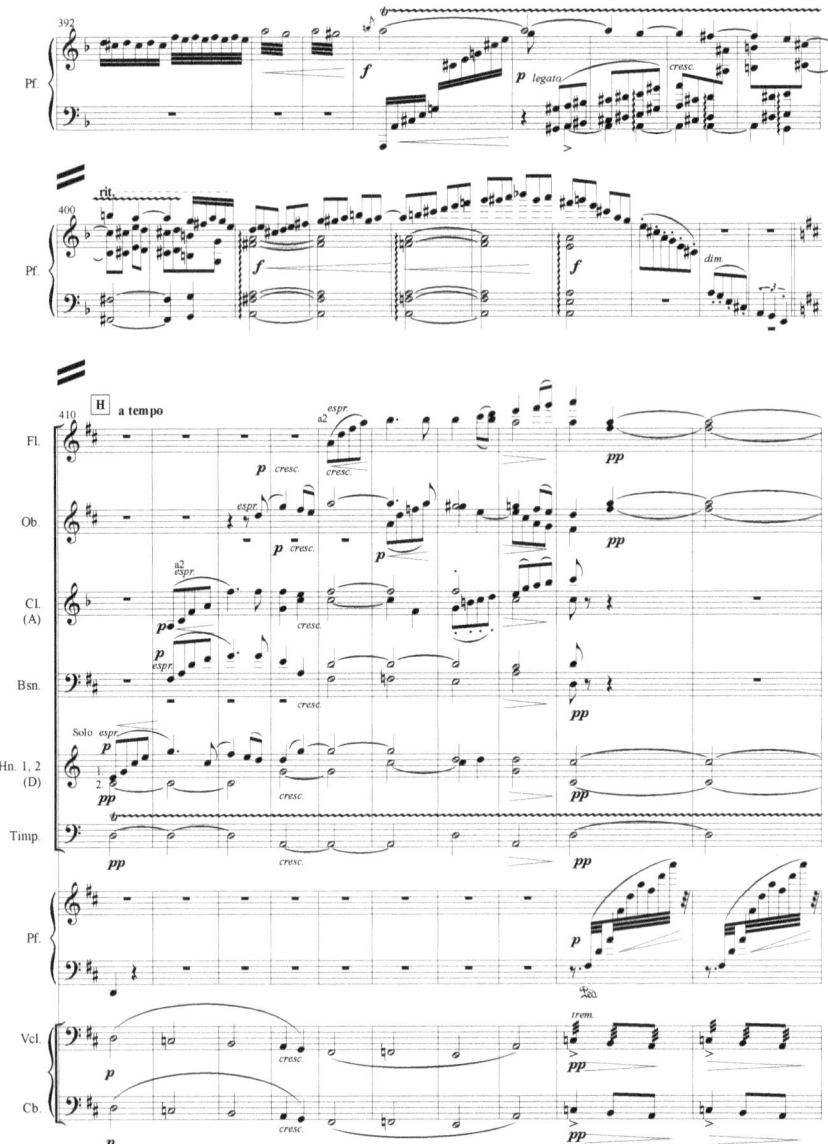

material heard in the tonic major, the theme that begins the coda, is not the refrain (as we would expect, since the initial cadenza is preceded by episodic material) but the theme of the second episode, by far the most idyllic of the movement's themes. Now that D major has arrived, the second-episode theme becomes even more idealized, with an emphasis on the "pastoral" winds and brass and on the upper registers; the melodic line continues upward where it previously turned down (cf. mm. 185–88 and 414–18); and a syncopated passage from the episode's original statement (mm. 189ff.) is replaced with more flowing material, including additional flowering of the theme in the winds (mm. 426ff.). Even the refrain material, when appearing for the final time (beginning in D major at mm. 442), is notably lighter, more relaxed, and less brusque than previously.

The sense of transcendence associated with the establishment of D major and the arrival of the idyllic theme in this key coincides with the soloist's gradual loosening of grip, his ceding of melodic material, voluntarily and without resistance, to the orchestra. The soloist, having single-handedly brought the music around to D major, drops out entirely for a time, almost as if to conserve energy, while the orchestra launches the coda, initiating the movement's first tonic-major passage with the one main theme of the movement not originally introduced by—nor, in fact, ever clearly stated in—the solo part. This is, however, merely the denouement of a process that has already been progressing more subtly for some time, as the piano has gradually become less predominant; it is almost as if, the closer the soloist comes to attaining D major (and, correspondingly, self-actualization), the less he feels compelled to exert himself as though responding to an orchestral threat, and the more soloist and orchestra are able to combine without contention or resistance, approaching the ideal glimpsed in the D-major movement. When D major finally arrives in the finale, the piano, having assertively declared its autonomy, is finally free of adolescent angst, emerging with a mature sense of self that allows it to coexist with the ensemble in the manner of a true adult, neither submitting to the orchestra's power nor straining to dominate. By the final measures of the Concerto, it is as though the soloist has actually transcended the *need* for melodic control—has, in fact, been altogether liberated from the constraints and limitations of thematic articulation—and is now released into the realm of free-flowing figuration, where he can do as he pleases. He even launches into a *second cadenza*, this one entirely in the major mode. (Thus, each movement of the Concerto contains one cadenza more than the preceding movement.) Although the soloist becomes somewhat troubled as the cadenza progresses, getting caught up in circular motion, with chromaticism and dissonance, he emerges triumphant, with a rapid, *fortissimo* sweep upward and a sequence of victorious trills. The ensemble, however, adopts the off-to-on-the-beat pattern–the "stutter" once associated with the hesitant soloist (mm. 526–27). Unlike the D-major conclusion of the slow movement, that of the finale is loud and emphatic, matching the dynamic levels of the disturbed opening and minor-mode close of the first movement. The soloist, with his loud, bold ascending sweeps, remains assertive to the end, leading the way to the work's conclusion.

The Signal Call

The final melodic ascents in the piano in fact represent the culmination of a third cross-movement process, this one involving motivic evolution. Here at the end of the finale, we find a transformation of the fanfare-like figure that heralded the soloist's initial appearance in the work. As the piece concludes and the soloist becomes "liberated," the call resurfaces and is freed of tensions it exhibited in the first movement, coming to represent a sort of "victory cry." The ultimate victory with which the call is associated is foreshadowed in the ways in which the figure is antithetical to the work's troubled opening: the call not only coincides with the initial arrival of D major in the first movement (m. 82; ex. 4.9), but it also begins with an inversion of the work's initial gesture.

Yet, in the first movement, the call itself is associated with tension and frustration. Unsteadiness is conveyed by stress on the weak beats of the measure and by the melodic wavering that restricts the melody to three pitches. The melody seems to want to continue its ascent beyond the tonic pitch, but never surpasses the upper neighbor. When the motive returns in the solo part in the F-major second theme group (mm. 166ff.; ex. 4.10), its initial fourth leaps no longer reach the work's tonic pitch. This time, the melody grows louder and climbs by step, and the music moves chromatically through harmonies of secondary function, conveying a sense of yearning and striving. Perhaps this is an attempt to once again reach the movement's tonic pitch, for it is when the melody attains a high D that the rising ceases (m. 170)—and yet the yearning remains unfulfilled, for the high D now appears not within a D-major context, but within a subdominant chord in F major. As if frustrated, the piano becomes louder, its melodic line eventually settling into a circular pattern in which the yearned-for D continually clashes with the A-flat a tritone below, until the D moves down chromatically (m. 175). As the movement continues, the motive remains associated with the frustrations of an unattainable goal. For example, at the beginning of the development section (ex. 4.11), the soloist forcefully attempts to reinstate the figure—repeatedly pounding out the leap from C up to F in *fortissimo* octaves—but the piano falters and then loses its grip entirely, leading to the orchestra's resumption of the troubled movement-opening motive (m. 231–32), modulation to a distant key (mm. 232–33), rapid scalar undulation, and the ensuing developmental material, with all its traditional markers of instability and ferment. And when the "horn call" surfaces for the last time in the movement, now actually in the horn, it does so in D major, but the figure's final note marks the precise point at which the music reverts to

Example 4.9. Brahms, Piano Concerto No. 1 in D Minor, op. 15, First Movement, mm. 82–86

D minor, not to return to the major tonic for the remainder of the movement. As the movement draws to a close, the piano begins to invoke the passage that once culminated in the first arrival of D major and the "horn call" (mm. 467–72). Although summoned, the D-major call does not reappear. As the final measures of the movement approach, the accents in the piano part emphasize ascending fourths, perhaps invoking those of the call (ex. 4.12), but these are ultimately countered by the emphasis on downward fourths in the orchestra (mm. 478–79, intensified in m. 481), confirming the work's opening gesture.[18]

In the Concerto's second movement, just as the struggle to permanently establish D major is temporarily suspended, so too is there a temporary suspension of progress in reestablishing the call and resolving its associated tensions. The call itself is not clearly invoked in this movement; any possible reference

Example 4.10. Brahms, Piano Concerto No. 1 in D Minor, op. 15, First Movement, mm. 164–77

to it would lie in the emphasis on ascending fourth leaps, particularly those so prominently featured in the movement's opening phrase (ex. 4.13; see also mm. 79–84, shown in part in ex. 4.14). Frustrated fourth ascents and descending fourth leaps are prominent also in the movement's cadenza and conclusion (see mm. 93–95 and the bassoon in m. 100, recalling the close of the previous movement).[19] And yet the music remains peaceful and resigned, transferring to the finale the onus of resurrecting the call and relieving its tensions.

Indeed, the solo piano takes up this task immediately upon beginning the finale. The initial gesture of the refrain (ex. 4.2) echoes the ascending fourth

Example 4.11. Brahms, Piano Concerto No. 1 in D Minor, op. 15, First Movement, mm. 226–30

leap from the end of the previous movement. Here in the finale, however, the soloist restores the pitch level of the original call, beginning on the fifth scale degree of D and landing, with defiant, off-beat emphasis, on the tonic. Unlike the first-movement call, in which attempts to ascend from the tonic pitch were immediately thwarted, the finale's opening gesture results in an optimistic, determined climb.[20] Following the first episode, the finale's opening gesture is transformed into a true, recognizable horn call, summoning back the refrain and the tonic key. At m. 119, a pair of horns cries out *marcato*, recalling, both melodically and

158 | *Allusion as Narrative Premise in Brahms*

Example 4.12. Brahms, Piano Concerto No. 1 in D Minor, op. 15, First Movement, mm. 473–78

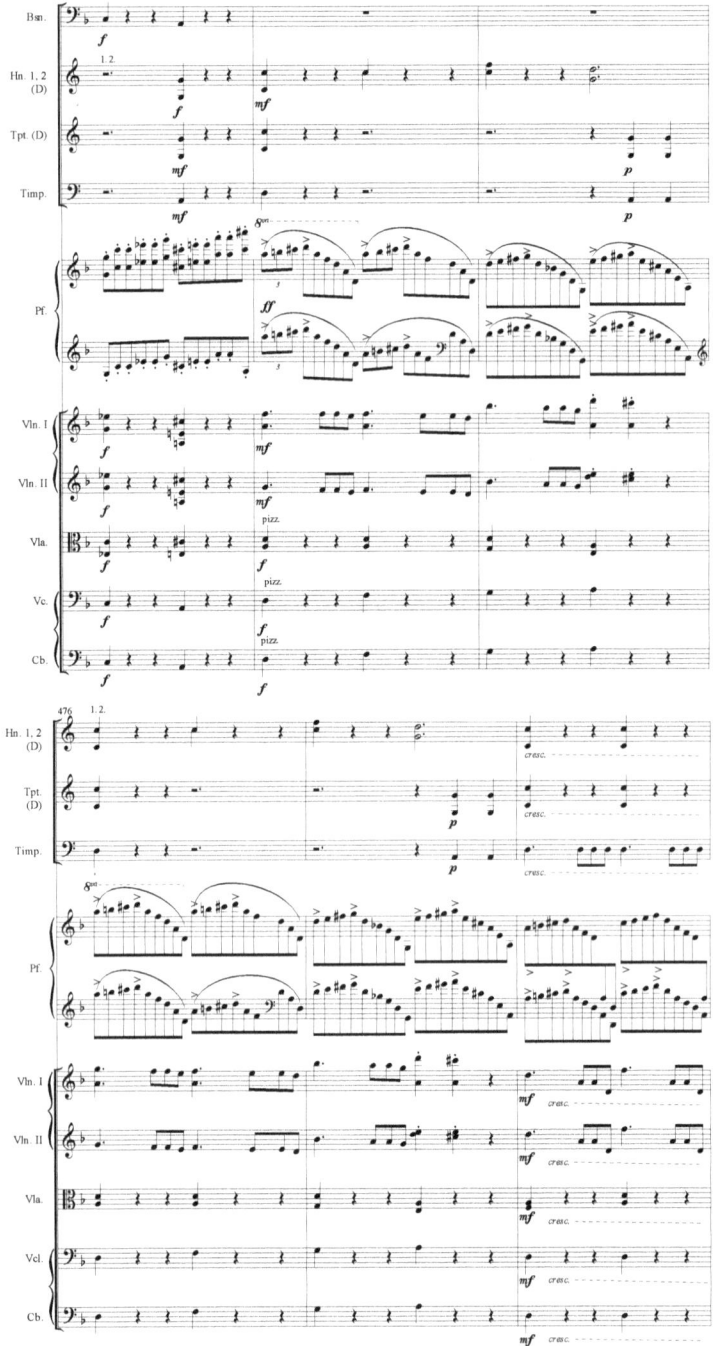

Example 4.13. Brahms, Piano Concerto No. 1 in D Minor, op. 15, Second Movement, mm. 1–5

rhythmically, the initial measure of the refrain theme and then leaping up, again by fourth, creating a $\hat{5}$-$\hat{1}$-$\hat{2}$-$\hat{5}$ ascent in D (ex. 4.15). This call retains the underlying shape of those heard in the first movement, which can be reduced to $\hat{5}$-$\hat{1}$-$\hat{2}$-$\hat{1}$ (e.g., the last one of the first movement, in m. 434) and, sometimes, to the $\hat{5}$-$\hat{1}$-$\hat{2}$-$\hat{5}$ we find here (e.g., in the penultimate appearance, beginning at m. 423 of the first movement). Here in the finale, however, the gesture has been streamlined, the

Example 4.14. Brahms, Piano Concerto No. 1 in D Minor, op. 15, Second Movement, mm. 79–82

Example 4.15. Brahms, Piano Concerto No. 1 in D Minor, op. 15, Third Movement, mm. 114–23

oscillations entirely removed so that the ascent progresses with determined directedness, free of setbacks. Yet, any resolution of tension is incomplete, for not only does the figure exhibit syncopation and end inconclusively on the dominant, but the horn call has not yet been recalled, streamlined, nor extended in D major. The four-note version of the call reappears, *forte* (although at the wrong pitch level), at the end of the first episode's recapitulation (m. 370), marking not only the ultimate establishment of D major, but also the movement's first cadenza, the soloist's most extended opportunity yet for virtuosic display. When the refrain material surfaces for the last time in the coda (in the passage starting at m. 442), finally in D major, the last note of its opening ascent is sustained, creating a greater sense of satisfaction, while the melody is continued in other voices (ex. 4.16a). With the onset of the "*più animato*" (m. 463), the melody is abbreviated to this victoriously ascending motive, which sounds imitatively in the strings, jubilant, in overlapping, major-mode statements (ex. 4.16b).

It is not until the very end of the work (m. 520; ex. 4.17) that the call returns both in the horn and in D major simultaneously, contributing to the sense of triumph and resolution at the Concerto's close, where it is supported by an extended series of celebratory piano trills. (Compare the chain of assertively ascending fourth and fifth leaps at mm. 526ff. with the resigned descending chains at the conclusions of the previous two movements.) As the texture thickens and the dynamic level rises, the call becomes increasingly directed and assertive: its melody is streamlined, and its off-kilter rhythm evened out. In the final measures, the soloist, emitting his last cries of victory, brings the signal call home, for the first time in the entire work, to precisely the same elevated register (and thus the same

Example 4.16a–b. Brahms, Piano Concerto No. 1 in D Minor, op. 15, Third Movement
(a) mm. 440–45

(b) mm. 463–69

pitches) in which the calls were initially heard in the first movement. The soloist further streamlines the figure, twice carrying it straight upward—$\hat{5}$-$\hat{1}$-$\hat{2}$-$\hat{3}$-$\hat{5}$, as the culmination of an extended ascent—each time, doubling the value of the high note and concluding with a decisive leap to F-sharp, thereby emphasizing, in triumph, both the height attained and the signifying pitch of the hard-won tonic major (mm. 528–32). At last, rising steadily in D major, the ascents are free of oscillation and syncopation. The trajectory of each call opposes the initial gesture of the Concerto, as if symbolically conquering the agitation and oppression associated with the work's opening orchestral theme. Embedded in the determined-sounding, minor-mode opening of the finale, then—and, before that, in the unsteadily oscillating, syncopated fanfare that announced the first, anticlimactic, timid arrival of the soloist—are the seeds of the joyous victory calls that celebrate the assertive emergence of the work's main protagonist, and, correspondingly, the permanent establishment of the tonic major.

Example 4.17. Brahms, Piano Concerto No. 1 in D Minor, op. 15, Third Movement, mm. 518–36

Example 4.17. *(Continued)*

Identification of Brahms with Soloist

Although the issue of extramusical meaning remains a thorny one (particularly in this concerto, whose first two movements have already been subjected to much programmatic interpretation), we would be remiss not to consider the metaphorical ties between the main protagonist of the Concerto—whose gradual emergence and transcendence of impediment coincides with the permanent establishment of D major and with the proliferation of such triumphant horn calls—and the young Brahms himself. As Botstein observes, "the concerto in the nineteenth century provided composer, performer and audience with an ideal … paradigm of music as a mirror of the struggle for individuality … as a solo instrument worked against, resisted, displaced, led and triumphed over orchestral sound. The concerto's solo instrument functioned as a metaphor of the individual's engagement with the conflict between freedom and order."[21] As Gál points out, Brahms, being a pianist, may well have been "incapable of thinking of a piano concerto without identifying himself with the soloist and of reshaping the concept accordingly."[22] Although Gál's statement would potentially apply to any concerto Brahms set out to perform, in no concerto could this be more the case than one actually composed by Brahms and for which he planned to be the original soloist.

Furthermore, as the protracted genesis of this work reminds us, in the 1850s, Brahms was struggling to emerge from adolescence as an artistically mature, autonomous individual capable of making his own unique and lasting musical contribution. In the Concerto's massive first movement, the soloist's struggle to assert himself against overwhelming odds is paralleled by the composer's own strain to produce a substantial, imposing artistic statement.

The work's finale represents a victory and a resolution not only for the soloist, but for the composer himself. The significant compositional problems and delays Brahms experienced in producing this piece reflect psychological and emotional challenges, personal insecurities, inexperience—what Walter Frisch refers to as "the composer's agitated state of mind in this period."[23] From the work's inception as a two-piano sonata in the spring of 1854 until approximately mid-December 1856, Brahms had remained unable to compose a finale for the piece. That he was, at last, able to complete the final movement, and thus the Concerto, represented a real triumph. Unlike material earlier in the work, the finale originated as a concerto movement and thus, as Musgrave observes, its "scheme and style are completely free of the conflict of genres inherent in the first movement. The soloist's relation to the orchestra is now entirely in accord with the tradition of the concerto rondo."[24] The finale's freedom from generic conflict corresponds directly to Brahms's own resolution—however temporary—of compositional indecision and dissatisfaction.

What is more, there is evidence that may link this concerto with E. T. A. Hoffmann's fictional character Johannes Kreisler—which is suggestive in light of the fact that Brahms strongly identified with this character from Hoffmann, even signing his early works "Kreisler, Jr."[25] First of all, the eleventh-spanning gesture at the opening of the Concerto's finale (where the soloist really begins to assert himself) bears a resemblance to a motive from Schumann's *Kreisleriana*—a gesture that furthermore appears prominently in the parallel position of that work, at the head of its final movement (ex. 4.18).[26] If this is a deliberate allusion, then the finale of op. 15 seems to begin all the more literally with the emergence of "Kreisler," with whom Brahms so happily advertised his strong identification—and, therefore, with that of Brahms himself. As we have seen, this motive in the Concerto appears in various forms throughout that work, generally embedded in versions of the signal call. The motive's transformation into triumphant D-major horn calls at the work's close would then appear to correspond all the more to a victorious transformation of the protagonist himself.

A mysterious notation in the autograph score of the Concerto may also have to do with Kreisler: under the opening melody of the *Adagio*, Brahms inscribed the phrase "*benedictus qui venit in nomine Domini.*"[27] There are various possible interpretations of this annotation (including that it refers to Robert Schumann—whom Brahms is known to have called "*Mynheer Domine*"—or, by extension, to his wife), and it was once even thought that the movement may have originated as part of a lost mass setting, although this is now known not to have been the case.[28] However, Kross proposes that "the real answer is ... to be found in [E. T. A.] Hoffmann. In *Kater Murr* this verse is written on the portal of the Abbey Kanzheim where Johannes Kreisler ultimately finds himself and achieves piece of mind" and that, furthermore, "if we recall how Brahms struggled over the proper form for his op. 15 ... the finishing of the first movement and the beginning of the second may very plausibly be seen in connection with the figure of Kreisler. The '*benedictus*' ... would then mark Brahms's passage ... [to] secure knowledge of his own artistry. It would characterize the emotional content of this movement only to a limited extent, and would not refer at all to Robert (or Clara) Schumann."[29] In Hoffmann's novel, Brahms's alter-ego, Johannes Kreisler, is in fact addressed several times by Father Hilarius as "*Domine.*"[30] Bozarth builds on this interpretation: "in the finale the solo piano takes the lead.... Our pianist/composer (Kreisler/Brahms) seems at last to be emerging as an individual, taking control over his musical fate, and moving in a determined fashion, free of the *Maestoso*'s problems."[31]

Whether or not we are convinced of the Concerto's relationship to Kreisler, if we accept the basic premise that the work is revelatory of Brahms's own struggles to assert himself artistically—that the Concerto is, in essence, a vehicle through which Brahms plays out, whether consciously or subconsciously or something in

Example 4.18. Schumann, *Kreisleriana*, op. 16, Eighth Movement, mm. 1–2

between, his artistic emergence and the establishment of his autonomy—then there remains an important matter with which we must deal: what is the significance of Brahms's having modeled the final movement of his Concerto on a movement by Beethoven? This is an issue to which we will return shortly.

A Closer Look at the Differences between the Brahms and Beethoven Movements

Despite the correspondences between the Brahms and Beethoven movements, there are important differences in general character and in aspects of structure through which Brahms distinguishes his concerto finale from his predecessor's. Although both movements begin with a good deal of momentum and with striking opening gestures in the solo part, certain features suggest that Brahms's soloist is the more intensely restless and strained of the two. Beethoven's refrain, with its lightly bouncing repeated notes, playful seventh leaps, and frolicky descending lines, sounds like child's play. The opening section of Brahms's finale more immediately exhibits circular tendencies and repetition in the melodic line, as well as a heavier texture and greater emphasis on syncopation than Beethoven's relatively square-cut opening. Beethoven begins his first two four-measure phrases identically in the tonic key, whereas Brahms is more restless, moving his opening gesture into the subdominant after four measures, transposing it up an eleventh, thickening the texture, and further emphasizing the syncopation with accent marks. As Michael Collier has observed, the continuous-sixteenth-note accompaniment in Beethoven's refrain is "steady, moving within … an octave" and "stabilized by the pedal note G," whereas that in op. 15 is "agitated," spanning two octaves "with frequent and abrupt changes of direction."[32] Transitions, for instance between the refrain and first episode, tend to be longer and melodically and harmonically more complicated with Brahms, and, unlike Beethoven, Brahms avoids strong cadences in his first episode, despite preparing the listener for them on several occasions.[33] Furthermore, Beethoven's fugato is based simply on his refrain theme, whose first two-and-a-half measures, although transposed, remain essentially intact. The fugato in Brahms's finale is more complex, developing both the refrain and a version of the second episode (whose common origin with the refrain is thus highlighted), and subjecting them to a greater degree of thematic transformation, including a healthy dose of chromaticism.

In the passages surrounding the establishment of the tonic major, discrepancies between the two movements become most pronounced—and most interesting. Brahms begins to deviate more substantially from the Beethovenian model in the recapitulation of the first episode (beginning at m. 348). In Beethoven's finale, the recapitulation is complete. In Brahms's recapitulation, however, only the first eight measures of the episode return; Brahms continues on with new material, but, even so, ends the section nearly twenty measures earlier than in the exposition, breaking from his model.[34] That this represents a triumph of sorts is suggested by the brief but clear reference to the signal call at the culmination of Brahms's recapitulatory episode. More thoroughly than Beethoven, Brahms keeps the primary focus on the soloist here, allowing him to retain the melody, accompanied only lightly, so that this triumph is not only that of Brahms himself but is identified with the assertion of the work's main protagonist.

Brahms rejects his model in another important respect here as well: by recapitulating the episode not in the major tonic, as we would expect, but in the *minor* mode. Brahms thus delays the arrival of D major until the elision between the cadenza and coda—where, as we have seen, the mode shift signals a sort of transcendence, coinciding with the ultimate liberation of the soloist. Indeed, Brahms reserves the tonic major for the moment when he is liberated from the confines of his model, for, with the arrival of the cadenza and then the long, triumphant coda, he breaks away from the mould most dramatically. Brahms's cadenza immediately follows the abbreviated recapitulation of the first episode, whereas Beethoven brings a greater sense of closure to the movement before the cadenza begins by first returning to refrain material. Brahms's cadenza thus appears as a further interruption of the modeled structure; the composer/soloist has seized control and, heralded by the signal call at the end of the first episode's recapitulation, he makes his ultimate emergence, stealing the opportunity for soloistic display without waiting his turn and marking his triumph by finally establishing the tonic major.

Brahms then celebrates this victory, flaunting his newly declared independence in a triumphant coda of highly unconventional structure. Beethoven ends his finale simply, with a brief, almost perfunctory coda, an afterthought, a true "tail" section. What remains of Brahms's finale, however, is far more substantive; having broken away from his Beethovenian model, the composer/soloist has much left to say on his own terms. Brahms's expansive coda consists of a series of a subsections that, totaling 127 measures, comprises nearly a quarter of the movement's material and provides additional opportunity for solo display in the form of a second cadenza. Also defiantly unconventional is Brahms's decision to begin the coda not with a return to refrain material—by now, certainly overdue—but with a recapitulation of the second episode, reinvoking the refrain only subsequently. In this context, the horn calls at the work's conclusion become the composer's own cries of liberation. (Might the melodic oscillations of Brahms's first-movement horn calls even be related to the repeated leaps between dominant and tonic at the close of the very first phrase of Beethoven's own Concerto? In the ascending gestures of his closing measures, Brahms seems to contradict not only the initial gesture of this work, but also the opening of Beethoven's Ninth Symphony, for the ascending open-fifth arpeggiation in sixteenths in mm. 526ff., are nearly exact inversions of the gestures with which the first violins are occupied in the first several measures of the Symphony).

Furthermore, the emergence of the piano over the course of the work originates with Brahms himself, for Beethoven's soloist (like that in Brahms's Second Piano Concerto) is far more assertive from the outset. Beethoven's initial solo entrance is, in fact, strikingly more assertive than the entrance of the orchestra, and whereas Brahms's first movement contains no cadenza, Beethoven's features a long, highly virtuosic one. Brahms waits until the finale to allow his soloist to initiate a movement alone, whereas Beethoven's soloist takes the initiating role as early as the second movement. Even within the finale itself, Beethoven's soloist has many more opportunities than Brahms's for free-flowing virtuosic display (e.g., in mm. 26 and 152) before the movement's main cadenza.

Reinterpreting the Significance of the Beethovenian Model

If the D-Minor Concerto is concerned with its composer's struggles for autonomy and maturity, then why would Brahms choose to model his music so closely on that of another composer—particularly when the composer is such an imposing role model, and especially in the finale, where, presumably, autonomy must be most clearly demonstrated? Indeed, as Moseley suggests, if op. 15 "composes out a fierce struggle for autonomy from Beethoven, then it seems strange that the rondo finale unabashedly lifts its formal template" from one of Beethoven's works.[35]

Moseley attempts to reconcile this apparent paradox by underplaying the relevance of Beethoven to any declaration of autonomy that may be embedded in Brahms's Concerto and proposing that it was primarily Robert Schumann, not Beethoven, from whom Brahms felt a need to distinguish himself at the time of the Concerto's composition.[36] Although Moseley concedes that there are similarities between the Concerto's opening and the *Schreckensfanfare*, he nonetheless proposes that the Concerto reaches back to Beethoven mainly by way of the opening of Schumann's D-Minor Symphony, op. 120, "itself composed in the shadow of Beethoven's Ninth."[37] "Beethoven," Moseley argues, "is thus invoked as a topos ... more than he is engaged in dialectical combat; it would take Brahms decades to summon up the courage for that. It was only when he began to nurture his ambitions for a lofty place in the canon that Beethoven would become a real cause for anxiety. In the 1850s, it was a closer figure that sparked a Bloomian fusion of homage and disparagement, emulation and competition: ... Robert Schumann."[38] Yet, regardless of the Concerto's possible associations with Schumann, Moseley is rather too hasty in dismissing the possibility that Beethoven himself—who of course clearly induced in Brahms a signifcant, "Bloomian" "anxiety of influence" in this period and later—is more directly involved in any meaning the work might bear.[39] This is especially so in light of all that is known about the psychological significance of Beethoven to Brahms's development of an artistic sense of self even during the *"Neue Bahnen"* period, in light of the fact that Brahms's opening indeed seems to recall one of the most memorable moments of Beethoven's Ninth, and especially given Brahms's use of a Beethovenian model for the Concerto's final movement. Brahms even assigns to his First Piano Concerto the same opus number that Beethoven used for his own.

Brahms indeed appears to engage in "dialectical combat" with Beethoven in this work, if not at the beginning of the Concerto, then in the finale, where the work's protagonist wages his ultimate battle for autonomy. For it is precisely Brahms's employment of a Beethovenian model for the finale that sets up the framework, the backdrop, against which such a dialectical battle may take place. The particular way in which Brahms's handles his model suggests that the modeling results not necessarily from a lack of inspiration, but from Brahms's need to demonstrate his own *departure* from Beethoven. It is suggestive that Brahms's finale begins with angst-filled determination and striving on the part of the pianist-composer and shifts to triumphant celebration— complete with jubilant horn calls—in the long-awaited major mode precisely where the young composer most clearly differentiates himself from Beethoven. The soloist's transcendence of a concerto-long struggle to assert his independence parallels Brahms's own transcendence of the Beethovenian model, his own assertion of autonomy. Thus, *Brahms's handling of the model reflects the same concern for the gradual emergence of the soloist/composer that is exhibited over the course of the work as a whole.* Perhaps Brahms's decision to model the majority of his finale so closely upon Beethoven's was motivated by his desire ultimately to demonstrate his breaking away from the model, to act out his own declaration of independence at the culmination of this big work, as though illustrating (for himself) his ability to cast out on his own artistically. Although Brahms was to remain in Beethoven's shadow, perhaps never quite outpacing it, this concerto may thus have been an attempt—whether fully conscious or not— to grapple with conflicting feelings of admiration, reverence, indebtedness, angst, and even resentment toward Beethoven and, more broadly, toward the tradition and standards he represented. Such meaning would certainly have been intensely private, not something that Brahms would have intended his audiences to perceive. Indeed, that Brahms employed a model at all is difficult enough to detect that it appears to have remained unnoticed until well into the twentieth century.

Furthermore, the fact that Brahms's fugato demonstrates a higher level of structural complexity than Beethoven's may bear hermeneutic significance. By associating Brahms's refrain with the protagonist and his attempts to assert himself, and by linking the second episode with idyllic transcendence, we may view the fugato's unification of the two themes and revelation of their common origin as in some sense foreshadowing the protagonist's transcendence of the struggle to assert himself. Now in the minor mode and twisting in circular chromatic motion, the episode theme no longer sounds idyllic, but the orchestral "working out" of the fugato's tangles (while, remarkably, the soloist is silent) clears the way for the piano's emergence in the tonic major, an event to culminate in the restoration and enhancement of the idyllicism already associated with the second episode. As we know, the immediate outcome of the fugato is a significant advance along this path to "transcendence": upon his initial reentry after the fugato, Brahms's soloist presents the refrain theme for the first time in the major mode, without the hesitation of Beethoven's soloist, who, at the parallel spot, stalls for a full eight measures before beginning the melody. If the restlessness of Brahms's protagonist within the borrowed structure of this movement is indicative of Brahms's own restlessness in Beethoven's shadow, then this pivotal "working out" in the fugato is all the more relevant to Brahms's own struggles for independence: it occurs in the very portion of the movement that most distinctively reveals a structural linkage between Brahms's finale and Beethoven's.

Tovey has suggested that it is from Joachim's Violin Concerto, op. 11, "that Brahms has derived the main points in which his form differs from Beethoven"; this must be addressed here, for Brahms does not effectively declare his autonomy if he merely resorts to a second model in deviating from the first.[40] Indeed, the periods of composition for the Brahms and Joachim concertos did overlap; both works are in D minor, ending in the parallel major; and the basic structure of Joachim's finale, like that of Brahms's final movement, seems to have been strongly influenced by the structure of the final movement of Beethoven's C-Minor Concerto.[41] Yet, it appears that Brahms neither saw nor heard Joachim's finale until several months after his own concerto was premiered, and thus it is more likely that Joachim was influenced by Brahms rather than the other way around.[42] (Joachim's Concerto is, in fact, dedicated to Brahms.) There are, in any case, highly relevant differences between the ways in which the two composers handle their model. Unlike Brahms, Joachim recapitulates his first episode as expected, in the tonic major, rather than delaying the mode shift; Joachim's coda is less substantial than that of Brahms; and Joachim's finale, although virtuosic throughout, contains no cadenza—let alone two.

Reconciling Our Interpretation with Other Possible Meanings

How, then, does our interpretation interact with other extramusical programs that have been suggested for op. 15? We have good reasons to believe that the work—particularly its first two movements—contains programmatic associations with the Schumanns. For instance, Joachim claimed that the powerful opening of the work represented a reaction to Schumann's suicide attempt of February 1854.[43] (It remains debatable, however, whether Schumann's breakdown could actually have inspired the opening of the Concerto, for the suicide attempt did not occur until February 27, and already, by April 9, when Grimm wrote of the work to Joachim, the entire piece had been finished and the parts copied out, and Brahms had also been traveling during the intervening time.[44]) As for the second movement of the Concerto, Brahms himself wrote to Clara Schumann that the *Adagio* was a "tender portrait" of which she was the subject.[45] There is also the mysterious "*benedictus*" notation discussed above, sometimes taken to be a reference to Robert Schumann (for whom the movement could have been conceived as a requiem of sorts) or to his wife, who bore his name. If Brahms meant to represent himself either as the one who had come "in the name of the Lord" or as "*Domine*" himself, then the second movement could, in turn, represent Brahms's idyllic vision of his ability to be "at peace" with the lofty role prescribed for him by the Schumanns. Ultimately, however, given what we know of Brahms's self-effacing personality, it is unlikely that the young composer would have portrayed himself in such terms. In the case of the finale alone, there is no testimonial evidence to suggest a clear programmatic link with the Schumanns, nor, for that matter, any other programmatic intentions; Reynolds suggests that, by combining the "Kreisler" motive from Schumann's *Kreisleriana* with Schumann's supposed "Clara cipher" at the opening of the finale, Brahms depicts his yearned-for union with Clara, although the evidence for this is tenuous.[46]

While it is impossible to determine conclusively what extramusical meaning the work may bear, neither is it necessary to dismiss one theory to entertain another, for the Concerto may well contain layers of meaning that co-exist and even enrich one another. The need to establish his own musical voice and historical position, the need to come to terms with his feelings for Clara Schumann, and the need to cope with her husband's nervous breakdown all weighed heavily on Brahms during the period in which this concerto was written, intermingling in his mind in ways that must remain at least partially indiscernible to us and that, in all likelihood, may not have been entirely discernible even to him—but that surely caused the young man to question deeply who he was and where he was headed. It is not at all implausible that all of these concerns are intertwined in op. 15. As Bozarth suggests, even if the opening of the Concerto represented a reaction to Schumann's suicide attempt, "the issues raised in Brahms's mind by [this event] were surely the larger ones" of "the composer in conflict, on both professional and personal levels, with the world around him, and the devastating effects of this tension on his life," and thus the emotion expressed in the work's opening need not relate specifically to Schumann but may represent more generally the "existential turmoil" experienced by creative artists.[47]

To whatever extent this work is has to do with the Schumanns, it is also, inevitably, concerned with Brahms himself, for any meaning the Concerto may hold is necessarily filtered through the composer's own subjective lens. We have every reason to believe that Clara and Robert Schumann were, in fact, inseparably linked in Brahms's mind with his need to establish himself professionally. As his mentors and promoters, they both encouraged his development and contributed to his anxieties—and thus it is not incongruous that their images should be superimposed here on the same canvas on which Brahms expresses his struggle for artistic independence.

In the Concerto's last movement, as the soloist finally asserts himself and as Brahms breaks away from Beethoven's structural model, arriving on his own terms in the tonic major and embarking on an unconventional, extensive coda replete with victorious horn calls, Brahms appears to act out a triumphant establishment of self. Perhaps he attempts, thereby, to metaphorically overcome the various, yet interrelated, psychological challenges involved not only in reconciling his complicated feelings about the Schumanns, but also in finding his own artistic voice and seeking to determine his own historical significance and position.

Notes

1. Brahms to Joachim, Düsseldorf, June 19, 1854, as published in Brahms, *Briefwechsel*, ed. Max Kalbeck (Berlin: Deutsche Brahms-Gesellschaft, 1919; repr. Tutzing: Hans Schneider, 1974), 5:47. Max Kalbeck (*Johannes Brahms*, 4th ed. (Berlin: Deutsche Brahms-Gesellschaft, 1921; repr. Tutzing: Hans Schneider, 1976), 1:164–65) suggested that the work began as a symphony inspired by Brahms's first hearing of Beethoven's Ninth Symphony. This idea is supported by Christopher Reynolds ("A Choral Symphony by Brahms?," *19th-Century Music* 9/1 (1985): 3–25), who argues that the piece may even have been conceived as a "choral" symphony in the manner of Beethoven's. Although the early piano version could have been simply a sketch for an intended symphony not yet orchestrated, members of Brahms's immediate circle clearly refer to it as a sonata in their correspondence.

2. See Brahms to Joachim, Düsseldorf, June 19, 1854, and Brahms to Joachim, Düsseldorf, July 27, 1854, as published in Brahms, *Briefwechsel*, 5:47 and 55–56, respectively; George S. Bozarth, "Brahms's First Piano Concerto, op. 15: Genesis and Meaning," *Beiträge zur Geschichte des Konzerts: Festschrift Siegfried Kross zum 60. Geburstag*, ed. Reinmar Emans and Matthias Wendt (Bonn: G. Schroeder, 1990), 211–12; and Roger Scott Moseley, "Brief Immortality: Recasting History in the Music of Brahms" (PhD diss., University of California, Berkeley, 2004), 114–15.

3. Brahms to Robert Schumann, Düsseldorf, January 30, 1855, in *Johannes Brahms: Life and Letters*, ed. Styra Avins, trans. Josef Eisinger and Styra Avins (Oxford: Oxford University Press, 1997), 85.

4. Bozarth, "Brahms's First Piano Concerto," 215, 216, 241.

5. Reynolds, "A Choral Symphony by Brahms?," 5; Bozarth, "Brahms's First Piano Concerto," 216, fn. 28, 241; and John Daverio, *Crossing Paths: Schubert, Schumann, and Brahms* (Oxford: Oxford University Press, 2002), 148.

6. Kalbeck, *Johannes Brahms*, 1:292–93.

7. Malcolm MacDonald, *Brahms, Master Musicians Series*, ed. Stanley Sadie (Oxford: Oxford University Press, 2001; originally published in New York by Schirmer Books, 1990), 99.

8. See Jan Swafford, *Johannes Brahms: A Biography* (New York: Alfred A. Knopf, 1997), 171; Michael Musgrave, *The Music of Brahms, Companions to the Great Composers* (London: Routledge & Kegan Paul, 1985), 124; and Moseley, "Brief Immortality," 118.

9. Donald Tovey (*Essays in Musical Analysis* (London: Oxford University Press, 1935), 3:74, 118–19) seems to have been among the first to suggest an underlying similarity between the finales. Charles Rosen demonstrates the modeling more thoroughly in "Influence: Plagiarism and Inspiration," *19th-Century Music* 4/2 (1980): 91–93.

10. Rosen, "Influence: Plagiarism and Inspiration," 93.

11. Swafford, *Johannes Brahms*, 169.

12. Walter Niemann (*Brahms*, trans. Catherine Alison Phillips (New York: Alfred A. Knopf, 1941; originally published in 1920 in Berlin by Schuster & Loeffler), 282) suggests that, for Brahms, the key of D minor generally signifies "hard, pitiless struggle, daemonic, supernatural shapes, sinister defiance, steely energy, dramatic intensity of passion, darkly fantastic, grisly humor." Consider, for instance, the "Edward" Ballade, op. 10/1 (1854), and the "Tragic" Overture, op. 81 (1880).

13. This "stutter" pattern is also prominent near the beginning of Beethoven's Ninth Symphony (e.g., mm. 13ff.).

14. I use the pronoun "he" in referring to the soloist here only because Brahms himself was the work's original intended soloist.

15. See Edwin Evans, *Handbook to the Pianoforte Works of Johannes Brahms* (New York: Burt Franklin, 1970); originally published as vol. 4 of Evans's *Historical, Descriptive and Analytical Accounts of the Entire Works of Johannes Brahms* (London: W. Reeves, 1912), 121.

16. See MacDonald, *Brahms*, 159–60.

17. Niemann, *Brahms*, 315.

18. Cf. the descending fourths here with the first violin part in the first several measures of Beethoven's Ninth Symphony (and note also the "Fate Motive" rhythm in Brahms's timpani). My thanks to an anonymous reviewer for the observation about the accents in the piano in this passage.

19. Again, cf. the first several measures of Beethoven's Ninth Symphony.

20. The beginning of the finale recalls not only the opening gesture of the call itself, but also the initial $\hat{5}$-$\hat{1}$-$\hat{2}$-$\hat{3}$ of the first movement's second theme. As it was only a number of measures into the first movement's second theme group that the solo piano clearly invoked the signal call, this troubled reminiscence at the beginning of the finale may suggest the soloist's struggle to reinstate the call in some form—and, by extension, to reestablish the tonic major, in which that second theme was last heard. The same $\hat{5}$-$\hat{1}$-$\hat{2}$-$\hat{3}$ also initiates the finale's own, impassioned second theme (which, like that of the first movement, first appears in F major in the solo piano). Taking this into account, MacDonald (*Brahms*, 103–4) suggests that perhaps the "'academically' verbatim" recapitulation of the first movement's second subject was intended "to fix its shape more strongly in the listener's mind so that the finale might at length be sensed as the true fulfillment of a promise made in [that subject]." Yet the promise is not truly to be fulfilled until the horn call returns, its tensions are released, and D major is permanently reestablished.

21. Leon Botstein, "Concerto—Section 4: The Nineteenth Century—Subsection ii: The Place of Virtuosity," *Grove Music Online*. Accessed June 17, 2007. www.grovemusic.com

22. Hans Gál, *Johannes Brahms: His Work and Personality*, trans. Joseph Stein (New York: Knopf, 1963), 215.

23. Walter Frisch, *Brahms and the Principle of Developing Variation*, California Studies in Nineteenth-Century Music 2 (Berkeley: University of California Press, 1984), 65.

24. Musgrave, *The Music of Brahms*, 123.

25. For a facsimile of Brahms's signature ("*Kreisler jun.*") on the F-Minor Piano Sonata, see Constantin Floros, *Johannes Brahms, "Free but Alone": A Life for a Poetic Music*, trans. Ernest Bernhardt-Kabisch (Frankfurt am Main: Peter Lang, 2010); originally published as *Johannes Brahms, "frei aber einsam": Ein Leben für eine poetische Musik* (Zürich: Arche Zürich, 1997), 20. See also 21.

26. See Christopher Reynolds, *Motives for Allusion: Context and Content in Nineteenth-Century Music* (Cambridge, MA: Harvard University Press, 2003), 122–23. See also Reynolds, "A Choral Symphony by Brahms?," 15. It is worth noting that there is also a clear, recognized allusion to this motive in the finale of Schumann's own First Symphony.

27. For a facsimile of the autograph page, see Bozarth, "Brahms's First Piano Concerto," 224.

28. See Tovey, *Essays in Musical Analysis*, 3:117–18; MacDonald, *Brahms*, 195; Bozarth, "Brahms's First Piano Concerto," 215; and Reynolds, "A Choral Symphony by Brahms?," 6, as well as Malcolm MacDonald, "'Veiled Symphonies'?: The Concertos," in *The Cambridge Companion to Brahms*, ed. Michael Musgrave (Cambridge: Cambridge University Press, 1999), 161.

29. Siegfried Kross, "Brahms and E.T.A. Hoffmann," *19th-Century Music* 5/3 (1982): 200. On Brahms's nickname for Schumann, see Kalbeck, *Johannes Brahms*, 1:166. See also Bozarth, "Brahms's First Piano Concerto," 245; Kalbeck, *Johannes Brahms*, 1:166; Burnett James, *Brahms: A Critical Study* (London: Dent, 1972), 74; Constantin Floros, *Brahms and Bruckner: Studien zur Musikalischen Exegetik* (Wiesbaden: Breitkopf & Härtel, 1980), 145; and Floros, *Johannes Brahms, "Free but Alone*," 42–43.

30. E. T. A. Hoffmann, *The Life and Opinions of the Tomcat Murr, Together with a Fragmentary Biography of Kapellmeister Johannes Kreisler on Random Sheets of Waste Paper*, trans. and annotated by Anthea Bell (London: Penguin Books, 1999), 261–62.

31. Bozarth, "Brahms's First Piano Concerto," 242.

32. Michael Collier, "The Rondo Movements of Beethoven's Concerto No. 3 in C Minor, op. 37, and Brahms's Concerto No. 1 in D Minor, op. 15: A Comparative Analysis," *Theory and Practice: Journal of the Music Theory Society of New York State* 3/1 (1978): 5.

33. See Collier, "The Rondo Movements of Beethoven's Concerto No. 3 in C Minor, op. 37, and Brahms's Concerto No. 1 in D Minor, op. 15," 11 and William Hussey, "Compositional Modeling, Quotation, and Multiple Influence Analysis in the Works of Johannes Brahms: An Application of Harold Bloom's Theory of Influence to Music" (PhD diss., University of Texas, Austin, 1997), 49.

34. Hussey observes that "Brahms separates himself from those before him, including Beethoven, since the return is normally complete or at least more substantial" ("Compositional Modeling," 54).

35. Moseley, "Brief Immortality," 110.

36. Moseley, "Brief Immortality," 110–12.

37. Moseley, "Brief Immortality," 111–12. See also Bozarth, "Brahms's First Concerto," 227–28, fn. 62 and Steven Lubin, "Transforming Reheard Themes: Brahms and the Legacy of Beethoven's Ninth," *American Brahms Society Newsletter* 17/1 (1999): 2.

38. Moseley, "Brief Immortality," 112.

39. On Harold Bloom and his notion of an "anxiety of influence," see chapter 1, n. 14.

40. Tovey, *Essays in Musical Analysis*, 3:108.

41. Tovey, *Essays in Musical Analysis*, 3:118. See also MacDonald, "'Veiled Symphonies'?," 160–61; and Daverio, *Crossing Paths*, 236.

42. See Daverio, *Crossing Paths*, 296–97, n. 92; and MacDonald, "'Veiled Symphonies'?," 301, n. 13.

43. See Bozarth, "Brahms's First Piano Concerto," 212, fn. 6. On possible reminiscences of Schumann's music in the first movement of op. 15, see also Moseley, "Brief Immortality," 110–11; Reynolds, "A Choral Symphony by Brahms?," 7; and John Horton, *Brahms Orchestral Music*, BBC Music Guides (Seattle, WA: University of Washington Press, 1978), 29. For more on meaning in the Concerto's first movement, see also James Hepokoski, "Monumentality and Formal Processes in the First Movement of Brahms's Piano Concerto No. 1 in D Minor, op. 15," in *Expressive Intersections in Brahms: Essays in Analysis and Meaning*, ed. Heather Platt and Peter H. Smith (Bloomington: Indiana University Press, 2012), 217–51.

44. Gustav Ernst, *Johannes Brahms: Persönlichkeit, Leben und Schaffen* (Berlin: Deutsche Brahms-Gesellschaft, 1930), 78. Grimm's letter is actually dated "March 9," but nearly all scholars since Kalbeck (*Johannes Brahms*, 1:166) have realized that Grimm must have meant "April 9," for, as Bozarth points out, "the letter mentions Brahms's trip to Cologne in late March as having already taken place" ("Brahms's First Piano Concerto," 212, fn. 8). Raymond Knapp, however, suggests that "März" may actually have been intended to read "Mai" (*Brahms and the Challenge of the Symphony* (Stuyvesant, NY: Pendragon Press, 1997), 5, fn. 13).

45. Brahms to Clara Schumann, Hamburg, December 30, 1856, cited in Jan Swafford, *Johannes Brahms*, 168. Some have identified, in this movement, resemblances to certain song melodies and/or an apparent reference to the moment in Beethoven's *Fidelio* when Leonora is reunited with Florestan, linking these with Clara Schumann. (See Bozarth "Brahms's First Piano Concerto," 218–20, 229; Carl Dahlhaus, *Johannes Brahms: Klavierkonzert Nr. 1*, Meisterwerke der Musik: Werkmonographien zur Musikgeschichte 3, ed. Ernst Ludwig Wältner (München: Fink, 1965), 19; Hussey, "Compositional Modeling," 65–68 and 72; and Reynolds, "A Choral Symphony by Brahms?," 6–7).

46. Reynolds also identifies the fugato subject (at m. 181) as a reference to Robert Schumann and proposes that Brahms thus "implants a representation of Robert into a movement that begins and ends by thematically binding Kreisler to Clara" and that, "while

waiting for Robert to die," Brahms wrote his finale "with a motivic anticipation of the day when Clara would be his." (See Reynolds, "A Choral Symphony by Brahms?," 19–21.) This scenario has been taken less than seriously—particularly as the appearance, here, of the so-called "Clara cipher" (a five-note motive whose identification with Clara has been touted especially by Eric Sams, e.g., in "Brahms and His Musical Love Letters, *The Musical Times* 112/1538 (1971): 329–30) is certainly not clear, and, indeed, the very existence of such a cipher in Brahms's works has been called into question. See Bozarth, "Brahms's First Piano Concerto," 218, fn. 39 and 240, fn. 87. Although even Daverio, who is generally cautious about ciphers, acknowledges that these can appear in retrograde, Bozarth (240, fn. 87) points out that the use of the five-note cipher in retrograde would be "an unlikely way in which to" actually introduce this motive into the work for the first time. See also Daverio, *Crossing Paths*, 112–13.

47. Bozarth, "Brahms's First Piano Concerto," 237–38.

5 A Later Example: Tragic Antiquarianism in Brahms's Fourth Symphony

> *"To the resigned, elegiac character of the Fourth Symphony, its note of quiet tragedy and uncanny merriment, and its epic ballad quality, may be added a strong tendency to archaism. There is no other Symphony of Brahms's which has so individual, strong, or consciously archaistic a character."*
>
> —Walter Niemann, *Brahms*, 345
>
> *"The finale of the Fourth Symphony is a technical tour de force in an archaic genre, expressed in terms of a personal and cultural tragedy."*
>
> —Jan Swafford, *Johannes Brahms: A Biography*, 523

"Tragic" and "archaic" have always been two of the most frequently recurring themes in interpretations of Brahms's fourth and final symphony, a work composed during the summers of 1884 and 1885 while Brahms vacationed in Mürzzuschlag.[1] It has even been suggested that the piece may have been inspired by the tragedies of Sophocles, which Brahms read at around this time in a German translation by his friend, Gustav Wendt.[2]

The Symphony's somber atmosphere is attributable in part to Brahms's unusual choice of the "dark" tonality of E minor for its tonic key.[3] There are relatively few precedents for this choice of key among the standard symphonic repertory of the Classical and Romantic periods. Haydn's "*Trauer*" ("Mourning") Symphony, by far the most well-known of these, was clearly a work that Brahms had in mind, for he rather remarkably referred to his own Fourth Symphony as his "neue traurige Symphonie."[4]

The finale of the Fourth Symphony is one of the work's most "tragic" movements, especially due to Brahms's decision to conclude the work in the minor mode rather than in the parallel major; a "transcendent" shift to the major had come to be expected in minor-mode symphonies, particularly following the examples set by Beethoven's Fifth and Ninth, and this is indeed what occurs at the conclusion to Brahms's other minor-mode symphony, No. 1.[5] As Tovey observes, the piece is "one of the rarest things in classical music, a symphony which ends tragically."⁶ Indeed, Hans Gál goes so far as to characterize the finale as exhibiting the "merciless horror of a death dance."⁷ And Kalbeck writes that, in this movement, "death is ushered into the midst of life … Brahms celebrates the destroying angel of darkness as the lord and master of a symphony of the world's destruction.… Fire and murder, war and pestilence, flash flood and earthquake have inspired in him the theme that is varied in the giant passacaglia, and the events of millennia have laid the groundwork for this … series of commemorative columns to things and martyrs."⁸

Pointing to a greater number of E-minor symphonic precedents from the Baroque Era, Raymond Knapp has suggested that this tonality itself is "an emblem of the Baroque," and Brahms's intention to evoke music of the past—particularly of the Baroque Era—in this work is certainly obvious in other respects.⁹ Among these are Brahms's mixing of the major and minor scales and use of the "archaic" Phrygian mode (with its lowered second scale degree) and plagal harmony in the slow second movement and, to some extent, in the third movement as well.¹⁰ Additionally, scholars have identified a number of possible references or models for the Symphony's opening, noting resemblances to Bach and Handel, to Lully and Mendelssohn, to Beethoven's "Hammerklavier" Sonata, and to the opening of Mozart's Symphony No. 40 in G Minor, K. 550, as well as a possible reference to Beethoven's Fifth Symphony near the close of the second movement.¹¹

And yet Brahms's sense of historicism is most blatant in the Symphony's final movement: the finale is a chaconne, a form generally associated with the Baroque Era (Tovey calls it "one of the most ancient of musical forms").¹² The finale consists of a simple eight-bar ostinato theme, followed by a series of thirty variations and a coda (also related to the ostinato). (The variations may be grouped into a broad ternary form, with a central "B" section coinciding with Var. 10, and Var. 16 representing the beginning of a recapitulation at m. 129.)¹³ The ostinato appears not in the bass at first, but in the melody until Variation 4 (beginning at m. 33) and sometimes moves back up to the melody to serve as the basis for elaboration (e.g., in Variation 12, beginning at m. 97).

This chapter will demonstrate that, given the very real possibility that the ostinato served as a motivic kernel for the Symphony's opening and for other thematic materials in the piece, we can find in this symphony further evidence of the interrelationship of historical reference and intermovement motivic connections in Brahms's music. The ostinato is, at the very least, a clear stylistic reference to times gone by, but it is most likely an allusory reference to a specific work as well: it is thought to have been inspired by a theme from a cantata attributed to J. S. Bach. The following discussion begins with an examination of the relevance of the ostinato theme and its relationship to the Fourth Symphony as a whole. I will then demonstrate that Brahms's symphonic finale may contain another, heretofore unacknowledged, thematic allusion to a familiar passage from Wagner—a passage whose text resonates closely with that of the Cantata, thereby helping to confirm the work's own ties to the Brahms piece and thus the relationship between allusion and intermovement thematic connections in this piece. This discovery will be considered in the context of Brahms's handling of related musical materials in his other works, as well as what we know of Brahms's personal and aesthetic relationship with Wagner. Ultimately, I will argue that what emerges when these factors are taken into account are deeper insights into the work's allusions in terms of Brahms's historical outlook in the 1880s and into the composer's unofficial moniker for the work: "Neue Traurige Symphonie."

Some Possible Influences and a Bach Connection

A variety of models and musical sources have been proposed for the Symphony's finale. These include a number of Baroque works with which Brahms is known to have been familiar, particularly the chaconne from Bach's D-minor partita for solo violin (BWV 1004), Buxtehude's E-minor *ciacona*, the B-minor *passacaille* of Couperin, and Georg Muffat's G-minor passacaglia for organ, as well as the "Crucifixus" from Bach's B-minor Mass.[14] There is also a possibility of some influence from other nineteenth-century works that likewise employ ostinato technique, such as Beethoven's Thirty-Two Variations in C Minor, WoO 80; the variation movement that concludes the "Eroica" Symphony; the "Ocean" Symphony of Rubinstein; and the B-Minor Symphony of Schubert.[15] Kenneth Hull has suggested that Brahms's finale alludes to the last movement of Beethoven's Fifth Symphony and has also attempted to link Brahms's finale with the Schumanns by identifying, in the movement, a network of allusions to melodies associated with Clara and Robert Schumann, including the "Clara cipher," as well as Robert Schumann's song "Süsser Freund," Schumann's *Fantasie*, op. 17, and a song from Beethoven's *An die ferne Geliebte*.[16] Although Robert Ricks has recently made the interesting suggestion that the E-minor aria sung by Theone in Act II, Scene ii of Lully's tragic opera *Phaëton* may have served as a source for the ostinato theme of Brahms's finale, he admits that there is no concrete evidence that Brahms was even familiar with this opera.[17] As the palette of possible sources for Brahms's finale grows richer, the relevance of any particular would-be source becomes all the more questionable.

There is, however, one work whose status as a model for Brahms's finale is most widely accepted, largely on the basis of an account from a member of Brahms's own "circle." It has long been thought that the final movement's ostinato theme is derived from that of the chaconne finale of J. S. Bach's Cantata No. 150, *Nach dir, Herr, verlanget mich* (ex. 5.1a–b). The association between the two ostinatos is based not only on thematic resemblance, but also on Siegfried Ochs's recollection of a discussion between himself, Brahms, and Hans von Bülow in January 1882 (two and half years before Brahms's finale was completed), in which Brahms asked

Example 5.1a–b. Brahms and Bach Chaconne Themes
(a) Brahms, Symphony No. 4 in E Minor, op. 98, Fourth Movement, mm. 1–8

(b) J. S. Bach, *Nach dir, Herr, verlanget mich*, BWV 150, Seventh Movement, mm. 1–5

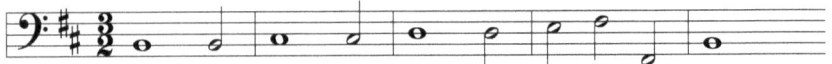

the others what they would think of a symphonic movement based on that theme from Cantata 150. Brahms reportedly commented to Ochs and von Bülow that, if employed for such a movement, Bach's theme would need to be chromatically altered because it was too straightforward in its original state.[18] Brahms's ostinato theme indeed deviates from Bach's not only by the transposition from B minor to E minor, but also in the addition of the raised fourth scale degree (the chromatic A-sharp in Brahms's ostinato). Although the Cantata was not published in the complete Bach edition until 1884, Brahms already had at his disposal in 1882 a manuscript copy of the work, obtained from Philipp Spitta in 1874.[19]

The Falling Third Motive

The main thematic material of the final movement, very possibly derived from the Cantata, is connected to themes of the earlier movements of Brahms's Symphony by a particular emphasis on the motive of the falling third, a kernel from which much of the work is generated.[20] The beginning of the Symphony (ex. 5.2), is constructed substantially from thirds; a chain of falling thirds (B-G-E-C-A-F-sharp-D-sharp-B) accounts for the work's opening melody (in thirds and rising sixths), followed by series of rising and falling thirds, with accompaniment often doubling at the third.[21] Chains of descending thirds are featured later in the movement as well, not only in the development, retransition (especially mm. 240–44), and recapitulation, but also serving as a link between this opening and other passages, as in the accompaniment of the passage beginning at m. 57 (recapitulated at m. 302), at mm. 122ff. (recapitulated and extended at mm. 366ff.), and at mm. 190–92 and 208–10.[22]

Thirds are also prominent in the Symphony's other movements. They pervade the andante in both ascending and descending stepwise form from the initial gesture, which ascends and then descends a third from the pitch E. Mm. 30ff. (especially in the violins), as well as the new theme at m. 41, also emphasize third-based gestures.[23] The opening gesture of the scherzo begins with a stepwise descending fifth that is then reiterated and extended (mm. 3–4) to a longer third-chain as a stepwise descending third plus two descending third leaps. Leading

Tragic Antiquarianism in Brahms's Fourth Symphony | 183

Example 5.2. Brahms, Symphony No. 4 in E Minor, op. 98, First Movement, mm. 1–13

Example 5.2. *(Continued)*

into the scherzo's second theme, descending thirds in the strings are followed by a descending-third chain in the winds at mm. 48–51. (The second theme itself (beginning at m. 52) is not only partly comprised of consecutive descending thirds (after all, merely arpeggios), but is momentarily, in the second violin and viola parts, reminiscent of the Symphony's opening theme (see especially mm. 58–61).[24]) In the finale, at the conclusion of Variation 12 (mm. 102–4), the flute solo outlines the same chain of falling thirds found at the opening of the Symphony, now decorated with appoggiaturas; here, the gesture closes on the first scale degree rather than the fifth, bringing a greater degree of closure here, in the work's final movement, than at the Symphony's opening.[25]

Even more striking, though, is the relationship of the Symphony's opening falling-thirds theme to the main subject of the chaconne finale. This correspondence is revealed toward the end of the finale, as if in culmination, in the second-to-last variation before the coda (Statement 30; mm. 233–36 in ex.

Example 5.3. Brahms, Symphony No. 4 in E Minor, op. 98, Fourth Movement, mm. 233–36 (Beginning of Ostinato Statement 30)

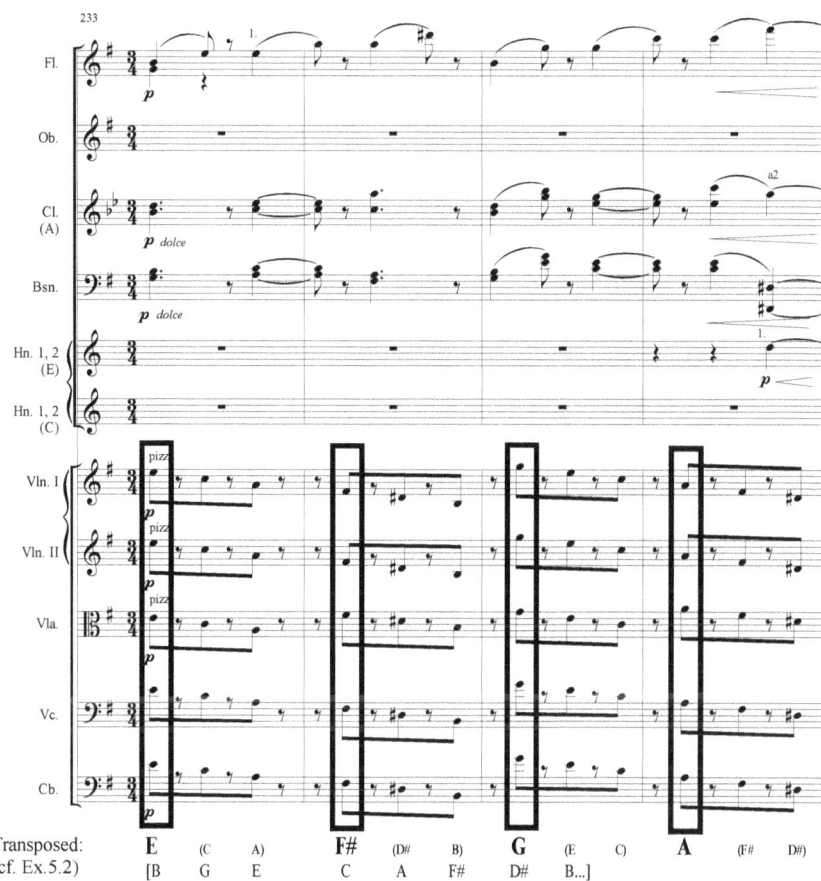

5.3), where Brahms capitalizes on the ability of the first half of the ostinato to combine contrapuntally with a chain of descending thirds. The potential for this is demonstrated early in the movement, with the bassline that accompanies the second ostinato statement (mm. 9–12).[26] In this variation, each of the first four pitches of the ostinato appears, in turn, as the fifth in a falling arpeggiated triad, producing what is, allowing for octave displacement, an extensive series of falling thirds in unison in the strings. As shown in the example, if this entire series of thirds is transposed up a fifth to start on B, then its initial eight pitches constitute a precise match with the first eight pitches of the Symphony's opening theme.[27] In short, as Walter Frisch puts it, this variation allows us to "recognize all at once the relationship between the first theme and the chaconne subject:

when every fourth note from a chain of descending thirds is abstracted or given metrical stress, the result is a rising stepwise line—hence the first four notes of the chaconne."[28] Series of falling thirds continue to feature prominently in the finale once this relation is revealed, both at the beginning of the final variation before the coda (mm. 241–44) and in the coda itself (starting at m. 253).

The finale's ostinato theme is foreshadowed additionally in the third movement of the Symphony. The stepwise motion (A-B-natural-C-D-E-flat) beginning at m. 317 in the third movement's coda presages the first five notes of the chaconne theme; Frisch argues further that this third-movement figure has, itself, evolved out the material from that movement's opening (m. 5) and development section (beginning at m. 93).[29]

Judging by Ochs's account of events in January 1882, Brahms may have had the borrowed ostinato theme in mind for some time before beginning work on the Symphony in 1884, and, given its motivic relationship to the work's other thematic materials, the allusion to Bach in the finale may well have served as an initiating, generative concept for the Symphony, inspiring not only the final movement, but also the work's opening theme and other materials based on or incorporating chains of falling thirds. As Knapp writes, Brahms "clearly began [his conception of the Symphony] with the careful construction of the [chaconne] subject itself.... For it would surely have been a much simpler task to exploit thematic possibilities latent within an ostinato subject than to devise a subject so as to embody already elaborated thematic material."[30]

The influence of the finale on earlier movements may extend not only to the motivic links, but also to the significance of the technique of variation itself. Brahms's use of chaconne form in the work's finale has been linked to his employment of variation technique in some of the work's earlier movements, with some going so far as to interpret not only the finale but also the opening movement as a combination of the sonata-allegro and chaconne forms.[31]

Chaconne Form, the Falling Third, and BWV 150: Fate and Death?

The "tragic" quality of the Symphony's finale is enhanced by the sense of inevitability and relentless progress inherent in its structure as a series of variations on an ostinato, a form that has been associated with the inescapable progress of Fate.[32] Indeed, as the finale draws to a close, Brahms even evokes the "Fate Motive" from Beethoven's Fifth Symphony in the incessant, emphatic repetitions of the triplet-quarter-note figure in Variations 22–25 (mm. 177–208), particularly in the last of these (starting at m. 201; ex. 5.4), with the repetition of single notes on each triplet. Just as the minor-mode ending shakes loose an aspect of Beethovenian symphonic precedent, so too is the figure Brahms uses here a rhythmic displacement of Beethoven's actual

Example 5.4. Brahms, Symphony No. 4 in E Minor, op. 98, Fourth Movement, mm. 201–8 (Variation 25)

motive, for Brahms's quarter-notes fall on the final beat of the measure rather than on the downbeat.

Another aspect of the work of potential relevance to the Symphony's associations with the "tragic" is the prominent incorporation of chains of falling thirds, as these have sometimes been linked with the idea of "death" in Brahms's late music. Several Brahms songs that are concerned with death also feature prominent falling-thirds gestures—particularly songs composed from 1879 on, the period to which the Fourth Symphony dates.[33] Examples include "Feldeinsamkeit," op. 86/2 (by 1882); "Gestillte Sehnsucht," op. 91/1 (1884); "Mit vierzig Jahren," op. 94/1 (1883); "Auf dem Kirchhofe," op. 105/4 (by 1888); and "Ich wandte mich und sahe an alle" and "O Tod, wie bitter bist du" the second and third of the *Vier Ernste Gesänge*, op. 121 (1896).[34] We will return to the last of these examples shortly.

Turning back, for now, to the Fourth Symphony and the would-be source of the finale's ostinato theme, the text of Cantata 150 (author unknown, but based in part on Psalm 25) deals explicitly with death. Its main idea is that mankind is rescued from the struggles of life by eternal salvation resulting from faith in God, and that death is therefore not to be feared but to be viewed as a source of consolation. The text reads as follows:

Nach dir, Herr, verlanget mich.	For you, Lord, do I yearn
Mein Gott, ich hoffe auf dich.	My God, I place my hopes in You.
Lass mich nicht zuschanden werden,	Let me not be shamed,
Dass sich meine Feinde nicht freuen über mich.	That my enemies do not rejoice over me.
Doch bin und bleibe ich vergnügt,	Yet I am and remain content
Obgleich hier zeitlich toben	Although here at the moment riot
Kreuz, Sturm und andre Proben,	Cross, storm, and other trials,
Tod, Höll und was sich fügt.	Death, hell and what goes along with them.
Ob Unfall schlägt den treuen Knecht,	If mishap strikes the faithful servant,
Recht ist und bleibet ewig Recht.	What is right is and remains forever right.
Leite mich in deiner Wahrheit und lehre mich;	Lead me in Your truth and teach me;
Den du bist der Gott, der mir hilft,	for you are the God, who helps me,
Täglich harre ich dein.	Daily I await You.
Zedern müssen von den Winden	Cedars must from the winds
Oft viel Ungemach empfinden,	Often feel much adversity
Oftmals werden sie verkehrt.	Oftentimes they are uprooted.
Rat und Tat auf Gott gestellet	Counsel and deed based on God
Achtet nicht, was widerbellet,	Regard not what howls against them,
Denn sein Wort ganz anders lehrt.	For His word teaches entirely otherwise.
Meine Augen sehen stets zu dem Herrn;	My eyes look always to the Lord;
Denn er wird meinen Fuss aus dem Netze ziehen.	For he will pull my foot from the net.

[Bach's finale begins here:]

Meine Tage in dem Leide	My days in suffering
Endet Gott dennoch zur Freude;	God ends yet in joy;
Christen auf den Dornenwegen	Christians on their thorny paths
Führen Himmels Kraft und Segen.	Are led by heaven's strength and blessing.
Bleibet Gott mein treuer Schutz,	God remains my true protection,
Achte ich nicht Menschentrutz,	So I heed not the suffering of humankind.
Christus, der uns steht zur Seiten,	Christ, who remains at our side,
Hilft mir täglich sieghaft straiten.	Helps me every day victoriously to strive.[35]

How, if at all, do the themes of this text relate to Brahms's music? Hull has suggested that Brahms's employment of "an ascending stepwise ostinato ... a kind of inverted ... lament figure" may represent "the joyful anticipation of death" reflected in the text of the Cantata.[36] The bassline does seem to "yearn" upward (towards heaven?). Brahms's addition of the chromatic A-sharp (forming a tritone with the tonic pitch, E, and thus as far from "home" as possible) makes the anticipation seem that much more difficult. Julian Littlewood interprets the ostinato's "octave drop on the fifth degree" as a denial of the yearned-for fulfillment, which doesn't arrive until the coda, when the music is "at last free of the passacaglia process."[37] Hull suggests that the text's first three couplets each "presents a pair of opposites: sorrow/joy, thorny path/strength and blessing and suffering/treasure" and that "the opening theme of Brahms's first movement offers a musical analogue for this oscillation between opposites, both in its use alternately of falling thirds and rising sixths and in its use of a falling third chain followed immediately by a rising chain."[38]

I now turn to a passage from Brahms's finale: Statements 13–16 of the ostinato (Vars. 12–15, mm. 97–128) and then especially Statement 15 (Var. 14, beginning at m. 105). Statements 13–16 have attracted the attention of listeners and commentators, being distinguished from the preceding material by such features as a shift from 3/4 time to 3/2 and the resulting halving of the pace; the almost chorale-like texture (starting in Statement 15); a particular emphasis on winds and brass, especially trombones, which, as in Brahms's First Symphony and Beethoven's Ninth, had been withheld until the beginning of the finale and have now been absent since the conclusion of Variation Three (in m. 33); and the turn from E minor to E major. The passage is also placed centrally in the movement, with the close of Statement 16 ushering in a return to a full orchestral texture in E minor and 3/4 for a recapitulation of sorts (beginning at m. 129), a hearkening back to the opening of the movement.

Elisabeth von Herzogenberg, Brahms's good friend and herself a talented musician to whom Brahms often sent his compositions for review, is one of many to identify this passage as one distinctively expressive in weight and effect. She writes that, of all of the finale's variations, "most impressive of all" is the "trombone effort in the golden key of E major."³⁹ Hull writes of Statements 13–16 that "the greater breadth [here], the intimacy created by the quiet dynamic and solo writing, the air of stillness which they create all serve to set this passage apart, and to suggest that a special meaning is to be found in them. They are not only the structural centre of the movement, they seem to be its 'expressive core' as well."⁴⁰ Others have explicitly associated the passage with death. Hermann Kretzschmar, for example, hears in the trombones in this solemn passage "the elevated ideas of a requiem," and Pestelli writes of the "processional solemnity" of Statements 15 and 16, envisioning a "cortege" and remarking on "the 'mordore' colouring of the trombones."⁴¹ Hull suggests that these variations "have the character of an elegy," noting the prominent use of trombones, whose association with death and the supernatural is a long-standing one" and whose "main function in the Fourth Symphony is their role in these two statements."⁴²

This especially distinctive moment in Brahms's final symphonic movement possibly represents a musical allusion of some sort. This is consistent with David Brodbeck's observation that several of Brahms's other symphonic movements are "marked by ... 'digressive' allusions, in which, as Robert Bailey has put it, Brahms seems 'for a moment ... to depart from the context of the movement, bringing in a short section apparently different from anything else in the movement, and then allowing the original context to resume.'"⁴³ This particular passage of the Fourth Symphony's final movement has suggested, to some, hints of the finale of Schumann's "Rhenish" Symphony No. 3 or of Schumann's song cycle *Frauenliebe und-Leben*.⁴⁴ Hull suggests that the opening of the sixth song of Schumann's cycle, "Süsser Freund" (which itself alludes to "Nimm sie hin den diese Lieder," the final song of Beethoven's *An die ferne Geliebte*), served as a model for Statement 14 in Brahms's finale, and that the "the chordal texture, slow tempo, and repeated sarabande-like rhythm in the postlude" to the cycle, in which a wife grieves for her deceased husband, may have influenced Statements 15–16 of Brahms's finale.⁴⁵ Although the latter reference would fit thematically with a focus on death in Brahms's symphonic movement, a reference to "Süsser Freund," in which the protagonist happily anticipates the birth of her child, does not; Hull attempts to explain this by suggesting that "the joyful tears" [shed in "Süsser Freund"] are transformed by Brahms into "tears of sorrow" that "do not lead forward expectantly to new life, but to the inevitability of death, and backwards in time through remembrance and elegy."⁴⁶ Given the associations between the song cycle and Clara Schumann (the cycle was written during Schumann's "Song Year," 1840, a year in which the composer's separation from and romantic longing for Clara Wieck culminated in his marriage to her), Hull proposes that Brahms's Statements 13–16 actually represent "a portrait of Clara," with "the initial five notes of Statement 13 present[ing] her name [in a cipher] ... and the unvarying use of five-note phrases throughout these four statements suggest[ing] that she is the 'subject' throughout."[47]

This is an interesting idea, but a problematic one. Not only is the sufficiency of the musical link questionable, but the idea ostensibly relates to death or tragedy only insofar as Brahms continued to envision Clara (who, herself, lived for several years beyond the completion of Brahms's Fourth Symphony) mourning the death of her husband, and, by the mid-1880s, Robert's death was already a good thirty years in the past. Although Clara dressed in black for the remainder of her days, we cannot presume, without further evidence, that Schumann's death was still a focal point for Brahms as he constructed this symphony so many decades later. Much had taken place in the intervening years, including the deaths of many other people of importance to Brahms. Under the circumstances, it makes sense to consider other possibilities as to the source material and significance of this passage—and as to how else these may relate to the themes of tragedy and death in Brahms's final symphonic movement.

Wagner and the Finale

Although the number of sources already proposed for Brahms's final symphonic movement surely exceeds what he could have had in mind, there is compelling evidence of yet another possible allusion in the finale that has been surprisingly overlooked. Its relevance to the Symphony is both supported by textual connections to the Bach Cantata and implicative of extramusical significance.

The fourteenth variation in Brahms's chaconne (beginning at m. 113 and elaborated upon in Variation 15, which begins in m. 121) bears a striking resemblance to the "Pilgrim's Chorus" from the third act (and overture) of Wagner's *Tannhäuser* (ex. 5.5a–b). Brahms's distinctive turn to E major and focus on the winds both bring this passage of the finale closer to Wagner's chorus. Both triple-meter themes are played at a low dynamic level, with a degree of solemnity. It is significant, as well, that Brahms brings the trombones in at this particular point and entrusts them with this melody, as Wagner ultimately places his own melody in the trombone part, as in mm. 36ff. of the overture, where it is in fact preceded immediately by a "Fate Motive"-like figure that appears elsewhere in the Wagner example as well, and which serves as another link to the Brahms finale (ex. 5.5c). The melodic similarity between the Wagner and Brahms passages is remarkable. Wagner's opening anacrustic leap from B to E corresponds to Brahms's stepwise ascent between the same pitches in the uppermost trombone part (mm. 113–15). Elided with this in Brahms's variation (mm. 115–16; D-sharp-E-D-sharp-D-sharp-C-sharp) is a gesture that melodically and rhythmically recalls mm. 3–4

Example 5.5a–c. Brahms and Wagner Themes
(a) Brahms, Symphony No. 4 in E Minor, op. 98, Fourth Movement, mm. 113–285

Tragic Antiquarianism in Brahms's Fourth Symphony | 193

(a) Brahms, Symphony No. 4 in E Minor, op. 98, Fourth Movement, mm. 113–285 *(Continued)*

(b) Wagner, *Tannhäuser*, Overture, mm. 1–18 ("Pilgrim's Chorus" Theme)

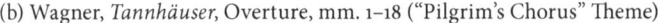

of Wagner's overture, but with the pitches a third higher than in Wagner. As Brahms moves the melody into the horns in E (mm. 117–19), emulating Wagner's own instrumentation, he echoes Wagner's mm. 4-6, retaining the downbeat repetition of the passing tone in the descending third (F-sharp-D-sharp-D-sharp-C-sharp) as at the end of Wagner's first phrase, and then continuing the pattern with another descending third—C-sharp-B-B-A—rather than continuing Wagner's second phrase. The recollection may be fragmentary, but it lingers: as if to emphasize its importance, Brahms not only slows the pace for this portion of the movement, but he retains the melody for his retransitional Variation 15.

In Variations 14–15, then, Brahms seems to demonstrate the musical compatibility of the ostinato theme (which remains in the strings in elaborated form)

(c) Wagner, *Tannhäuser*, Overture, mm. 36–41 ("Pilgrim's Chorus" Theme Entering in Trombones)

(c) Wagner, *Tannhäuser*, Overture, mm. 36–41 ("Pilgrim's Chorus" Theme Entering in Trombones) *(Continued)*

and his version of the Wagner melody. The latter, it may be mentioned, also contains its own share of ascending and descending stepwise thirds (and Wagner also employs the triplet-quarter-note rhythm that appears towards the end of Brahms's finale). In helping by means of textual correspondences to confirm the Cantata as a source for Brahms's ostinato (which is thematically linked to other movements), this apparent Wagner reference is not only in keeping with Brahms's tendency to weave allusive "webs" by drawing on multiple sources, but it is also certainly pertinent to the relationship between allusion and intermovement motivic connections in this work.[48]

Textual Relationships between the Bach and Wagner Works

The *textual* resonances between Wagner's "Pilgrim's Chorus" and BWV 150, are similarly striking. Wagner's text reads as follows:

Beglückt dar nun dich, o Heimat,	Happy, may I now look on you,
Ich schauen,	O homeland,
Und grüssen froh deine lieblichen Auen;	And gladly greet your lovely meadows;
Nun lass' ich ruhn den Wanderstab,	Now I let rest my wanderer's staff,
Weil Gott getreu ich gepilgert hab'.	For, true to God, I have made my pilgrimage.
Durch Sühn' und Buss' hab' ich versöhnt	Through penance and repentance have I propitiated
Der Herren, dem mein herze frönt,	The Lord, whom my heart indulges,
Der meine Reu' mit Segen krönt,	Who crowns my remorse with blessing,
Den Herren, dem mein Lied ertönt.	The Lord, to whom my song sounds.
Der Gnade Heil ist dem Büsser beschieden,	The grace of salvation is granted the penitent,
Er geht einst ein in der Seilgen Frieden!	He goes one day into the blessed peace!
Vor Höll' und Tod ist ihm nicht bang,	Before hell and death he is not afraid,
Drum preis' ich Gott mein Lebelang.	Therefore I praise God all my life.
Halleluja	Hallelujah
Halleluja in Ewigkeit, in Ewigkeit!	Hallelujah in eternity, in eternity!

This text, like that of the Cantata (and, for that matter, the texts of Brahms's German Requiem), is concerned with death as a welcome respite from suffering, with faith in the eternal joy of heaven, a positive perspective that is paralleled by Brahms's shift to the major mode for the portion of the finale in which this second apparent allusion occurs. The similarities between the texts strongly suggest that Brahms in fact had both the Cantata and the passage from *Tannhäuser*, in mind while writing this piece.[49]

The presence of these shared textual themes, as well as the other possible associations between Brahms's Fourth Symphony and the concept of death, indicate that the purpose behind such allusions may well have been more than purely musical. We must not forget that Brahms, still in good health and years from his own death when his final symphony was completed, designated this piece a "new mourning symphony."[50] This leaves us, then, to question what he might have been trying to say.

Returning to "O Tod," op. 121/3

The third of Brahms's *Vier Ernste Gesänge*, op. 121, "O Tod, wie bitter bist du," although composed more than ten years after the Fourth Symphony, shares with the Symphony not only the key of E minor, but an opening melody based on the same series of falling thirds, from B to G to E to C, here on the words "*O Tod, o Tod*" (Oh Death, oh Death). These words and this falling-third chain coincide several

Example 5.6a–b. Brahms, *Vier Ernste Gesänge*, op. 121, No. 3 ("Oh Tod, wie bitter bist du")
(a) Mm. 1–3: "O Tod" on descending thirds

(b) Mm. 31–36: "O Tod" on ascending sixths

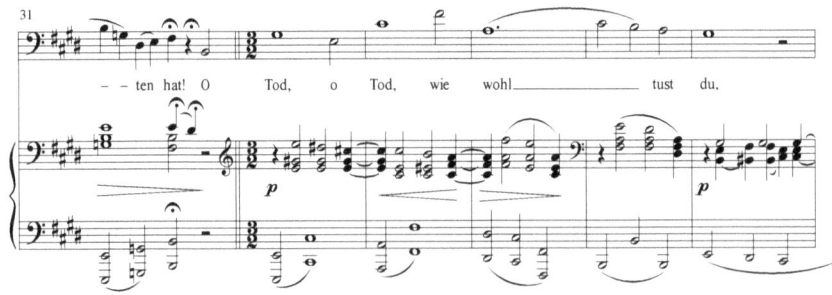

more times in the song [mm. 13–15, 20–21 (partial statement), and 31–33]; in the last two instances, the interval on each "O Tod" is inverted to form an ascending sixth, so that the resulting gesture matches that at the opening of the Symphony in its last three rather than in its first three of the four notes (ex. 5.6a–b).[51] Whereas the initial "O Tod" statements, employing the falling-third interval, correspond to a characterization of death as bitter, the final one, inverted to rise a sixth, corresponds by contrast to a positive characterization of death as a welcome end to earthly sufferings.[52] In the Symphony's opening, we find the equivalent of the descending-third "O Tod" in alternation with that of the ascending-sixth version; if the song and the Symphony's opening were connected in Brahms's mind, the alternation of these two versions at the opening of the Symphony may represent an ambivalence between the optimistic view of death, suggested by the texts of the Bach and Wagner works, and the tragic view, suggested by the ominous character of the finale with its minor-mode ending.[53] It is interesting that the song's final and most positive invocation of death (mm. 31–33), the only one with a repeated sixth-ascent, coincides with a shift into 3/2 time, the meter into which Brahms's finale shifts during the E-major passage that evokes the Wagner theme, with its positive characterization of death. And yet the song began in that meter also, with a characterization of death as bitter. Given the Symphony's harmonic trajectory, as well as the overwhelming emphasis on the descending interval in the finale's last variations, if a single view ultimately proves decisive, it appears to be the tragic one.

Meaning in the Fourth Symphony

From the work's earliest performances, critics and scholars have suspected that Brahms's final symphony may contain hidden programmatic content, but it has never been clear exactly what extramusical meaning the work might conceal. A critic who had attended the premiere in Cologne in 1885 concluded, "it is often said that Brahms is a closet program musician; no work proves this more than this new symphony," and in reviewing the work's Viennese premiere the following year, Ludwig Speidel found that the symphony "practically shouts for a program to tell us in dry words what is actually meant here, for we get no answer in a purely musical way to this question."[54] Brahms himself refuted a rumor in 1885 that the finale had been inspired by a frieze at a villa on Lake Como depicting the Alexander Procession.[55] Brahms's own description of the Symphony as "a sort of No. 4 ... that fits no text at all" at first seems to suggest that he did not have a program in mind.[56] Perhaps, though, he meant by this simply that the music carries a message more profound, deeper, more complex than words could convey—for elsewhere, he not only refers to the work as a "Mourning Symphony," but evokes dramaturgical associations, referring to the work as "a few entr'actes ... lying here."[57]

One rather obvious interpretation of Brahms's label "Traurige Symphonie" is that Brahms's "mourning" was a metaphorical reflection on the state of artistic culture, and particularly symphonic music, as the nineteenth century drew towards its close—in which case, it would also naturally have reflected Brahms's concerns about the historical significance and continuing relevance of his own works at this time in his career. Readings of this symphony have tended to focus on the work's "lateness"—lateness within Brahms's career, within the nineteenth century, within the history of the symphony as a genre, within the history of tonality, etc. Knapp, for example, suggests that, in the finale, an "inexorable advance to the tragic denouement, a layering of Wagnerian harmonic practice onto Baroque formal procedures, a range of allusive materials ... seemingly ... [suggest] a devastating perspective on [Brahms's] own situation, in which even happy memories were tinged with regret, a sense of irretrievable loss, and an ominous premonition of death."[58] The Symphony's most "tragic" movement, its finale, is also the most blatantly historicist.

The tragic, resigned conclusion of the work invites comparison with the triumphant finale of Beethoven's Ninth and final symphony. For Jan Swafford, the chaconne movement is Brahms's "dark answer and counterpart to Beethoven's joy. [Brahms] saw himself as the ... last-ditch embodiment of the great Germanic tradition.... The E-minor Symphony 'means' many things, but surely part of it is this: his funeral song for his heritage, for a world at peace, for an Austro-German middle class that honored and understood music like no other, for the sweet Vienna he knew, for his own lost loves."[59] Ludwig Finscher and Rheinhold Brinkmann characterize Brahms's Fourth Symphony as a "retraction" or "taking back" of Beethoven's Ninth and of the latter's triumphant ending and all that it stood for.[60] As such, Swafford writes, the Fourth Symphony created "an anti-archetype" that would apply to "Mahler's more tormented and grotesque symphonies" and then to "the shattering course of Viennese and German musical Expressionism."[61]

There is much to indicate that Brahms was in fact insecure about the symphony that he was producing—and even afraid that his creative powers had been exhausted and were failing.[62] Upon sending the first movement of the work in progress to Elisabeth von Herzogenberg, for instance, he wrote to her that "cherries never get ripe for eating in these parts, so don't be afraid to say if you don't like the taste. I am not at all eager to write a bad No. 4."[63] Similarly, he wrote to Joachim, "I wonder if [the Symphony] will ever have any other audience [i.e., than Joachim]! I rather fear that it has been influenced by this climate, where the cherries never ripen. You would never touch them!"[64] To Elisabeth, he wrote that, following the premiere at Meiningen, "it's very doubtful whether I shall inflict the piece on anybody else."[65] When she failed to respond within several weeks of his sending the Symphony to her, Brahms wrote to her husband Heinrich, "my last attack was evidently a complete failure—a symphony too! But I do beg your dear lady will not abuse her pretty talent for writing pretty letters by inventing any belated fibs for my benefit."[66] To his publisher, Simrock, Brahms proclaimed in early October 1885, "I have indeed, at the moment, no idea whether I will allow the thing to be published! ... It would be nonsense if you were to spend a groschen for it!"[67]

Although Brahms to some degree exhibited modesty and self-doubt throughout his career, the work was indeed met by others with some misgivings. Before the Symphony was premiered, Elisabeth and other of Brahms's intimates expressed doubts with regard to the unconventional structure and the dark character of the final movement. Elisabeth was concerned that the music was too cerebral, and Max Kalbeck encouraged Brahms to replace the last two movements with other material and to use the finale as a freestanding work instead.[68]

And although the work's highly successful Meiningen premiere proved prophetic of the positive reception that the work would ultimately garner, the Symphony was initially received with ambivalence by Viennese audiences and some critics.[69] That the composer's inventiveness may have run its course was not only a fear of Brahms himself, but an opinion expressed by members of the Viennese public who chanted the words "*es fiel ihm wieder mal nichts ein!*" ("once again he had no ideas") to the Fourth Symphony's motivically economical opening tune.[70] Viennese critic Ludwig Speidel writes in mid-January 1886 that,

> the most puzzling movement of all is the finale. One seems to hear an impassioned conversation from a distance, but unfortunately the words cannot be understood. Something seems to happen, but who is saying what? ... motifs are intensified to a level of energy that they originally had no notion of, and a broad, noisy rhetoric of passion is developed which is without actual content. 'A soldier's corpse,' said someone as he left the hall.... It was a lost battle, but the defeat was not held against the commander in chief. He had triumphed so many times before![71]

A degree of initial puzzlement is suggested even in the ostensibly positive review by another prominent Viennese critic, Eduard Hanslick, usually one of Brahms's staunchest supporters. Hanslick writes of the final movement that "the form is completely novel for a great symphonic finale, and every detail in it is novel too. It is the most ingenious of all, but it is also the least popular, possibly because its size is out of proportion to the melodic material.... It is," he writes, "like a dark well; the longer we look into it, the more brightly the stars shine back."[72]

Meanwhile, not everyone was willing to look into this well with the sustained intensity of Hanslick, or, perhaps lacking a certain predisposition, many simply did not find that a prolonged gaze yielded such celestial visions. In a review of a January 1887 performance by the New York Philharmonic, we read that the Fourth Symphony's

> antiquarian formalism and poverty of ideas are too conspicuous to be covered over by the composer's virtuosity in technical elaboration. Unlike most arts, music is still undergoing a process of evolution. In its latest phase it is distinguished by exquisite sensuous beauty of instrumentation, by great concentration of ideas, by a bond of organic unity between the different parts, and by dramatic definiteness of expression. In all these respects the conservative Brahms is behind the times. His music is born old. It seems a pity that such works of mere talent, allied with industry, should be continually inflicted upon an unwilling public, while the works of [Anton] Rubinstein, who concentrates more genius into one bar than Brahms does in ten pages, have been for years left in the cold.[73]

If Brahms were concerned, while writing this Symphony, with issues such as fate and death, the "lateness" of this work and of his own music-historical position more generally, if he were acknowledging a destined "twilight" of sorts—for himself, for his era, for his musical ideals—then composers like Wagner (and Liszt and Berlioz) are inextricably linked with such concerns. For it is such "New German" composers who—citing Beethoven's Ninth symphony, with its texted finale, as evidence that untexted, aprogrammatic orchestral music had exhausted its expressive limits—had heralded and helped to bring about the decline of traditional orchestral music by turning away from the "absolute" symphony to compose operas (or "music dramas") with enhanced roles for orchestra, as well as symphonic poems, and program symphonies.[74] By referring to Wagner immediately before what Felix Weingartner once referred to as the "veritable orgy of destruction" conveyed by the Symphony's conclusion, Brahms perhaps even acknowledges Wagner's role in the waning of the Western symphonic tradition of their forebears, to whom he glances back, here, as far as the Baroque Era.[75] Ironically, but consistently with the sense of resignation and mournfulness, if this is Brahms's meaning, then Brahms must ostensibly admit some degree of defeat in this arena, although, unlike in the music of the "New German" composers, any extramusical intent here does not override traditional musical forms, his highly structured chaconne contrasting starkly with Wagner's more open-ended forms.

The text of the "Pilgrim's Chorus," like that of Cantata 150, represents death as welcome respite from earthly sufferings—a characterization that seems to be negated by the work's tragic close. To Wagner, the developments in late-nineteenth-century symphonic music were fated, necessary, and signs of evolution; to him, the "death" of the Beethovenian or "absolute" symphony represented a new life for creativity in orchestral music. Brahms, however, much as he respected Wagner's operatic writing, clearly did not espouse such views and had reason to see the music of the New German School as the undoing of the symphonic genre and of the musical structures he valued so highly and so staunchly upheld in his own works. To Brahms, the "death" of the symphony represented no respite, no salvation. Perhaps the conclusion of his tragic finale represents his ultimate word on the matter, a rejection of and resistance to this by-now seemingly inevitable death, to the views and influence of Wagner in the symphonic sphere.

Brahms's sense of disturbance as he glanced backwards may even be reflected in his chromatic alteration of the Cantata's ostinato theme. As Knapp writes, "what is unusual about Brahms's subject is not that it combines well with a melodic pattern of descending thirds, but that, ultimately, it does not.... the regularity of the pattern ... necessitates a harsh clash with the A-sharp at the beginning of the fifth measure, forcing the pattern to break off ... the very changes that Brahms supposedly made in Bach's subject prohibit him from combining the full subject with a descending chain of thirds" and thus, by "devis[ing] a subject with a built-in obstruction to such a linkage," he "sets aside one of the most attractive features of [the Baroque ostinato] tradition—the graceful capacity to join seamlessly each phrase to the next—in favor of a subject with a closed-off phrase structure."[76] The past, in short, has not survived the nineteenth century unscathed.

On the other hand, the philosophical relationship between Brahms and the New German School (particularly Wagner) is not so clear as a simple aesthetic dichotomy: Brahms sincerely respected Wagner's work. Perhaps, rather than a metaphorical death, Brahms composed his so-called "mourning symphony" more literally in response to the loss of an actual human life. But whose? At least a couple of possibilities deserve special consideration.

It has been suggested that the Fourth Symphony may have represented a memorial tribute to Gustav Nottebohm.[77] Nottebohm, a composer and musicologist known especially for his groundbreaking studies of Beethoven's manuscripts and sketches, died on October 29, 1882. By that time, he and Brahms had enjoyed a twenty-year friendship, and it was through Nottebohm that Brahms obtained access to some of Beethoven's sketches.[78] Nottebohm, a bachelor, called for Brahms to care for him during his final illness. Brahms stayed with him and tended to him until his death; made the funeral arrangements; notified Nottebohm's close friend, Robert Volkmann, of Nottebohm's death; and was consulted by Breitkopf & Härtel about Nottebohm's final thoughts on the revised Complete Bach Edition, a project for which Nottebohm had been serving as general editor.[79]

Although a connection between Brahms's Fourth Symphony and Nottebohm's death certainly remains within the realm of possibility, the evidence for this is scant, consisting mainly of Brahms's incorporation of allusions to Beethoven and Bach, composers that Brahms and Nottebohm mutually revered. Nottebohm was not only editing the Bach edition, but had composed a set of variations on a Bach theme and was a respected Beethoven scholar who had also produced an edition of the "Hammerklavier."[80] Needless to say, however, Nottebohm and Brahms were by no means alone in their reverence for Bach and Beethoven, and these were composers to whom Brahms had referred throughout his career on numerous other occasions long preceding his relationship with Nottebohm.

It is also possible that the Symphony (which bears no formal dedication) responds to the death of another person of importance to Brahms: Richard Wagner himself, who had passed away on February 13, 1883, just a year before Brahms began composing the Fourth Symphony (and thus in greater proximity to the work's inception than Nottebohm). Before continuing in this vein, it will be useful to briefly examine the nature of the relationship between these two composers.

Brahms and Wagner: A Complicated Relationship

Although the artistic and personal relationships between Brahms and Wagner are more complex than sometimes characterized, they were certainly strained. The aesthetic differences between the two composers are clear enough from their respective works. Whereas Brahms preferred more traditional forms and maintained the continued viability of instrumental music as a form of expression autonomous from extramusical associations, Wagner's music, rife with chromaticism, modulation, sequential transpositions, resists not only the traditional formal structures, subjugated to extramusical narratives, but also the conventions of tonality up to his time. Despite these differences, however, much as Brahms railed against Wagner's views on the future of symphonic music, he was ultimately able to respect and even admire Wagner's accomplishments in the realm of opera.

The personal relationship between the two composers has its roots in the year 1860, when the young Brahms and Joseph Joachim composed a manifesto objecting to the aesthetics of the so-called New German School, which, in the minds of Brahms, Joachim, the Schumanns, and their colleagues, represented a grave threat to the independence and integrity of the art of music itself by allowing extramusical elements to undermine or dictate musical structure. It is significant that as they worked on the document, Brahms wrote to Joachim in May 1860 to indicate explicitly his intention that the statement not be read as an attack on Wagner: "no one can have Wagner in mind. In any case one must show the same concern for Berlioz and Franz. Only Liszt can be finished off as we are doing."[81] Liszt was to be the only representative of the New German School mentioned by name.[82] The document was intended to represent a substantial statement, and approximately twenty reputable musicians (including for example Carl Reinecke, Max Bruch, Woldemar Bargiel, Albert Dietrich, Carl Grädener, Theodor Kirchner, Franz Wüllner, Ferdinand Hiller, Emil Naumann, Gustav Schumann, Moritz Hauptmann, Julius Rietz, and Clara Schumann) had agreed to add their signatures in advance of the document's publication.[83] Unfortunately, the document proved a great embarrassment; it was leaked prematurely, and not only did the published version fail to name names (and thus it did not make clear that Liszt, not Wagner, was the primary target), but only Brahms, Joachim, and two of their friends, Julius Otto Grimm and Bernhard Scholz, had yet signed.[84]

Brahms's first and only in-person meeting with Wagner, arranged by the composers' mutual associate Dr. Josef Standhartner, occurred at Wagner's home on February 6, 1864.[85] The meeting was pleasant enough; Wagner listened to Brahms playing his own Handel Variations, among other works, and responded by commenting to Brahms, "one sees what may still be done in the old forms when someone comes along who knows how to use them."[86]

Nevertheless, subsequent developments enhanced whatever tensions initially existed between the two. Following his move to Vienna in 1862, Brahms had developed congenial relationships with two of Wagner's friends, Peter Cornelius and Carl Tausig. Cornelius and Tausig admired Brahms personally and artistically, and both men elicited Brahms's praise for their own musical works as well.[87] Tausig took it upon himself to give to Brahms as a token of friendship something that had fallen into his possession: the autograph of the "Venusberg" music from

Wagner's *Tannhäuser*. When a production of the opera was being mounted in Munich in 1865, Cornelius wrote to Brahms on behalf of Wagner, requesting that the manuscript be returned to its composer, who required it for practical purposes.[88] Brahms, who prized his manuscript collection (which also included the concert ending of the *Tristan* Prelude and a page of the *Rheingold* manuscript) and clearly found musical value in Wagner's work, refused to surrender the autograph.[89] The matter was dropped, but Wagner appears to have held a grudge.

In 1869, just around the time that Brahms was achieving his greatest critical success to date with his German Requiem, Wagner published a lengthy essay "On Conducting," in which he made several unfriendly remarks about Brahms. Although he concedes that "Brahms once had the kindness to play a composition of his own to me ... which I thought excellent," he adds the following: "His performance of other pianoforte music at a concert gave me less pleasure. I even thought it impertinent that the friends of this gentleman professed themselves unable to attribute anything beyond 'extraordinary technical power' to 'Liszt and his school,' whilst the execution for Herr Brahms appeared so painfully dry, inflexible, and wooden. I should have liked to see Herr Brahms'[s] technique anointed with a little of the oil of Liszt's school."[90] The essay sarcastically alludes several times to Schumann's characterization of Brahms as a musical "Messiah." He describes Brahms's playing as "a very respectable phenomenon; only it remains doubtful how such a phenomenon could be set up in a natural way as the Messiah ... unless, indeed, an affected enthusiasm for mediaeval wood-carvings should have induced us to accept those stiff wooden figures for the ideals of ecclesiastical sanctity. In any case we must protest against any presentation of our great warm-hearted Beethoven in the guise of such sanctity."[91] Later in the essay, he refers to the "silly title" of the "'Liebeslieder-Walzer' of the blessed Johannes."[92] Wagner concludes the entire commentary with the following jab at Brahms and Joseph Joachim (and "the Jews"):

> Yet another thing appears dubious. I am told that Herr J. Brahms expects all possible good to result from a return to the melody of Schubert's songs, and that Herr Joachim ... expects a *new Messiah* for music in general. Ought he not to leave such expectations to those who have chosen him [for an appointment at the Hochschüle für Musik in Berlin]?' I, for my part, say to him 'go in, and win!' If it should come to pass that he himself is the Messiah, he may, at all events, rest assured that the Jews will not crucify him.[93]

Another factor in determining Wagner's attitude toward Brahms during the 1860s may have been Brahms's dealings with Wagner's former intimate, Mathilde Wesendonck. Wagner's relationship with Mathilde had begun in 1857 when Mathilde and her husband Otto, a silk merchant and patron of Wagner, began sheltering Wagner and his wife Minna in a small cottage alongside their own villa in Zurich. Wagner had fled to Zurich in early 1852 in search of asylum from the German authorities, who held a warrant for his arrest due to his involvement in the revolutionary activities at Dresden. It is during this time that a love affair (not clearly consummated) evolved between Wagner and Mathilde, and it continued until Minna confronted her husband about it in April 1858, prompting Wagner to depart alone for Venice, effectively bringing an end to both the affair and his marriage.[94] Although Wagner and Mathilde Wesendonck remained in touch, the Wesendoncks would turn down Wagner's request for a loan in 1863, and within another year, he was no longer welcome in their home.[95] The relationship, however, had left its mark on his work: it is generally recognized as an inspiration for *Tristan und Isolde* (composed between 1857 and 1859), and Wagner had set some of Mathilde's poetry as his *Wesendonck Lieder* (1857–58); earlier, in 1853, he had dedicated to her his *Sonate für das Album von Frau M. W.*

Remarkably, once her relationship with Wagner had cooled, Mathilde became an admirer and personal acquaintance of Johannes Brahms and began a correspondence with him that was to last for several years (1867–74), during which she attempted to foster their relationship on both personal and artistic levels. During this period, Brahms came into repeated contact with the Wesendoncks, and Mathilde had even offered to let him stay in the cottage that had once housed Wagner.[96] (Brahms declined, much to the approval of Clara Schumann, who wrote, "that you did not accept the Wesendoncks' offer I found very prudent; that would have imposed on you an obligation with regard to these people that would often enough have been a burden to you.")[97] The deterioration in Wagner's attitude toward Brahms in the mid-to-late 1860s may have been influenced by this shift in Mathilde's loyalties.[98]

Mathilde was not, of course, the only one to experience such a shift; most famous among the others is Hans von Bülow, whose loyalties changed after Wagner won away von Bülow's wife Cosima. Another is Friedrich Nietzsche, a one-time friend and admirer who also grew alienated by Wagner's persona, ideologies, and aesthetics before the 1870s were out.[99] In August 1874, when Nietzsche was staying at Bayreuth, he attempted to share with Wagner his enthusiasm for Brahms's *Triumphlied* by playing through the piece at the keyboard. Wagner would later recall:

> When I entered [Nietzsche's] room at the hotel I saw a suspicious-looking little red book, some songlet of triumph or of destiny by Brahms, with which he made ready to attack me. But I was not going to have any of it. Towards the evening the Professor came to Wahnfried and behold, he had the accursed red book under his arm. He now had a mind to put it on the piano desk and play it to me in all seriousness. He thought that I ought to know this work to appreciate the composer as he deserved. I declined; he would not cease to urge me. At last I became violent ... I was rude and—Heaven knows how—Nietzsche was kicked out.[100]

The following year, in 1875, Wagner wrote to Brahms personally to request the return of the manuscript of the "Venusberg" music from *Tannhäuser*. This time, Brahms complied. In return, Wagner sent a deluxe copy of the score for *Rheingold* and then attended a concert at which Brahms played in his own Piano Quartet, op. 60. Nonetheless, Wagner's public criticism of Brahms, no doubt inspired in part by the hostility directed toward Wagner by Vienna's Brahmsian critics (especially Eduard Hanslick) worsened as the 1870s drew to a close due to the bestowal upon Brahms on March 1, 1879, of an honorary doctorate from the University of Breslau, an honor of which Wagner, a generation older and with conflicting aesthetic ideals, had reason to be resentful.[101] That July, Wagner had the following to say in the *Bayreuther Blätter*:

> I know renowned composers you shall meet to-day at concert-masquerades in garb of a street-minstrel … tomorrow in the Hallelujah-perruque [i.e., Baroque wig] of a Handel, the day after as a Jewish tuner-up of Czardas, and later as a solemn symphonist disguised in a number ten! [N. B.: Hans von Bülow's had dubbed Brahms's First Symphony "Beethoven's Tenth."] … But those gentlemen themselves take things so seriously, nay, strictly, that it became necessary to pick out one of them and diploma him the Prince of Serious Music of our day, expressly to stop your laughter. Perhaps, however, that only adds to it? For this serious music-prince would long ago have struck you as most wearisome, had you sly ones not taken a peep behind the mask, and discovered that it hid no such mighty dignitary, but just a person like yourselves; so you now can go on playing masks again, pretending that you marvel at him, while it amuses you to see the mouths he makes as if he quite believed you.[102]

Despite the public attacks and the artistic and personal differences that accounted for them, Brahms clearly retained a level of respect for Wagner's work, even attending or planning to attend performances of his works, including an 1869 production of *Rheingold* in Munich that he had intended to attend with the Wesendoncks, a plan that was ultimately abandoned only upon Brahms's learning that Wagner himself disapproved of the production.[103]

In July 1882, about six months before Wagner's death, as former Wagnerian Hans von Bülow and his Meiningen Orchestra championed Brahms on well-received concert tours, Wagner published an "Open Letter to Friedrich Schön" in the *Bayreuther Blätter*, which included the following comments, clearly made with Brahms in mind: "but as the Gospel has faded since the cross of the Redeemer has been hawked like merchandise on every street corner, so has the genius of German music grown silent ever since it has been hauled around the world-mart by the métier, and pseudo-professional gutter-witlessness celebrates its progress."[104] More explicitly, he registers here the following bitter complaint:

had anyone set up a school for me, most probably I should have confined myself to [Beethoven's symphonies,] my favourite works ... only, these obstinately conservative efforts would have booted nothing, with that Asiatic hurricane soon sweeping over us: for things would then fare as with those who came after the great folk-migration—to whom but few of Sophocles' and Aeschylus' tragedies were saved, but most of the works of Euripides—and our posterity would be left with about nine symphonies by Brahms to two at most of Beethoven's; for the copyists have always marched with the times.[105]

Despite the strained relations between the two composers, Brahms, clearly moved by Wagner's death, was among the first to send a funeral wreath.[106] As of the mid-to-late 1880s, Brahms was very much preoccupied with Wagner's works, even contradicting those who criticized Wagner, advising conductor Arthur Nikisch to play Wagner at his Leipzig debut, and, according to Richard Specht, claiming to understand Wagner's music better than other musicians of the time; remarkably, following Brahms's own death, Wagner's wife (and Liszt's daughter) Cosima, who had previously been outspoken against Brahms, would in turn praise him for his attitude toward Wagner's music.[107]

Wagner and the Third Symphony

If Brahms's Fourth Symphony responds to the death of Wagner, it is not necessarily the first of his symphonic works to do so. In his recent book, *Wagner, Schumann, and the Lessons of Beethoven's Ninth*, Christopher Reynolds not only provides additional perspective on the responses of both Wagner and Schumann to Beethoven's symphonic legacy, but also explores the possible influence of Wagner's *Faust* Overture, *Der fliegende Holländer*, and *Tristan und Isolde* (particularly where these works appear themselves to allude to Beethoven's Ninth) on the first movement of Brahms's First Symphony.[108] Somewhat more established in the literature, however, and perhaps of greater relevance to us here, is a relationship between the music of Wagner and Brahms's Third Symphony.

In the opening movement of the Third Symphony—a work composed in the summer of 1883, only months after Wagner passed away (and, considering Ochs's anecdote, not necessarily preceding the conceptual origins of the Fourth Symphony)—there appears to be an allusion to the "Venusberg" music from the same opera (at m. 31; ex. 5.7a–b).[109] What is more, this reference is introduced by a transitional passage whose progressive modulations by descending major third (beginning from F major at m. 15; ex. 5.7c) seem to recall the musical language of Wagner and his "New German" peers.[110]

Wagner was clearly in Brahms's thoughts anyway in the summer of 1883, as he wrote to Billroth from Wiesbaden that summer, "I live here quite charmingly, almost as if I were trying to imitate Wagner!," and, notably, the reference here in the Third Symphony is to the "Venusberg" music, the very portion of the opera whose manuscript Brahms had once withheld from its composer.[111]

Brodbeck suggests, furthermore, that "Brahms could scarcely have failed to see how [*Tannhäuser*'s] contest between the two Minnesänger of the thirteenth century parallels the real-life struggle over aesthetic matters waged in the music of nineteenth-century Germany's two greatest composers," and even that Brahms may have "felt a kinship toward the ... opera's Wolfram, whose ambivalent

Example 5.7a–c. Brahms's Third Symphony and *Tannhäuser*
(a) Brahms, Symphony No. 3 in F Major, op. 90, First Movement, mm. 29–39

(b) Wagner, *Tannhäuser*, Act I, Scene 1, mm. 113–20 ("Naht euch dem Strande"): Vocal and String Parts

(c) Brahms, Symphony No. 3 in F Major, op. 90, First Movement, mm. 13–18

feeling toward Tannhäuser mirrors that of Brahms toward Wagner's music: devotion mixed with repulsion."[112] In any case, whatever significance a reference to *Tannhäuser* may hold in the Third Symphony it may, by extension, hold in the Fourth, a work with an overlapping period of genesis.[113]

A Wagnerian influence on Brahms's Fourth Symphony has been noted from the beginning. Clara Schumann herself observed in her diary the "influence of Wagner in the way [the Symphony] is orchestrated, the often odd tone colors, except perhaps with the difference that here it serves something beautiful and noble, there something ugly and trivial," and Speidel even wrote suggestively in 1886 that, with this piece, "one can almost assume that Brahms wanted to musically outdo the prelude to *Tristan und Isolde*, at the same time making it redundant and getting rid of it."[114]

Tannhäuser, in particular, played a key role in the degradation of the personal relationship between the two composers, something that Brahms may well have come to regret. One might even hypothesize that the allusion to the "Pilgrim's Chorus," following so closely upon Wagner's death, represents Brahms's regret for the fouled relations that arose in part from his having withheld the "Venusberg" manuscript from its composer for so long. (Admittedly, it is not to the "Venusberg" music itself that Brahms alludes in his Fourth Symphony finale, but this may be because he had already referred to that music in his *Third Symphony*.) In this sense, the Fourth Symphony might be viewed as a tribute to Wagner and as an attempt to return his *Tannhäuser* to him yet again, a concession, even an apology. Considering the text of the "Pilgrim's Chorus," Brahms's music perhaps even reflects a hope that Wagner, in death, had transcended earthly cares and had been absolved, like Tannhäuser himself, from his sins, both personal and aesthetic.

It is true that Ochs's anecdote dates from January 1882, suggesting that Brahms's decision to draw on Cantata 150 in a work of his own predated Wagner's death by some time. This does not, however, preclude the possibility that, following the death of Wagner, or perhaps the death of someone else of importance to Brahms, Brahms decided that his previously conceived notion of basing a movement or a work on this ostinato could be put to good use within the context of a musical response to this death: a "mourning symphony."

Conclusions

What, then, can we conclude about the relationship between intermovement motivic connections and historical reference and awareness in Brahms's Fourth Symphony? The most significant original contributions this chapter makes are the identification and interpretation of an apparent reference to the "Pilgrim's Chorus" from *Tannhäuser* in the E-major passage of Brahms's finale. What light does this shed on the work?

To begin with, given the relatively close overlapping of textual themes, the idea that Brahms refers to BWV 150 in the work's finale both supports and is supported by the identification of an allusion to the "Pilgrim's Chorus" in the same movement. Although many scholars have agreed that the ostinato is drawn from Cantata 150, this has not been universally accepted.[115] This chapter provides strong evidence for the notion that the ostinato was actually drawn from the Cantata. Furthermore, our findings help to confirm the continuing relevance, in a "late" work, of historical reference to Brahms's drawing of intermovement motivic connections. As we have seen, the ostinato subject in the finale, which appears to be derived from Cantata 150 but is at the very least historically referential in hearkening back to the form and style of the Baroque Era, is motivically related to material in the Symphony's earlier movement (most notably the work's opening theme), arguably serving as the thematic starting point of the Symphony.[116] Finally, a reference to the "Pilgrim's Chorus" would help to support the notion that the Symphony—and thus perhaps the motive of the falling-third chain—was associated with death in Brahms's mind.

Nonetheless, although Brahms referred to the work as his "Traurige Symphonie," the reason or reasons for and the extent of this association with death ultimately remains something that we cannot definitively determine. It may have had something to do with the historical standing of symphonic music or of Brahms's own oeuvre at the time; it could have been a response to the death of a specific person; or perhaps it was some combination of these.

Certainly, Brahms was all too aware that he was standing at a historical crossroads. His final symphony totters on the brink of past and future. It employs Phrygian modality, chaconne form, and apparent thematic allusions to specific works of past masters; even Wagner lay in the past by the time of this work's composition.[117] At the same time, Brahms produces a work whose harmonic and formal language is in other ways quite modern (e.g., in the use of chromaticism, the rhythmic sophistication, and the innovative handling of the chaconne form, in which the subject is heard first in the treble voices, not in the bass, and in which we find grouping of variations, changes in meter and mode, a bridge between the final variation and coda, etc.).[118] This is a symphony in which Brahms deliberately subverts an expected, conclusive, Beethovenian shift to the major mode. It is a work that would serve as source material for later pieces by other composers, for example, Reger's "Resignation," op. 26/5 (1898, with a subtitle explicitly indicating that the piece was written in response to Brahms's death in the previous year), and which has been cited as a model for the finales of Reger's Organ Suite in E minor, op. 16 (1895) and Zemlinsky's Symphony in B-flat (1897) and for Webern's Passacaglia for Orchestra, op. 1 (1908).[119] Furthermore, the Fourth Symphony's opening theme—which, almost in the manner of a "tone row" employs its first seven pitches (here, one for each letter name) precisely once each before any is heard again—was cited by Arnold Schoenberg in his article "Brahms the Progressive" as an example of Brahms's motivically economical technique of developing variation in which Schoenberg, proclaimed that his own techniques had roots.[120]

If Brahms's view of death in this Symphony is ambivalent, characterized simultaneously as tragic and as a respite from earthly cares, perhaps this reflects Brahms's awareness that, while his own aesthetics may have seemed to be passing gradually into obsolescence, they were bound to have paved the way for something new that would hold some artistic merit. Perhaps it simply reflects a self-righteous satisfaction that he had stood by those principles and that what would happen after him would be beyond his control or his care. Perhaps it reflects the combination of sorrow over the death of a colleague and/or friend with the hope that the deceased was now resting in peace. Ultimately, we can never know with certainty.

Notes

Portions of this chapter were presented at a meeting of the Mid-Atlantic Chapter of the American Musicological Society at the University of Pennsylvania on October 6, 2012, in a paper entitled "Tragic Antiquarianism in the Finale of Brahms's Fourth Symphony."

1. The first two movements were written in 1884, and the fourth and third movements (likely in that order) were composed during the following summer. On this chronology, see Walter Frisch, *Brahms: The Four Symphonies* (New Haven, CT: Yale University Press, 2003; previously published in New York by Schirmer Books in 1996), 115. The work was premiered under the composer's baton at Meiningen in October 1885 and was published by Simrock during the following year.

2. See Karl Geiringer, in collaboration with Irene Geiringer, *Brahms: His Life and Work*, 3rd enlarged ed. (New York; Da Capo Press, 1982), 262.

3. In his discussion of the work, Hugo Riemann, for example, characterizes the key of E minor as "pale, washed-out," and autumnal. Riemann's comments were originally published in *Musikführer No. 120* (Leipzig: Hermann Seeman, n.d.) which was reprinted in C. Beyer et al. *Johannes Brahms: Erlauterung seiner bedeutendsten Werke* (Frankfurt am Main: H. Bechhold, 1898), 116–32. The passage to which I refer here is given in English translation on p. 200 of Hull's edition of the Fourth Symphony (cited above).

4. See Kenneth Ross Hull, "Brahms the Allusive: Extra-Compositional Reference in the Instrumental Music of Johannes Brahms" (PhD diss., Princeton University, 1989), 96 and Kalbeck, *Johannes Brahms* 3/2:447, citing a letter of October 24, 1885, from Brahms to his friends, the von Beckeraths. The slow movement of Haydn's Symphony No. 44 ("*Trauer-Symphonie*") of 1772 was designated by its composer as a work that indicated that he wanted played at his own funeral. See Karl Geiringer, *Haydn: A Creative Life in Music*, 3rd rev. and enlarged ed. (Berkeley: University of California Press, 1982), 260.

5. On the use of minor-mode endings to minor-key symphonies in the eighteenth and nineteenth centuries, see for example Raymond Knapp, "The Finale of Brahms's Fourth Symphony: The Tale of the Subject," *19th-Century Music* 13/1 (1989), 13, fn. 31.

6. Donald Francis Tovey, *Essays in Musical Analysis* (London: Oxford University Press, 1935), 1: 115. See also Frisch, *Brahms: The Four Symphonies*, 127. On "melancholia" in Brahms's Fourth Symphony, see also Horst Weber, "Melancholia—Versuch über Brahms' Vierte," in *Neue Musik und Tradition: Festschrift Rudolf Stephan zum 65. Geburtstag*, ed. Joseph Kuckertz (Laaber: Laaber-Verlag, 1990), 281–95.

7. Hans Gál, *Johannes Brahms: His Work and Personality*, trans. Joseph Stein (New York: Alfred A. Knopf, 1963), 175.

8. See English translation by Susan Gillespie as appearing in *Johannes Brahms, Symphony No. 4 in E Minor, op. 98: Authoritative Score, Background Context, Criticism, Analysis*, ed. Kenneth Ross Hull (New York: W. W. Norton, 2000), 214, 229; Max Kalbeck's original discussion of the Symphony appears in his *Johannes Brahms* (Berlin; Deutsche Brahms-Gesellschaft, 1912), 3/2:459–86.

9. Raymond Knapp, *Brahms and the Challenge of the Symphony* (Stuyvesant, NY: Pendragon Press, 1997), 96.

10. For a detailed discussion of plagal harmony and the role of plagal harmony and the Phrygian mode in this Symphony's second movement, see especially Margaret Notley, "Plagal Harmony as Other: Asymmetrical Dualism and Instrumental Music by Brahms," *Journal of Musicology* 22/1 (2005): 90–105. See also Michael Musgrave, *The Music of Brahms* (London: Routledge & Kegan Paul, 1985), 227; Karen Painter, "Symphony No. 4 in E Minor, opus 98," in *The Compleat Brahms: A Guide to the Musical Works of Johannes Brahms*, ed. Leon Botstein (New York: W. W. Norton, 1999), 74; and Hermann Kretzschmar, "The Brahms Symphonies," trans. Susan Gillespie, in *Brahms and His World*, ed. Walter Frisch (Princeton, NJ: Princeton University Press, 1990), 141. Kretzschmar's discussion of Brahms's four symphonies was previously published in *Führer durch den Concertsaal*, I. Abteilung: Sinfonie und Suite (Leipzig: A. G. Liebeskind, 1887), 276–93.

11. The Bach reference will be discussed thoroughly in this chapter. On a proposed reference to "Behold and See" from Handel's *Messiah*, see Hugo Riemann, "'Johannes Brahms, Fourth Symphony (E minor)' (1897)," in Hull's edition of the Fourth Symphony, 201, 205. On Lully, see Robert Ricks, "A Possible Source for a Brahms Ground," *American Brahms Society Newsletter* 23/1 (2005), 1–5. Constantin Floros [*Johannes Brahms, "Free but Alone": A Life for a Poetic Music*, trans. Ernest Bernhardt-Kabisch (Frankfurt am Main: Peter Lang, 2010); originally published as *Johannes Brahms, "frei aber einsam": Ein Leben für eine poetische Musik* (Zürich: Arche Zürich, 1997), 151] connects the first movement with Mendelssohn's Hebrides Overture. The "Hammerklavier" Sonata is addressed below. On Mozart, see Kalbeck, *Johannes Brahms* 3/2:461; Benjamin Boretz, "Meta-Variations, Part 4: Analytic Fallout (II): 6. Example 3: The First Eighteen Measures of Brahms's Fourth Symphony," *Perspectives of New Music* 11/2 (1973), 161; and Hull, "Brahms the Allusive," 121, 152–53. On Beethoven's Fifth Symphony, see Hull, "Brahms the Allusive," 97–114. Raymond Knapp ("The Finale of Brahms's Fourth Symphony," 10) notes that "as Brahms would have known from the work of his friend [the Beethoven scholar] Gustav Nottebohm, it was once Beethoven's intention to make the opening theme of his Fifth Symphony an unbroken chain of descending thirds"; the opening of Brahms's Fourth Symphony is built of a series of descending thirds and inverted descending thirds, that is, ascending sixths.

12. Tovey, *Essays in Musical Analysis*, 1:115. Although Brahms composed no other chaconne finales for "multi-movement, sonata-style" works [Walter Frisch, *Brahms and the Principle of Developing Variation* (Berkeley: University of California Press, 1984), 144], he had

written a piano transcription of Bach's D-minor violin Chaconne from BWV 1004 (1877?) and had already composed in the form himself, as in his Haydn Variations (1873). See also Giorgio Pestelli, "On the Finale of Brahms's Fourth Symphony," *Brahms Studien* 15 (2008), 129. For more on the historical context for Brahms's choice of form, see also Knapp, *Brahms and the Challenge of the Symphony*, 173-74; and Robert Pascall, "Genre and the Finale of Brahms's Fourth Symphony," *Music Analysis* 8/3 (1989), 233-45.

13. On the movement's melding of chaconne form with ternary or sonata-allegro structure, see Johnathan Dunsby, *Structural Ambiguity in Brahms: Analytical Approaches to Four Works* (Ann Arbor, MI: UMI Research Press, 1981), 76-83; Hull, "Brahms the Allusive," 165-73; A. Peter Brown, *The Symphonic Repertoire, 4: The Second Golden Age of the Viennese Symphony: Brahms, Bruckner, Dvorak, Mahler, and Selected Contemporaries* (Bloomington: Indiana University Press, 2002), 112; David Brodbeck, "Brahms," in *The Nineteenth-Century Symphony*, ed. D. Kern Holoman (New York: Schirmer Books, 1997), 262-63; Pascall, "Genre and the Finale," 237-43; Byron Cantrell, "Three B's—Three Chaconnes," *Current Musicology* 12 (1971), 70-72; and Pestelli, "On the Finale," 134-35. On the grouping of variations into units and for a slightly different interpretation of how the movement is superimposed with sonata form, see also Frisch, *Brahms: The Four Symphonies*, 131-37.

14. On the possible structural influence of BWV 1004, a movement for which Brahms expressed admiration and which he arranged for piano left hand, see for example Michael Musgrave, *The Music of Brahms*, 225-26; Robert Pascall, "Musikalische Einflüsse auf Brahms," *Östereischische Musikzeitschrift* 38/4-5 (1983), 231; and Jan Swafford, *Johannes Brahms: A Biography* (New York: Alfred A. Knopf, 1997), 523-24. On the possible relevance of the Buxtehude work, see for example, Knapp, "The Finale of Brahms's Fourth Symphony," 6-8. Regarding the Couperin piece and Brahms's assistance in the 1870s-80s with Chrysander's Couperin edition, see Musgrave, *The Music of Brahms*, 225; Knapp, "The Finale of Brahms's Fourth Symphony," 8; and Julian Littlewood, *The Variations of Johannes Brahms* (London: Plumbago Books, 2004), 210-11. The connection to Muffat is observed by, for example, Robert Pascall, "Genre and the Finale of the Fourth Symphony," 237; Michael Musgrave, *The Music of Brahms*, 225; and John Horton, *Brahms Orchestral Music* (Seattle, WA: University of Washington Press, 1978; originally published by the BBC in 1968), 57. On the B-Minor Mass, see Hull, "Brahms the Allusive," 199-200.

15. See Cantrell, "Three B's—Three Chaconnes," 70; Knapp, *Brahms and the Challenge of the Symphony*, 132-33; Hull, "Brahms the Allusive," 186-88; and Peter Petersen, "Die Variationen-Finale aus Brahms' e-Moll-Sinfonie und die c-Moll-Chaconne von Beethoven (WoO 80)," *Archiv für Musikwissenschaft* 70 (2013), 105-18.

16. Kenneth Ross Hull, "Allusive Irony in Brahms's Fourth Symphony," *Brahms Studies*, vol. 2, ed. David Brodbeck (Lincoln, NE: University of Nebraska Press, 1998), 146-47 and 153-68.

17. Ricks, "A Possible Source." 1-5.

18. This anecdote was originally reported in Siegfried Ochs, *Geschehenes, Gesehenes* (Leipzig: Grethlein, 1922), 299-300.

19. See Knapp, "The Finale of Brahms's Fourth Symphony," 5, fn. 7 and Brown, *The Symphonic Repertoire*, 4:111. Bach's authorship of this cantata has been called into question, but, as Alfred Dürr asserts, "there are no convincing grounds for such doubts beyond a certain weakness of invention and occasional technical errors" (it may be among his earliest cantatas), and in any case as far as Brahms was aware, it was a genuine Bach work. See Alfred

Dürr, *The Cantatas of J. S. Bach, with Their Librettos in German-English Parallel Text*, rev. and trans. Richard D. P. Jones (Oxford: Oxford University Press, 2005), 774.

20. This motive may also reflect the influence of Beethoven's "Hammerklavier" Sonata. For example, cf. the opening of Brahms's Symphony with mm. 76–86 of Beethoven's slow movement. See Littlewood, *The Variations of Johannes Brahms*, 213 and Musgrave, *The Music of Brahms*, 224. See also MacDonald, *Brahms*, 311–12 and Hull, "Allusive Irony," 136. Additionally, Knapp ("The Finale of Brahms's Fourth Symphony," 12, fn. 29) points to the descending thirds in the development section of Beethoven's first movement (mm. 139ff.).

21. Rule ("The Allure of Beethoven's 'Terzen-Ketten': Third-Chains in Studies by Nottebohm and Music by Brahms" (PhD diss., University of Illinois at Urbana-Champaign, 2011), 144–45, citing Hull, "Allusive Irony in Brahms's Fourth Symphony," 141–53) has noted a possible connection to Beethoven's Fifth Symphony, which, she observes, was originally conceived as a series of falling thirds, as Brahms might have been aware through his connection with Beethoven scholar Gustav Nottebohm. Furthermore, as MacDonald has pointed out (*Brahms*, 312, fn. 7), the first movement of BWV 150 also contains a falling-thirds chain (on "Lass mich nicht zu Schanden warden"). Additionally, as David Brodbeck (among others) has observed, "the two triads that can be formed from the first four notes" of this opening thirds-chain, E minor and C major, represent the primary tonalities of the Symphony's four-movement scheme, with the first and fourth movements in E minor, the second in a Phrygian-inflected E major that is "strongly inclined toward" C, and the third in C major. See Brodbeck, "Brahms," 255.

22. On the falling-third chain as a motive that helps to unify the thematic materials of the movement, see Marie Rivers Rule, "The Allure of Beethoven's 'Terzen-Ketten,'" 146–50. See also Brodbeck, "Brahms," 255.

23. See David Osmond-Smith, "The Retreat from Dynamism: A Study of Brahms's Fourth Symphony," in *Brahms: Biographical, Documentary, and Analytical Studies*, ed. Robert Pascall (Cambridge: Cambridge University Press, 1983), 156. See also Knapp, *Brahms and the Challenge of the Symphony*, 185.

24. Horton, *Brahms Orchestral Music*, 55.

25. My thanks to an anonymous reviewer for pointing this out.

26. See Arnold Schoenberg, "Brahms the Progressive (1947)," in *Style and Idea*, ed. Leonard Stein, 1st paperback edition with revisions (Berkeley: University of California Press, 1984), 405–6. See also Tovey, *Essays in Musical Analysis* 1:122; Brown, *The Symphonic Repertoire*, 4:114; Knapp, "The Finale of Brahms's Fourth Symphony," 15–16. As Knapp ("The Finale of Brahms's Fourth Symphony," 12) points out, however, "what has traditionally been seen as the most important ... aspect of the subject: its ability to combine with and even to be generated by, descending chains of thirds" is hardly unique to Brahms's subject, as "typical ostinato subjects consist primarily of scales, which are easily combined with descending chains of thirds; thus, almost any ostinato subject could have been used." See also Knapp's fn. 29 and his *Brahms and the Challenge of the Symphony*, 292; as well as Riemann, "Johannes Brahms, Fourth Symphony (E minor) (1897)," 213, ex. 27.

27. Schoenberg, "Brahms the Progressive" 406.

28. Frisch, *Brahms: The Four Symphonies*, 139. Since Schoenberg's time, the motivic link between the passacaglia subject and the Symphony's opening theme has been discussed in detail by several scholars, some of whom have cited examples in which the revelation of this relationship is foreshadowed earlier in the Symphony. See especially the detailed discussion

of intermovement connections in Knapp, "The Finale of Brahms's Fourth Symphony," 14–17, as well as Rudolf Klein, "Die Doppelgerüsttechnik in der Passacaglia der IV. Symphonie von Brahms," *Österreichische Musikzeitschrift* 27/12 (1972): 641–48 and Sigfried Kross, "Brahms the Symphonist," in *Brahms: Biographical, Documentary, and Analytical Studies*, ed. Robert Pascall (Cambridge: Cambridge University Press, 1983), 143–44. Other intermovement thematic relationships have also been observed in this work; see, for example, Brodbeck, "Brahms," 255–56 and 263; Edwin Evans, *Handbook to the Chamber and Orchestral Music of Johannes Brahms* (London: W. Reeves, Ltd., 1912; repr. New York: Burt Franklin, 1970), 2:155, 159–60; Walter Frisch, *Brahms and the Principle of Developing Variation*, 143; and *Brahms: The Four Symphonies*, 127; Hull, "Brahms the Allusive," 256; and Brown, "The Symphonies of Brahms," 108.

29. Frisch, *Brahms: The Four Symphonies*, 127. See also Frisch's corresponding example 6–11 on his p. 128. There are other potential motivic connections between the Symphony's third and fourth movements. For example, the descending lines in the finale's mm. 120 (Horn I), 128 (Flute I), and 132–36 (strings) may not only counterbalance that movement's ostinato ascending line, but perhaps also recall the third movement's opening gesture. The figure is associated more strongly with closure in these later instances, where it is used cadentially, rather than as an initiating gesture—and where its goal is the tonic pitch, rather than the fifth scale degree. In fact, if the finale's descending version is transposed into the third movement's C-major tonality, it appears that the fourth-movement figure actually completes the gesture that opens the third movement, bringing closure with arrival on the tonic. My thanks to an anonymous reader for pointing this out.

30. Knapp, "The Finale of Brahms's Fourth Symphony," 17. See also Knapp's *Brahms and the Challenge of the Symphony*, 21–22; Musgrave, *The Music of Brahms*, 224; Littlewood, *The Variations of Johannes Brahms*, 211, 215; Evans, *Handbook to the Chamber and Orchestral Music of Johannes Brahms*, 2:163.

31. On the use of variation technique in the first movement, see, for example, Evans, *Handbook to the Chamber and Orchestral Music of Johannes Brahms*, 2:147–52; Knapp, *Brahms and the Challenge of the Symphony*, 176–80, 295; Horton, *Brahms Orchestral Music*, 55; Brown, *The Symphonic Repertoire*, 4:110; Brodbeck, "Brahms," 257; and Musgrave, *The Music of Brahms*, 227–28. On the second movement, see Knapp, *Brahms and the Challenge of the Symphony*, 181; and Brown, *The Symphonic Repertoire*, 4:100, 106. On variation technique in the third movement, see Osmond-Smith, "The Retreat from Dynamism," 158.

32. See Felix Weingartner, "The Symphony Since Beethoven," in *Weingartner on Music and Conducting: Three Essays by Felix Weingartner*, trans. H. M. Schott (New York: Dover, 1969), 275–76; Knapp, *Brahms and the Challenge of the Symphony*, 185, 249; and Littlewood, *The Variations of Johannes Brahms*, 214. See also Ludwig Finscher, "The Struggle with Tradition: Johannes Brahms," trans. Eugene Hartzell, in *The Symphony*, ed. Ursula von Rauchhaupt (London: Thames and Hudson, 1973), 174.

33. Hull, "Brahms the Allusive," 123–24, 137. A chapter on Brahms's use of third chains in later works other than the Fourth Symphony is also included in Rule, "The Allure of Beethoven's 'Terzen-Ketten.'"

34. Composition dates given here are from George S. Bozarth and Walter Frisch, "Brahms, Johannes," *Grove Music Online / Oxford Music Online*. Accessed June 23, 2012, oxfordmusiconline.com. Op. 121/3 will be discussed in more detail here; on the other examples,

see Hull, "Brahms the Allusive," 124–34; Peter Latham, *Brahms* (London: J. M Dent and Sons, 1966), 153–54; and Max Harrison, *The Lieder of Brahms* (London: Cassell, 1972), 123–24.

35. Translation based in part on that appearing in Dürr, *The Cantatas of J. S. Bach*, 773–74.

36. Hull, "Brahms the Allusive," 178.

37. Littlewood, *The Variations of Johannes Brahms*, 214.

38. Hull, "Allusive Irony in Brahms's Fourth Symphony," 152, fn. 25.

39. Elisabeth von Herzogenberg to Brahms, Berlin, October 30, 1885, in *Johannes Brahms: The Herzogenberg Correspondence*, ed. Max Kalbeck, trans. Hannah Bryant (New York: E. P. Dutton and Company, 1909), 263–64.

40. Hull, "Brahms the Allusive," 204. Similarly, Knapp (*Brahms and the Challenge of the Symphony*, 294) identifies this as a key turning point in the final movement and in the work, stating that "the events just after the nostalgic central section of the finale [i.e., the 'tragic' minor-mode conclusion] may be understood as the linchpin to the larger dynamic of the work." See also Tovey, *Essays in Musical Analysis*, 1:122.

41. Kretzschmar, "The Brahms Symphonies," 142 and Pestelli, "On the Finale of Brahms's Fourth Symphony," 140–41. See also Kalbeck, *Johannes Brahms* 3/2:459–86.

42. Hull, "Brahms the Allusive," 220 and 221. Hull (231, fn. 17) provides Mozart's Requiem and *Don Giovanni* as examples. On the symbolism of the trombone in the nineteenth century, see also Floros, *Johannes Brahms, "Free but Alone,"* 153–54.

43. David Brodbeck, "Medium and Meaning: New Aspects of the Chamber Music," in *The Cambridge Companion to Brahms*, ed. Michael Musgrave (Cambridge: Cambridge University Press, 1999), 297, fn. 24, with quotation from Robert Bailey, "Musical Language and Structure in the Third Symphony," in *Brahms Studies: Analytical and Historical Perspectives*, ed. George Bozarth (Oxford: Oxford University Press, 1990), 405.

44. Brown, *The Symphonic Repertoire*, 4:114; and Hull, "Brahms the Allusive," 168.

45. Hull, "Brahms the Allusive," 205–20, 221–23.

46. See Hull, "Brahms the Allusive," 223–24.

47. Hull, "Brahms the Allusive," 224–25.

48. On Brahms's allusive "webs," see for example Raymond Knapp, "Utopian Agendas: Variation, Allusion, and Referential Meaning in Brahms's Symphonies," *Brahms Studies 3*, ed. David Brodbeck (Lincoln, NE: University of Nebraska Press, 2001), 144.

49. Although the musical connection to Schumann's "Süsser Freund" is not as strong, it is interesting to note that Wagner's text also resonates with that of the song, which is drawn from the poetry of Adelbert von Chamisso. Like the "Pilgrim's Chorus," Schumann's song begins with reference to gazing at someone or something that is loved: "*Süsser Freund, du blickest / Mich verwundert an*" ("Sweet friend, you look/At me with wonder"). My thanks to Christopher Reynolds for pointing this out to me in a personal communication.

50. Brahms does, however, make reference to his own mortality in a letter to Fritz Simrock from Vienna on October 2, 1885: "If the most human thing [i.e., death] should happen to me (so that I could have no more say in the matter), then the symphony should belong to you without further ado, that is, as a gift, both the score and the piano version, just as they stand." (Quoted in English translation, with bracketed editorial comment, in the "Historical Background" section of Hull's edition of the Symphony, p. 123. The original German appears in Johannes Brahms, *Briefe an Fritz Simrock*, ed. Max Kalbeck [Berlin: Deutsche Brahms-Gesellschaft, 1919; repr. Tutzing: Hans Schneider, 1974], 3:103–4.)

51. On the song and its construction from falling thirds, see Arnold Schoenberg, "Brahms the Progressive," 430–35.

52. See Hull, "Brahms the Allusive," 136. See also Floros, *Johannes Brahms, "Free but Alone,"* 154.

53. See Hull, "Brahms the Allusive," 148.

54. Floros, *Johannes Brahms, "Free but Alone,"* 149–50, citing a reviewer in the *Neue Musikzeitung* 6 (1885), 293 and Ludwig Speidel in the *Wiener Fremden-Blatt*, January 19, 1886, 6.

55. See Floros, *Johannes Brahms, "Free but Alone,"* 150.

56. Brahms to Franz Wüllner, Vienna, October 4, 1885, in *Johannes Brahms Briefwechsel*, vol. 15: *Johannes Brahms im Briefwechsel mit Franz Wüllner*, ed. Ernst Wolff (Berlin: Deutsche Brahms-Gesellschaft, 1922; repr. Tutzing: Hans Schneider, 1974), 121.

57. On the latter remark, see Kalbeck, *Johannes Brahms* 3/2: 447.

58. Knapp, *Brahms and the Challenge of the Symphony*, 297.

59. Swafford, *Johannes Brahms*, 526–27.

60. Ludwig Finscher, "The Struggle with Tradition," 174 and Reinhold Brinkmann, *Late Idyll: The Second Symphony of Johannes Brahms*, trans. Peter Palmer (Cambridge, MA: Harvard University Press, 1995), 221–26.

61. Swafford, *Johannes Brahms*, 526. See also Pestelli, "On the Finale of Brahms's Fourth Symphony," 145, 146–47. However, the minor-mode ending may also be interpreted as another element of historical reference, hearkening back to a pre-Beethovenian era in which minor-mode symphonic conclusions were common. (See Knapp, *Brahms and the Challenge of the Symphony*, 298, 299.)

62. See Brodbeck, "Brahms," 255. See also Swafford, *Johannes Brahms*, 512.

63. Brahms to Elisabeth von Herzogenberg, Mürzzuschlag, August 29, 1885, in *Johannes Brahms: The Herzogenberg Correspondence*, 238.

64. See Hull's edition of the Fourth Symphony, 137, fn. 5. See also 122–23 from this edition. Brahms wrote the same to Hans von Bülow; see *Hans von Bülow's Letters to Johannes Brahms: A Research Edition*, ed. Hans-Joachim Hinrichsen, trans. Cynthia Klohr (Lanham, MD: Scarecrow Press, 2011), 83.

65. Brahms to Elisabeth von Herzogenberg, October 10, 1885, as quoted in translation in Swafford, *Johannes Brahms*, 515.

66. See Hull's edition of Brahms, *Symphony No. 4 in E minor*, 139. Elisabeth then immediately responded in detail (see 141–43 from this edition), claiming to have been "deep in my letter just now when your strange post-card" arrived and asking, "what can you possibly mean by the 'complete failure' of your attack?"

67. Brahms to Fritz Simrock, October 2, 1885, in Brahms, *Briefe an Fritz Simrock*, 103–4.

68. See Brodbeck, "Brahms," 256–57; Painter, "Symphony No. 4 in E Minor," 72; and Swafford, *Johannes Brahms*, 514–16. On the responses of Brahms's friends, including Hans von Bülow and Clara Schumann, see also Hull's commentary in Brahms, *Symphony No. 4 in E Minor*, 118 and 123–27. Despite her initial reservations, upon hearing the work performed with the Berlin Philharmonic under the baton of Joachim on February 1, 1886, Elisabeth von Herzogenberg reported that the performance "was not good, but simply perfection ... The effect was *overpowering* ... I was moved to tears—happy tears—by the andante ... nothing in the whole symphony went wrong." English translation from Ivor Keys, *Johannes Brahms* (Portland, OR: Amadeus Press, 1989), 120.

69. On the reception at the Meiningen premiere, see Brown, *The Symphonic Repertoire*, 4:99 and Hull's commentary in Brahms, *Symphony No. 4 in E Minor*, 127. On the initial reception of the work in Vienna, see for example Swafford, *Johannes Brahms*, 517–18. It was not until shortly before Brahms's death in 1897 that the work received "substantial acclaim" in Vienna (Painter, "Symphony No. 4 in E Minor," 73).

70. Kross, "Brahms the Symphonist," 141.

71. This was originally published as "Konzert," *Fremden-Blatt*, January 19, 1886, 6. It is quoted here in translation as given by Hull in Brahms, *Symphony No. 4*, 171.

72. This review was originally published on January 19, 1886, on 1–3 of the *Neue Freie Presse*. It appears here in English translation as given in Eduard Hanslick, *Hanslick's Music Criticisms*, ed. and trans. Henry Pleasants (New York: Dover, 1988), 244–45.

73. This review by Henry Theophilus Finck of a New York Philharmonic concert conducted by Theodore Thomas was originally published on January 17, 1887 in the *New York Post*; this passage is reproduced on p. 188 of Hull's edition of the Fourth Symphony.

74. Wagner expressed his views on Beethoven's Ninth Symphony in his essay "Beethoven," originally published in Leipzig by E. W. Fritzsch in 1870.

75. This is all the more poignant in light of the fact that this was to be Brahms's final symphony—although apparently he did not conceive of it as his last at the time; he subsequently produced sketches for further symphonic work that remained unfinished. See Finscher, "The Struggle with Tradition," 174; Brodbeck, "Brahms," 263; and George S. Bozarth, "Brahms, Johannes—Section 5: Final Years and Legacy," *Grove Music Online / Oxford Music Online*. Accessed June 28, 2012. oxfordmusiconline.com. For the quotation from Weingartner, see "The Symphony Since Beethoven," 276.

76. Knapp, "The Finale of Brahms's Fourth Symphony," 12–13.

77. MacDonald, *Brahms*, 312, fn. 6. Similarly, Heather Platt has interpreted references to Haydn in Brahms's songs "Immer leiser wird mein Schlummer," op. 105/2, and "Im Herbst," op. 104/5, dating from the mid-1880s, as a response to the recent death of Brahms's friend, the Haydn biographer C. F. Pohl. See Platt's "Probing the Meaning of Brahms's Allusions to Haydn," *International Review for the Aesthetics and Sociology of Music* 42/1 (2011): 33–58.

78. See Rule, "The Allure of Beethoven's 'Terzen-Ketten,'" 212. For more on the relationship and correspondence between Nottebohm and Brahms, see also Rule's pp. 12–68.

79. See *Johannes Brahms: Life and Letters*, 598–600, 794.

80. See MacDonald, *Brahms*, 312, fn. 6.

81. Brahms to Joseph Joachim, Hamburg, ca. May 5, 1860, in *Johannes Brahms: Life and Letters*, ed. Styra Avins, trans. Josef Eisinger and Styra Avins (Oxford: Oxford University Press, 1997), 221.

82. See Karl Geiringer, "Wagner and Brahms, with Unpublished Letters," *Musical Quarterly* 22/2 (1936), 179 and Brodbeck, "Brahms, the Third Symphony, and the New German School," 72–73.

83. For a more complete list of names and more information on some of these figures, see Styra Avins's note in *Johannes Brahms: Life and Letters*, 749.

84. For the text of the manifesto in English translation, see David Brodbeck, "Brahms, the Third Symphony, and the New German School," *Brahms and His World*, ed. Walter Frisch (Princeton, NJ: Princeton University Press, 1990), 79. Appendix 2 of that volume is a translation of Carl Friedrich Weitzmann's parody of the manifesto (discussed in Brodbeck, 73).

85. Geiringer, "Wagner and Brahms," 181.

86. Geiringer, "Wagner and Brahms," 181.

87. See Geiringer, "Wagner and Brahms," 179–81.

88. For an English translation of Cornelius's letter to Brahms, see Karl Geiringer, "Wagner and Brahms," 181–82.

89. Klaus Kropfinger, "Wagner und Brahms," *Musica* 37/1 (1983), 13, citing Kurt Hofmann, *Die Bibliothek von Johannes Brahms: Bücher- und Musikalienverzeichnis* (Hamburg: Karl Dieter Wagner, 1974), 144.

90. This essay was originally published as "Über das Dirigiren" simultaneously in the *Neue Zeitschrift für Musik* and the *New-Yorker Musik-Zeitung* in 1869, and appeared in print immediately thereafter as a book by the same title (Leipzig: C. F. Kahnt, 1869–70). The quotation given here is drawn from the version subsequently published in English translation: Richard Wagner, *On Conducting (Über das Dirigiren): A Treatise on Style in the Execution of Classical Music*, trans. Edward Dannreuther (London: William Reeves, 1887), 83.

91. Wagner, *On Conducting*, 84.

92. Wagner, *On Conducting*, 86

93. Wagner, *On Conducting*, 106. Several of Brahms's good friends were Jewish, including Joachim.

94. See Chris Walton, *Wagner's Zurich: The Muse of Place* (Rochester, NY: Camden House, 2007), 203–4.

95. See *Johannes Brahms: Life and Letters*, 371.

96. Hofmann and Hofmann, "Zu den Beziehungen," 133–34.

97. Clara Schumann to Johannes Brahms, July 8, 1866, in *Clara Schumann–Johannes Brahms: Briefe aus den Jahren 1853–1896*, ed. Berthold Litzmann (Leipzig: Breifkopf & Härtel, 1927), 1:539. Translation from Geiringer, "Correspondence with Brahms: Richard Wagner," in *On Brahms and His Circle: The Collected Essays and Studies of Karl Geiringer*, ed. George S. Bozarth (Sterling, MI: Harmonie Park Press, 2006), 370, fn. 27.

98. Styra Avins, *Johannes Brahms: Life and Letters*, 370–71. For more on Brahms's relationship with Mathilde Wesendonck, including her attempts to have him set her poetry to music, see also Jacquelyn Sholes, "Brahms, Mathilde Wesendonck, and the Would-Be 'Cremation Cantata'," *American Brahms Society Newsletter* 30/2 (Fall 2012), 1–5; and Jacquelyn Sholes, "A 'Cremation Cantata'?: The Dramatic Conclusion of the Brahms-Wesendonck Correspondence," *Ars Lyrica* 21 (2012), 155–72, from which some of the material appearing here was drawn.

99. Nietzsche's conflicting feelings about Wagner are reflected in his own writings, including *Richard Wagner in Bayreuth* (1876), *Der Fall Wagner* (1888), and the essay "Nietzsche contra Wagner" (written 1888–89, first published 1895), which have been published together in a single volume: Friedrich Wilhelm Nietzsche, *Richard Wagner in Bayreuth; Der Fall Wagner; Nietzsche contra Wagner* (Stuttgart: Reclam, 1973). See also for example Alan Ryan, "The Will to Madness: The Story of Friedrich Nietzsche's Fateful Relationship with Richard and Cosima Wagner," *The New York Times* (January 24, 1999). Accessed January 30, 2017. www.nytimes.com/books/99/01/24/reviews/990124.24ryanlt.html; and Joachim Kohler, *Nietzsche and Wagner: A Lesson in Subjugation*, trans. Ronald Taylor (New Haven, CT: Yale University Press, 1998).

100. Wagner's account appears in English translation in Richard Specht, *Johannes Brahms*, trans. Eric Blom (London: J. M. Dent and Sons, 1930), 259, cited in David S. Thatcher, "Nietzsche and Brahms: A Forgotten Relationship," *Music & Letters* 54/3 (1973), 263–64.

101. See Karl Geiringer, "Wagner and Brahms," 186–87, 189.

102. These comments, originally published as part of an essay entitled "Über das Dichten und Komponieren" ("On Poetry and Composition"), appear here as translated in *Richard Wagner's Prose Works*, ed. and trans. William Ashton Ellis, vol. 6: Religion and Art (London: Kegan Paul, Trench, Trübner and Co., Ltd., 1897), 143–44. On von Bülow's nickname for Brahms's First Symphony, see *Hans von Bülow's Letters to Johannes Brahms*, 55–56.

103. Geiringer, "Correspondence with Brahms: Richard Wagner," 372. On Brahms's plans (which fell through) to visit Bayreuth in 1882, see also *Johannes Brahms: Life and Letters*, 594–95. See also Kropfinger, "Wagner und Brahms," 13.

104. English translation from Brodbeck, "Brahms, the Third Symphony, and the New German School," 66; the original German appears in Richard Wagner, *Gesammelte Schriften und Dichtungen*, 3rd ed. (Leipzig: E. W. Fritzsch, 1887–88), 10:292.

105. See *Richard Wagner's Prose Works*, 6:296–97.

106. Geiringer, "Wagner and Brahms," 188.

107. See Geiringer, "Wagner and Brahms," 188 and Peter A. Brown, "Brahms' Third Symphony and the New German School," *Journal of Musicology* 2/4 (1983): 437. Cosima's initial impressions of Brahms, upon having met him in Vienna in 1875, were rather less positive; upon having met him in Vienna in 1875, she described him in her day-book as "a red and rough-looking man" (*ein rot und roh aussehender Mann*). Kropfinger, "Wagner und Brahms," 13, citing Cosima Wagner, *Die Tagebücher*, ed. Martin Gregor-Dellin and Dietrich Mack (München: Piper, 1976), 1:949.

108. Christopher Alan Reynolds, *Wagner, Schumann, and the Lessons of Beethoven's Ninth* (Berkeley: University of California Press, 2015); see especially 145–54.

109. According to Kalbeck, the second and third movements of the Third Symphony (along with the "Tragic" Overture may have had their origins in 1880–81 as intended incidental music for a production of Goethe's *Faust*. See Brown, *The Symphonic Repertoire*, 4:81 and Kalbeck, *Johannes Brahms* 3/1:258. See also Knapp, "Utopian Agendas," 140ff.; Brodbeck, "Brahms, the Third Symphony, and the New German School," 67ff. and 154; Evans, *Handbook to the Chamber and Orchestral Music of Johannes Brahms*, 124–25; and Bailey, "Musical Language and Structure in the Third Symphony," 405–7. The allusion was also noted in John Fuller-Maitland, *Brahms* (New York: John Lane Co., 1911), 149 and was observed by Hugo Riemann in *Johannes Brahms: Erläuterung seiner bedeutendsten Werke* (Frankfurt am Main: H. Bechold, 1898), 101.

110. Knapp, "Utopian Agendas," 140. On the relationship between Brahms's harmonic language in this work and the harmonic language of Wagner and other possible aspects of "New German" influence in the Third Symphony, see also Brodbeck, "Brahms, the Third Symphony, and the New German School" 70–72; Knapp, "Utopian Agendas," 154; Brown, "Brahms' Third Symphony and the New German School," 434–52; and Brown, *The Symphonic Repertoire*, 4:94.

111. *Johannes Brahms and Theodor Billroth: Letters from a Musical Friendship*, trans. and ed. Hans Barkan (Norman, OK: University of Oklahoma Press, 1957, 132, quoted in Brodbeck, "Brahms, the Third Symphony, and the New German School," 67.

112. Brodbeck, "Brahms, the Third Symphony, and the New German School," 67, 76, fn. 11. See also pp. 66–70 and 75 of the same article, as well as Knapp, "Utopian Agendas," 154–57. Brodbeck (68–69) writes that, "this seductive song of the sirens, this invitation to enter into the 'Venusberg' realm may well be emblematic of the temptations which Wagner's

musical language must periodically have exerted on Brahms," but (70) that, "by juxtaposing chromatic and diatonic treatments of the same key, Brahms was able to demonstrate all the more effectively the rich possibilities remaining to be explored within the confines of traditional tonality."

113. It has also been proposed that the Third Symphony alludes to the conclusion of *Götterdämmerung* (Bailey, "Musical Language and Structure in the Third Symphony," 405–9), and Michael Musgrave (*The Music of Brahms*, 221–23) has suggested that the Third Symphony may pay tribute to Wagner through its employment of a Leitmotif-like F-A(b)-F motto. For more on Brahms's so-called "Frei aber Froh" (F-A-F) motive and its possible appearance in the Third Symphony, see also Brown, *The Symphonic Repertoire*, 4:83 and Peter A. Brown, "Brahms's Third Symphony and the New German School," *Journal of Musicology* 2/4 (1983): 445. Brodbeck ("Brahms, the Third Symphony, and the New German School," 67) suggests that "Brahms might well have been itching to requite Wagner's recent disparaging remarks about his place in music history, and to do so in his characteristic terms—through musical references that carry a point. But the role of the [F-A-F] motive ... should not be overstated; Brahms had previously deployed such cells in the first two symphonies ... as well as in other works." Brahms may have alluded to other Wagnerian operas in other works of his own as well. See Brodbeck, "Brahms, the Third Symphony, and the New German School," 77, fn. 12.

114. See Kalbeck, as appearing in English translation by Susan Gillespie in Hull's edition of the Fourth Symphony, 226. See also Clara's journal entry of March 5, 1886 as published in *Clara Schumann: Ein Künstlerleben nach Tagebüchern und Briefen*, ed. Berthold Litzmann (Leipzig: Breitkopf & Härtel, 1923), 475, cited in Knapp, *Brahms and the Challenge of the Symphony*, 294, fn. 101. Additionally, see Speidel, "Konzert," 6, appearing here in Hull's English translation from p. 171 of his own edition of the Fourth Symphony.

115. Knapp ("The Finale of Brahms's Fourth Symphony," 8) has asserted that "Buxtehude's ciacona is, in musical terms, more relevant to Brahms's symphony than Bach's Cantata." Hull ("Allusive Irony in Brahms's Fourth Symphony," 174, 151, fn. 24. See also 96–97) points out, for example, that that "external evidence" for the Cantata as a source, that is, Ochs's anecdote, is stronger than the musical evidence, for "the theme itself is not at all an unusual one to find as the basis of a chaconne ... the musical gesture ... is not a very singular one: a stepwise movement from tonic to dominant followed by a return to the tonic," and "the assumption that Brahms might have employed a particular model for the ostinato ... is ... dubious, since many similar examples exist in the musical literature." The status of the Cantata as a source has most recently been questioned by Ricks in his proposal (cited above) that the ostinato in Brahms's finale was actually derived from Lully. Some musical resemblance between the Lully theme and the Brahms does indeed exist, but, Lully seems a far less likely source than Bach, and the text of this passage from Lully deals with the torments of love and is thus not so clearly related to the Wagner text, nor to the theme of "death," as is the text of the Cantata.

116. Knapp ("The Finale of Brahms's Fourth Symphony," 3) refers to the finale's ostinato subject as "the integrative kernel for the Symphony as a whole," and Hull ("Allusive Irony in Brahms's Fourth Symphony," 168) writes that the extent to which some of the Fourth Symphony's allusions "have been integrated into the musical fabric that contains them implies that the decision to include them must have been both early and central to Brahms's conception of the symphony. Far from being a surface feature of marginal significance, as allusion is sometimes viewed, Brahms's allusive practice in the Fourth Symphony leads us to the heart of a work that challenges the symphonic norms of the later nineteenth century."

Swafford (*Johannes Brahms*, 523) asserts that "likely the conception of [the finale] was the beginning of the work" and "may have been its reason for being in the first place."

117. Margaret Notley points to essays in which Adorno writes about the use of archaic devices in late works by Beethoven and Goethe as a sign of artistic alienation. See Notley's *Lateness and Brahms: Music and Culture in the Twilight of Viennese Liberalism*, ed. Mary Hunter (Oxford: Oxford University Press, 2007), 64, citing Theodor Wiesengrund Adorno, "On the Final Scene of *Faust*" and "Alienated Masterpiece" in *Essays on Music*, ed. Richard Leppert, trans. Susan H. Gillespie (Berkeley: University of California Press, 2002). Perhaps there is some element of this phenomenon occurring here, although Brahms, as we have seen, always had a tendency to incorporate historical references into his works. Brahms was, of course, of a later generation than Beethoven and Goethe and, all too aware of this, seems to have felt his sense of artistic "lateness" even as a young man.

118. See Cantrell, "Three B's," 72; Knapp, "The Finale of Brahms's Fourth Symphony," 3, 9, fn. 20, 12; and Frisch, *Brahms the Four Symphonies*, 133–34. In *Brahms and the Challenge of the Symphony* (299), Knapp writes of a "Wagnerian harmonic manner" and "harmonic manipulations" in the Fourth Symphony's final movement that "Brahms uses to evoke a struggle against the authority of the ostinato subject," avoiding closure. "As each resistance to the closure demanded by the ostinato subject propels us into the next statement with its own demand for closure," he writes," the continued dominance of fate is assured by the very struggle against it."

119. See Walter Frisch, "The 'Brahms Fog': On Analyzing Brahmsian Influences at the Fin de Siècle," in *Brahms and His World*, ed. Walter Frisch (Princeton: Princeton University Press, 1990), 93–97; Frisch, *Brahms: The Four Symphonies*, 131; and Knapp, *Brahms and the Challenge of the Symphony*, 314–15.

120. Schoenberg, "Brahms the Progressive," 405–7.

Conclusion

In exploring historical reference and extramusical meaning in Brahms's multimovement instrumental works, this book has engaged with concerns that remain at the forefront of current Brahms scholarship—in particular, a growing acceptance of the idea that Brahms's instrumental music is not necessarily so devoid of extramusical meaning as it once appeared. The traditional idea of Brahms as "absolute" composer is coming to be recognized as the oversimplistic result of earlier critics' and scholars' attempts to neatly dichotomize the aesthetics of the "Brahmsians" versus those of the "Wagnerians" or the New German School; Eduard Hanslick was particularly influential in helping to reinforce this dichotomy.[1] As Raymond Knapp has observed, there is "on the one hand, an almost moralistic antipathy among Brahms's advocates to acknowledging his musical reminiscences, coupled with the widespread desire of many theorists and other absolutists to comprehend Brahms's music solely in terms of internal, musical criteria [that] has often blocked explorations of the more intimate ways Brahms's music connects to the past."[2] The present volume has been one of several recent studies (cited throughout) that attempts to redress this situation, demonstrating that, where Brahms as "absolutist" is concerned, things are not necessarily so "black and white" as we may once have believed.

Upon incorporating historical references into his music in the form of thematic or stylistic allusions or structural models, Brahms, famously among the most historically self-aware of composers, reveals through his musical handling of his source materials something of his attitude and orientation toward those sources and the past they represent. As Charles Rosen once observed,

> we cannot fully appreciate [Brahms's music] ... without becoming aware of the influence which went into its making.... Influence for Brahms was not merely a part of the compositional process, a necessary fact of creative life: he incorporated it as part of the symbolic structure of the work, its iconography. We might even conjecture that the overt references are there as signals, to call attention to others less obvious, almost undetectable.[3]

In Brahms's work, particularly early on, it frequently appears that thematic material with whose reminiscence, transformation, or disintegration a piece is concerned is actually a reference to a work of the musical past—generally a major work of special historical significance, often a piece by Beethoven, a figure well known to have born tremendous psychological significance for Brahms and for so many of his contemporaries. Although this occurs most markedly in works of the period following on the publication of Schumann's 1853 article "*Neue Bahnen*," it is true of music from Brahms's mid-career and later years as well, as we observed in chapters 1 and 5.

Brahms's historical awareness, although clearly acute throughout his career, was surely piqued in the mid-1850s as the young composer struggled to come to terms with the heavy burden of reconciling the terrific expectations expressed in and engendered by Schumann's article. Brahms faced the task of establishing his own position in music history as he sought to compose works worthy of one proclaimed a musical messiah and heir to the likes of Beethoven. Those works evidencing a concern with distorted recollection of or willful departure from music of the past appear to represent a means through which Brahms attempted to cope with insecurities and struggles regarding his relationship to the musical traditions and responsibilities he had inherited.

As Brahms's career progressed, his historicist sensitivity remained, but it evolved. During the middle decades of his career, the old issues were still of concern, especially in large milestone works with which Brahms struggled and that he knew would play an important role in solidifying his historical reputation, such as the First Symphony. However, over the course of this period, Brahms managed to establish himself quite solidly in an artistic sense. Not only do good examples of cross-movement allusory narratives appear to become less pervasive, but when they do occur, they at times seem to reflect other types of inner struggle, as with the folksong reference in the Horn Trio (see chapter 1), which seems to relate more directly to Brahms's conflicted but persistent bachelorhood than to any artistic or historicist insecurities.

And as we have seen with the Fourth Symphony (and, briefly, the Third), the late works reflect the evolving nature of the historicist concerns Brahms faced as a more mature composer. These concerns had just as much to do with the present and future as with the past, and Brahms draws on both "archaic" and progressive contemporary sources, including the music of Wagner. In the allusory narratives we have examined from earlier in his career, when Brahms employs a borrowed element—especially a Beethovenian element—it is very often so that he can gradually, over the course of the work, either break away from that element or at least modify it to make it more his own. This process often culminates in a triumphal close, as though Brahms, in taming or tempering the borrowed element, has overcome an artistic burden and has proven himself by establishing artistic autonomy. In the Fourth Symphony, when Brahms places his own "stamp" on historical elements, adding a chromatic element to Bach's ostinato theme and overturning the Beethovenian precedent of concluding a minor-mode symphony in the parallel major, the effect is quite different. Instead of victoriously proclaiming his artistic individuality, Brahms instead creates a sense of pessimistic defeat. The message is arguably less about self-absorbed artistic posturing than it is about more outward-looking topics, such as where music is headed stylistically and aesthetically, transience in life and art, the meaning of death, or perhaps even the passing of an associate. These things would certainly have had implications for Brahms himself, but Brahms is not at the very center of them. In this sense, the later allusory narrative, with its less strident, egocentric message, is decidedly less "adolescent" than those of the earlier periods. Further examination of such narratives in Brahms's later instrumental works will prove valuable in continuing to fill out this picture.

Another area that is ripe for additional research is the question of how Brahms's allusory practices compare to those of other composers of his time, particularly those by whom he is known to have been strongly influenced or upon whom he exerted a particular influence. Especially in need of further exploration are allusory relationships between Brahms's music and the works of a number of lesser-known composers active in Brahms's circle, including his only long-term compositional pupil, Gustav Jenner, his longtime friend Joseph Joachim (who eventually gave up composing to focus on his career as a violinist), and such composers as Franz Lachner, Heinrich and Elisabeth von Herzogenberg, Julius Stockhausen, Theodor Kirchner, Albert Dietrich, and many others.[4] Although still focusing primarily on Brahms's own allusions (especially in single-movement vocal works), Paul Berry has taken a first step in this direction with his recent book *Brahms Among Friends: Listening, Performance, and the Rhetoric of Allusion*, which examines mutual influences between Brahms and Heinrich von Herzogenberg, also touching on music of Joachim and Stockhausen.[5]

Any role played by allusions and historical models in the creation of inter-movement structures or narratives of the sort we have observed here does not detract in any way from the originality or importance of Brahms's own musical accomplishments. It does not, in other words, carry the same sort of stigma that might be associated with acts of borrowing or modeling as simple compositional crutches, born of a lack of new musical ideas. Brahms employs allusions and models because of meanings with which he associates the sources of these materials, and his music thereby comments on his relationship to these sources in ways that are not possible without actually referencing them. In this way, his works are in fact *enriched* by additional strata of psychological and historical depth, becoming more uniquely personal and, if anything, *more* creative and ingenious—not less so.[6]

Furthermore, as I have suggested several times in this book, to the extent that Brahms may have been conscious of imbuing his works with any meaning related to his own biography, it often appears that he did so for his own benefit and did not intend his meaning to be perceived by others.[7] In fact, composers of Brahms's time often seem to have taken care to conceal meaning from their listeners. Reynolds points out, for example, that Schumann

> discussed [thematic] transformation as a form of concealment, implicitly linking this process with the inclusion of poetic and dramatic content. Writing in 1832 ... he acknowledged that a composer "no longer persisted in developing a thematic idea within only one movement; one *concealed* this idea in other shapes and modifications in subsequent movements as well. In short, one wanted to integrate historical interest into the whole ... and as the age became more poetic, dramatic interest as well."[8]

Ultimately, of course, we cannot know what any of the works "really mean"— and, indeed should not warm to the idea that any piece (or any other thing, for that matter) contains only one fixed meaning. Works such as opp. 8 and 15, for instance, may contain meanings related to Brahms's historical position, to the Schumanns, to both, to neither, or to any number of other things within, partially within, or beyond Brahms's awareness. Psychoanalyst Stuart Feder points out that, "every symbol is capable of infinite representation ... A musical idea may bear multiple meanings ... simultaneously. More than this, other meanings may accrue over the course of time and others become obscured."[9] As he suggests, it is this potential for diverse meanings that allows listeners and performers alike to derive "a lifetime of fascination" from a familiar work.[10] And, in the end, we must not lose sight of the abstract meaning (or meanings) the work bears, most essentially, as musical expression on its own terms.

Notes

1. On Hanslick's influence, see Constantin Floros, *Johannes Brahms, "Free but Alone": A Life for a Poetic Music* (Frankfurt am Main: Peter Lang, 2010); originally published as *Johannes Brahms, "frei aber einsam": Ein Leben für eine poetische Musik* (Zürich: Arche Zürich, 1997), 194–202, especially 201–2.

2. Raymond Knapp, "Utopian Agendas: Variation, Allusion, and Referential Meaning in Brahms's Symphonies," in *Brahms Studies*, vol. 3, ed. David Brodbeck (Lincoln: University of Nebraska Press, 2001), 138.

3. Charles Rosen, "Influence: Plagiarism and Inspiration," *19th-Century Music* 4/2 (1980): 94. On hidden borrowings in the works of several majors composers, see also for example, a series of articles by Ellwood Derr: "Brahms' op. 38: Ein Beitrag zur Kunst der Komposition mit entlehnten Stoffen," in *Brahms-Kongress Wien 1983*, ed. Susanne Antonicek and Otto Biba (Tutzing: Hans Schneider, 1988), 95–124; "Beethoven's Long-Term Memory of C. P. E. Bach's Rondo in E Flat, W. 61/1 (1787), Manifest in the Variations in E Flat for Piano, op. 35 (1802)," *Musical Quarterly* 70 (1983), 45–76; "A Foretaste of the Borrowings from Haydn in Beethoven's op. 2," in *Joseph Haydn: Über den Internationalen Joseph Haydn Kongress,*

Wien, Hofburg, 5.-12. September 1982, ed. Eva Badura-Skoda (Munich: G. Henle, 1986), 159–70; "Mozart's Transfer of the Vocal 'Fermata Sospesa' to His Piano-Concerto First Movements," *Mozart-Jahrbuch* 1 (1991), 155–63; and "Handel's Procedures for Composing with Materials from Telemann's *Harmonischer Gottes-Dienst* in *Solomon*," in *Goettinger Händel-Beiträge*, ed. Hans Joachim Marx (Kassel: Bärenreiter, 1984), 1:116–47.

4. I am currently engaged in other work in this area. See for example Jacquelyn Sholes, "Gustav Jenner and the Music of Brahms: The Case of the Orchestral Serenades," *Nineteenth-Century Music Review*, forthcoming.

5. Paul Berry, *Brahms Among Friends: Listening, Performance, and the Rhetoric of Allusion* (Oxford: Oxford University Press, 2014).

6. Michael Vaillancourt has argued that, ca. 1860–85, Brahms's music seems to have played an important role in the growing critical acceptance of allusion as a "viable creative option"; see his "Brahms's 'Sinfonie-Serenade' and the Politics of Genre," *The Journal of Musicology* 26/3 (2009): 397.

7. Paul Berry (see *Brahms Among Friends*, 36) similarly argues that there are examples in which Brahms concealed allusions from friends for whom they would have had particular meanings.

8. Christopher Alan Reynolds, *Motives for Allusion: Context and Content in Nineteenth-Century Music* (Cambridge, MA: Harvard University Press, 2003), 164, citing Robert Schumann, *Gesammelte Schriften über Musik und Musiker*, 5th ed. (Leipzig: Breitkopf und Härtel, 1914), 1:159 as quoted in Mark Evan Bonds, *After Beethoven: Imperatives of Originality in the Symphony* (Cambridge, MA: Harvard University Press, 1996), 121. On concealment as an aspect of Romantic irony, see also Reynolds, *Motives for Allusion*, 164.

9. Stuart Feder, "'Promissory Notes': Method in Music and Applied Psychoanalysis," *Psychoanalytic Explorations in Music: Second Series*, ed. Stuart Feder, Richard L. Karmel, and George H. Pollock (Madison, CT: International Universities Press, 1993), 17, 12.

10. Feder, "'Promissory Notes,'" 18.

Bibliography

Abraham, Gerald. *A Hundred Years of Music*. 4th ed. London: Duckworth, 1974.
Agawu, Kofi. *Music as Discourse: Semiotic Adventures in Romantic Music*. New York: Oxford University Press, 2009.
Bach, Johann Sebastian. Cantate am fünften Sonntage nach Trinitatis über das Lied '*Wer nur den lieben Gott lässt walten*' von Georg Neumark, No. 93, BWV 93. *Bach-Gesellschaft Ausgabe*. Vol. 22. Edited by Wilhelm Rust. Leipzig: Breitkopf & Härtel, 1875.
———. *371 Four-Part Chorales*. Kalmus Classic Ed. Vol. 1. [S.l.]: Kalmus, 1985.
Bailey, Robert. "Musical Language and Structure in the Third Symphony." In *Brahms Studies: Analytical and Historical Perspectives: Papers Delivered at the International Brahms Conference, Washington, DC, 5–8 May 1983*, edited by George S. Bozarth, 405–21. Oxford: Oxford University Press, 1990.
Baldassarre, Antonio, "Johannes Brahms and Johannes Kreisler: Creativity and Aesthetics of the Young Brahms, Illustrated by the Piano Trio in B Major, op. 8." *Acta Musicologica* 72/2 (2000): 145–67.
Beethoven, Ludwig van. *Complete Piano Sonatas*. 2 vols. Edited by Heinrich Schenker. Vienna: Universal-Edition, 1923; repr. Mineola, NY: Dover Publications, 1975 with new introduction by Carl Schachter.
———. *Klavier-Sonaten*. 2 vols. Edited by B. A. Wallner, with fingering by Conrad Hansen. München: G. Henle Verlag, 1980.
———. *Complete Piano Concertos*. Mineola, NY: Dover, 1983. (Repr. of material originally published in Series 9 of *Ludwig van Beethoven's Werke; Vollständige kritisch durchgesehene überall berechtigte Ausgabe; mit Genehmigung aller Originalverleger*. Leipzig: Breitkopf & Härtel, [1862–65].)
———. *Symphonies Nos. 1, 2, 3, and 4*. Mineola, NY: Dover, 1989. (Repr. of the first four of the *Symphonies de Beethoven. Partitions d'Orchestre*. Braunschweig: Henry Litolff's Verlag, n.d.)
———. *Symphonies Nos. 5, 6, and 7*. Mineola, NY: Dover, 1989. (Repr. of three of the *Symphonies de Beethoven. Partitions d'Orchestre*. Braunschweig: Henry Litolff's Verlag, n.d.)
———. *Symphonies Nos. 8 and 9*. Mineola, NY: Dover, 1989. (Repr. of the last two of the *Symphonies de Beethoven. Partitions d'Orchestre*. Braunschweig: Henry Litolff's Verlag, n.d.)
———. *Lieder und Gesänge mit Klavierbegleitung*. Edited by Helga Lühning. Beethoven Werke, Series 12, Vol. 1. München: G. Henle Verlag, 1990.
Beller-McKenna, Daniel. *Brahms and the German Spirit*. Cambridge, MA: Harvard University Press, 2004.
———. "Distance and Disembodiment: Harps, Horns, and the Requiem Idea in Schumann and Brahms." *Journal of Musicology* 22/1 (2005): 47–89.
Berry, Paul. *Brahms Among Friends: Listening, Performance, and the Rhetoric of Allusion*. Oxford: Oxford University Press, 2014.

Bighley, Mark S. *The Lutheran Chorales in the Organ Works of J. S. Bach.* St. Louis, MO: Concordia Publishing House, 1986.

Blom, Eric. *Beethoven's Pianoforte Sonatas Discussed.* London: J.M. Dent & Sons Ltd., 1938.

Bloom, Harold. *The Anxiety of Influence: A Theory of Poetry.* London: Oxford University Press, 1973.

Boettinger, Peter. "Jahre der Krise, Krise der Form: Beobachtungen am 1. Satz des Klavierkonzertes op. 15 von Johannes Brahms." *Musik-Konzepte* 65 (1989): 41–68.

Bonds, Mark Evan. *After Beethoven: Imperatives of Originality in the Symphony.* Cambridge, MA: Harvard University Press, 1996.

Borchardt, Georg. "Ein Viertonmotif als melodische Komponente in Werken von Brahms." In *Brahms und seine Zeit: Bericht über das Symposion 1983 in Hamburg,* edited by Constantin Floros, Hans Joachim Marx, and P. Petersen, 101–12. Hamburg: Laaber-Verlag, 1984.

Boretz, Benjamin. "Meta-Variations, Part IV: Analytic Fallout (II): 6. Example 3: The First Eighteen Measures of Brahms's Fourth Symphony." *Perspectives of New Music* 11/2 (1973): 156–203.

Boyd, Malcolm. *Domenico Scarlatti—Master of Music.* New York: Schirmer Books, 1986.

Bozarth, George S. "Brahms's First Piano Concerto, op. 15: Genesis and Meaning." In *Beiträge zur Geschichte des Konzerts: Festschrift Siegfried Kross Zum 60. Geburtstag,* edited by Reinmar Emans and Matthias Wendt, 211–47. Bonn: G. Schröder, 1990.

———. "Brahms's *Lieder ohne Worte*: The 'Poetic' Andantes of the Piano Sonatas." In *Brahms Studies: Analytical and Historical Perspectives,* edited by George S. Bozarth, 345–78. Oxford: Clarendon Press, 1990.

Bozarth, George S., and Walter Frisch. "Brahms, Johannes." *Grove Music Online.* Accessed September 4, 2005 and April 12, 2006. www.grovemusic.com.

Brahms, Johannes. *Sämtliche Werke,* edited by Hans Gál and Eusebius Mandyczewski. Leipzig: Breitkopf & Härtel, 1926–27.

———. *Serenaden und Tänze für Orchester.* Leipzig: Breitkopf & Härtel, 1926; repr. as *Serenades and Dances for Orchestra.* Ann Arbor, MI: J. W. Edwards, 1949.

———. *Complete Chamber Music for Strings and Clarinet Quintet.* Edited by Hans Gál. Leipzig: Breitkopf & Härtel, n.d.; repr. Mineola, NY: Dover, 1968.

———. *Complete Symphonies in Full Orchestral Score.* Leipzig: Breitkopf & Härtel, n.d.; repr. Mineola, NY: Dover, 1974.

———. *Sonaten, Scherzo und Balladen, nach Eigenschriften und den Handexemplaren des Komponisten.* München: G. Henle Verlag, 1956; repr. 1977.

———. *Complete Songs for Solo Voice and Piano: Series I.* Edited by Eusebius Mandyczewski. Leipzig: Breitkopf & Härtel, n.d.; repr. Mineola, NY: Dover, 1979.

———. *Complete Concerti in Full Score.* Edited by Hans Gál. Leipzig: Breitkopf & Härtel, n.d.; repr. Mineola, NY: Dover, 1981.

———. *Complete Piano Trios.* Edited by Hans Gál. Leipzig: Breitkopf & Härtel, n.d.; repr. Mineola, NY: Dover, 1988.

———. *Complete Sonatas for Solo Instrument and Piano.* Edited by Hans Gál. Leipzig: Breitkopf & Härtel, n.d.; repr. Mineola, NY: Dover, 1989.

———. *Sämtliche Klavierwerke in 5 Bänden.* Urtext ed. 5 vols. Budapest, Hungary: Könemann Music Budapest, 1997.

———. *Serenades Nos. 1 & 2 in Full Score.* Leipzig: Breitkopf & Härtel, n.d.; repr. Mineola, NY: Dover, 1999.

———. *Symphony No. 4 in E Minor, op. 98: Authoritative Score, Background Context, Criticism, Analysis.* Edited by Kenneth Ross Hull. New York: W. W. Norton, 2000.
———. *Serenaden: Nr. 1 D-dur für grosses Orchester Opus 11, Nr. 2 A-dur für kleines Orchester Opus 16.* Edited by Michael Musgrave. Neue Ausgabe sämtlicher Werke, Series I: Orchesterwerke, vol. 5. München: G. Henle Verlag, 2006.
Brahms, Johannes, and Elisabeth and Heinrich von Herzogenberg. *Johannes Brahms: The Herzogenberg Correspondence.* Edited by Max Kalbeck, Translated by Hannah Bryant. New York: E. P. Dutton and Co., 1909.
Brahms, Johannes, and Theodor Billroth. *Johannes Brahms and Theodor Billroth: Letters from a Musical Friendship.* Edited and translated by Hans Barkan. Norman, OK: University of Oklahoma Press, 1957.
Brahms, Johannes, Albert Dietrich, and Robert Schumann. "F.A.E. Sonata." In Robert Schumann, *1. Sonate für Pianoforte und Violine, op. 105; 2. Sonate für Violine und Pianoforte, op. 121; F.A.E.-Sonate; 3. Violinsonate WoO 2.* Neue Ausgabe sämtlicher Werke. Series 2: Kammermusik, vol. 3. Edited by Ute Bär. Mainz: Schott, 2001.
Brahms, Johannes, et al. *Briefwechsel.* Edited by Max Kalbeck. 4th ed. 16 vols. Berlin: Deutsche Brahms-Gesellschaft, 1921; repr. Tutzing: Hans Schneider, 1974.
———. *Johannes Brahms: Life and Letters.* Edited by Styra Avins. Translated by Josef Eisinger and Styra Avins. Oxford: Oxford University Press, 1997.
Brahms-Handbuch. Edited by Wolfgang Sandberger. Kassel: Bärenreiter, 2009.
Brinkmann, Reinhold. "Anhand von Reprisen." In *Brahms-Analysen: Referate der Kieler Tagung 1983. Kieler Schriften zur Musikwissenschaft*; edited by Friedhelm Krummacher and Wolfram Steinbeck, vol. 28, 107–20. Kassel: Bärenreiter, 1984.
———. *Late Idyll: The Second Symphony of Johannes Brahms.* Translated by Peter Palmer. Cambridge, MA: Harvard University Press, 1995.
Brodbeck, David. "Brahms, the Third Symphony, and the New German School." *Brahms and His World*, edited by Walter Frisch, 65–80. Princeton, NJ: Princeton University Press, 1990.
———. "The Brahms-Joachim Counterpoint Exchange, or, Robert, Clara, and 'the Best Harmony between Jos. and Joh.'" In *Brahms Studies*, vol. 1, edited by David Lee Brodbeck, 30–80. Lincoln, NE: University of Nebraska, 1994.
———. *Brahms: Symphony No. 1.* Cambridge: Cambridge University Press, 1997.
———. "Brahms's Mendelssohn." In *Brahms Studies*, vol. 2, edited by David Brodbeck, 209–31. Lincoln, NE: University of Nebraska Press, 1998.
———. "Medium and Meaning: New Aspects of the Chamber Music." In *The Cambridge Companion to Brahms*, edited by Michael Musgrave, 98–132. Cambridge: Cambridge University Press, 1999.
Brown, A. Peter. "Brahms's Third Symphony and the New German School." *Journal of Musicology* 2/4 (1983): 434–52.
———. *The Symphonic Repertoire*, vol. 4: The Second Golden Age of the Viennese Symphony: Brahms, Bruckner, Dvorak, Mahler, and Selected Contemporaries. Bloomington: Indiana University Press, 2002.
Bülow, Hans von. *Hans von Bülow's Letters to Johannes Brahms: A Research Edition*, edited by Hans-Joachim Hinrichsen. Translated by Cynthia Klohr. Lanham, MD: Scarecrow Press, 2012. (Previously published as *Hans von Bülow: Die Briefe an Johannes Brahms.* Tutzing: Hans Schneider, 1994.)
Burk, John N. *Clara Schumann: A Romantic Biography.* New York: Random House, 1940.

Burkholder, J. Peter. "Brahms and Twentieth-Century Classical Music." *19th-Century Music* 8/1 (1984): 75–83.

Burnham, Scott G. "Our Sublime Ninth." *Beethoven Forum* 5 (1996): 155–63.

Calella, Michelle. "Gattung und Erwartung: Brahms, das Leipziger Gewandhaus und der Misserfolg des Klavierkonzerts op. 15." *Ad Parnassum: A Journal of Eighteenth- and Nineteenth-Century Instrumental Music* 2/3 (2004): 31–60.

Cantrell, Byron. "Three B's—Three Chaconnes." *Current Musicology* 12 (1971): 63–74.

Chissell, Joan. *Schumann Piano Music*. BBC Music Guides. Seattle: University of Washington Press, 1972.

———. *Clara Schumann, a Dedicated Spirit: A Study of Her Life and Work*. New York: Taplinger Publishing Co., 1983.

Collier, Michael. "The Rondo Movements of Beethoven's Concerto No. 3 in C Minor, op. 37, and Brahms's Concerto No. 1 in D Minor, op. 15: A Comparative Analysis." *Theory and Practice* 3/1 (1978): 5–15.

The Compleat Brahms: A Guide to the Musical Works of Johannes Brahms, edited by Leon Botstein. New York: W. W. Norton, 1999.

Cook, Nicholas. *Beethoven Symphony No. 9*. Cambridge Music Handbooks. Cambridge: Cambridge University Press, 1993.

———. "Performing Rewriting and Rewriting Performance: The First Movement of Brahms's Piano Trio, op. 8." *Tijdschrift voor Muziektheorie* 4/3 (1999): 227–34.

Czesla, Werner. "Studien zum Finale in der Kammermusik von Johannes Brahms." PhD diss., Rheinischen Friedrich-Wilhelms-Universität zu Bonn, 1968.

Dahlhaus, Carl. *Johannes Brahms: Klavierkonzert Nr. 1 D-Moll, op. 15*. Meisterwerke der Musik: Werkmonographien zur Musikgeschichte 3, edited by Ernst Ludwig Wältner. München: Fink, 1965.

———. *Nineteenth-Century Music*. California Studies in Nineteenth-Century Music; 5. Berkeley: University of California Press, 1989.

Daverio, John. *Robert Schumann: Herald of a "New Poetic Age."* New York: Oxford University Press, 1997.

———. *Crossing Paths: Schubert, Schumann and Brahms*. Oxford: Oxford University Press, 2002.

Daverio, John, and Eric Sams. "Schumann, Robert." *Grove Music Online*. Accessed April 5, 2005. http://www.grovemusic.com.

Dedel, Peter. *Johannes Brahms: A Guide to His Autograph in Facsimile*. MLA Index & Bibliography Series; 18. Ann Arbor, MI: Music Library Association, 1978.

Deiters, Hermann. *Johannes Brahms*. Sammlung Musikalischer Vorträge 23–24. Edited by Paul Graf Waldersee. Leipzig: Breitkopf & Härtel, 1880.

Derr, Ellwood. "Beethoven's Long-Term Memory of C. P. E. Bach's Rondo in E Flat, W. 61/1 (1787), Manifest in the Variations in E Flat for Piano, op. 35 (1802)." *Musical Quarterly* 70 (1983): 45–76.

———. "Handel's Procedures for Composing with Materials from Telemann's *Harmonischer Gottes-Dienst* in *Solomon*. In *Goettinger Händel-Beiträge*, edited by Hans Joachim Marx, 116–47. Kassel: Bärenreiter, 1984.

———. "A Foretaste of the Borrowings from Haydn in Beethoven's op. 2." In *Joseph Haydn: Über den Internationalen Joseph Haydn Kongress, Wien, Hofburg, 5.-12. September 1982*, edited by Eva Badura-Skoda, 159–70. Munich: G. Henle, 1986.

———. "Brahms' op. 38: Ein Beitrag zur Kunst der Komposition mit entlehnten Stoffen." In *Brahms-Kongress Wien 1983*, edited by Susanne Antonicek and Otto Biba, 95–124. Tutzing: Hans Schneider, 1988.
———. "Mozart's Transfer of the Vocal 'Fermata Sospesa' to His Piano-Concerto First Movements." *Mozart-Jahrbuch* 1 (1991): 155–63.
Deutsche Volkslieder mit ihren Original-Weisen. Edited by Eduard Baumstark, Anton Wilhelm Florentin von Zuccalmaglio, et al. 2 vols. Berlin: Vereinbuchhandlung, 1840.
Dietrich, Albert Hermann. *Recollections of Johannes Brahms*. Translated by Dora E. Hecht. Honolulu, HI: University Press of the Pacific, 2000. (Previously published as *Erringerungen an Johannes Brahms in Briefe besonders aus seiner Jugendzeit*. Leipzig: Otto Wigand, 1898.)
Dörffel, Alfred. *Geschichte der Gewandhausconcerte zu Leipzig vom 25. November 1781 bis 25. November 1881, im Auftrage der Concert-Direction verfasst von Alfred Dörffel*. Leipzig: [Breitkopf & Härtel], 1884.
Dubiel, Joseph. "Contradictory Criteria in a Work of Brahms." *Brahms Studies*, vol. 1, edited by David Lee Brodbeck, 81–110. Lincoln, NE: University of Nebraska Press in affiliation with the American Brahms Society, 1994.
Dunsby, Jonathan. *Structural Ambiguity in Brahms: Analytical Approaches to Four Works*. Ann Arbor, MI: UMI Research Press, 1981.
Dürr, Alfred. *The Cantatas of J. S. Bach, with Their Librettos in German-English Parallel Text*. Revised and translated by Richard D. P. Jones. Oxford: Oxford University Press, 2005.
Ehlert, Gero. Liner notes for Johannes Brahms, *Complete Piano Trios*. Vol. 3. Trio Parnassus. © 1996. Original sound recording made by Musikproduktion Dabringhaus und Grimm. MDG 303 0657-2 (1 compact disc). Liner notes translated by Susan Marie Praeder.
———. *Architektonik der Leidenschaften. Eine Studie zu den Klaviersonaten von Johannes Brahms*. Kieler Schriften zur Musikwissenschaft, 50. Kassel: Bärenreiter-Verlag, 2005.
Ehrmann, Alfred von. *Johannes Brahms: Weg, Werk und Welt. Mit zahlreichen Bildern und Dokumenten*. Leipzig: Breitkopf & Härtel, 1933; repr. Walluf: Sändig, 1974.
Ernest, Gustav. *Johannes Brahms: Persönlichkeit, Leben und Schaffen*. Berlin: Deutsche Brahms-Gesellschaft, 1930.
Evans, Edwin. *"The Immortal Nine": Beethoven's Nine Symphonies Fully Described & Analysed*. 2 vols. London: William Reeves, [1923–24].
———. *Handbook to the Chamber and Orchestral Music of Johannes Brahms*. London: William Reeves, 1912; repr. New York: Burt Franklin, 1970.
———. *Handbook to the Pianoforte Works of Johannes Brahms*. London: William Reeves, 1912; repr. New York: Burt Franklin, 1970.
Expressive Intersections in Brahms: Essays in Analysis and Meaning. Edited by Heather Platt and Peter H. Smith. Bloomington: Indiana University Press, 2012.
Feder, Stuart, et al. *Psychoanalytic Explorations in Music: Second Series*. Edited by Stuart Feder, Richard L. Karmel, and George H. Pollock. Madison, CT: International Universities Press, 1993.
Fellinger, Imogen. "Brahms und die Gattung des Instrumentalkonzerts." In *Beiträge zur Geschichte des Konzerts: Festschrift Siegfried Kross zum 60. Geburtstag*, edited by Reinmar Emans and Matthias Wendt, 201–9. Bonn, Germany: Schroeder, 1990.
Ferris, David. "Public Performance and Private Understanding: Clara Wieck's Concerts in Berlin." *Journal of the American Musicological Society* 56/2 (2003): 351–408.

Fink, Robert. "Desire, Repression, and Brahms's First Symphony." *Repercussions* 2 (1993): 75–103.
Finscher, Ludwig. "The Struggle with Tradition: Johannes Brahms." In *The Symphony*, edited by Ursula von Rauchhaupt, 165–74. London: Thames and Hudson, 1973.
Fischer, Edwin. *Beethoven's Pianoforte Sonatas: A Guide for Students & Amateurs*. London: Faber and Faber, 1959.
Fisk, Charles. *Returning Cycles: Contexts for the Interpretation of Schubert's Impromptus and Last Sonatas*. California Studies in Nineteenth-Century Music 11. Berkeley: University of California Press, 2001.
Floros, Constantin. *Johannes Brahms, "Free but Alone": A Life for a Poetic Music*. Frankfurt am Main: Peter Lang, 2010. (Originally published as *Johannes Brahms, "frei aber einsam": Ein Leben für eine poetische Musik*. Zürich: Arche Zürich, 1997.)
Frisch, Walter. "Brahms, Developing Variation, and the Schoenberg Critical Tradition." *19th-Century Music* 5/3 (1982): 215–32.
———. "Brahms and Schubring: Musical Criticism and Politics at Mid-Century." *19th-Century Music* 7/4 (1984): 271–81.
———. *Brahms and the Principle of Developing Variation*. California Studies in Nineteenth-Century Music 2. Berkeley: University of California Press, 1984.
———. *Brahms: The Four Symphonies*. New Haven, CT: Yale University Press, 2003. (Originally published in New York by Schirmer Books, 1996.)
———."The Snake Bites Its Tail: Cyclic Processes in Brahms's Third String Quartet, op. 67." *Journal of Musicology* 22/1 (2005): 154–72.
———. "Brahms, Johannes—Section 9: Orchestral Works and Concertos." *Grove Music Online*. Accessed April 12, 2006. www.grovemusic.com.
Frobenius, Wolf. "La Genèse du Premier Mouvement du Premier Concerto pour Piano de Brahms: Observations sûr le Manuscrit Autographe." *Ostinato Rigore: Revue Internationale d'Etudes Musicales* 13 (1999): 67–74.
Fuller-Maitland, John. *Brahms*. New York: John Lane Co., 1911.
Gál, Hans. *Johannes Brahms: His Work and Personality*. Translated by Joseph Stein. New York: Knopf, 1963. (Previously published as *Johannes Brahms: Sein Werk und Persönlichkeit*. Frankfurt am Main: Fischer Bücherei KG, 1961.)
da Silva, Fabio Roberto Gardenal. "Brahms' [sic] Piano Trio, op. 8, in B Major: A Comparison between the Early (1854) and Late (1860) [sic] Versions." PhD diss., New York University, 1993.
Garratt, James. *Palestrina and the German Romantic Imagination: Interpreting Historicism in Nineteenth-Century Music*. Cambridge: Cambridge University Press, 2002.
Geiringer, Karl. "Brahms as Musicologist." *Musical Quarterly* 69/4 (1983): 463–70.
———. *On Brahms and His Circle: The Collected Essays and Studies of Karl Geiringer*, edited by George S. Bozarth. Sterling, MI: Harmonie Park Press, 2006.
Geiringer, Karl (in collaboration with Irene Geiringer). *Brahms: His Life and Work*, 3rd ed. New York: Da Capo Press, 1982.
———. *Haydn: A Creative Life in Music*. 3rd rev. and enlarged ed. Berkeley: University of California Press, 1982.
Georgii, Walter. *Klaviermusik*. Zürich: Atlantis-Verlag, 1950.
Gerards, Marion. "Narrative Programme und Geschlechter-Identität in der 3. Sinfonie von Johannes Brahms: Zum Problem einer genderzentierten Interpretation absoluter Musik." *Frankfurter Zeitschrift für Musikwissenschaft* 8 (2005): 42–57.

Goebels, Franzpeter. "Scarlattiana: Bemerkungen zur Scarlatti-Rezeption von Johannes Brahms." *Musica* 40/4 (1986): 320–28.
Graybill, Roger. "Brahms' Integration of Traditional and Progressive Tendencies: A Look at Three Sonata Expositions." *The Journal of Musicological Research* 8/1–2 (1988): 141–68.
Grey, Thomas. "Metaphorical Models in Nineteenth-Century Criticism: Image, Narrative and Idea." In *Music and Text: Critical Inquiries*, edited by S. P. Scher, 93–117. Cambridge: Cambridge University Press, 1992.
Grove, George. *Beethoven and His Nine Symphonies*. 3rd ed. Mineola, NY: Dover Publications, 1962.
Hancock, Virginia. *Brahms's Choral Compositions and His Library of Early Music*. Studies in Musicology; 76. Ann Arbor, MI: UMI Research Press, 1983.
Hansen, Finn Egeland. *Layers of Musical Meaning*. København, Denmark: Museum Tusculanum Press, 2006.
Hanslick, Eduard. *Geschichte Des Concertwesens in Wien*. 2 vols. Vienna: Braumüller, 1869–70; repr. Farnborough: Gregg, 1971.
———. *Hanslick's Music Criticisms*. Edited and translated by Henry Pleasants. New York: Publications, 1988.
Hatten, Robert S. *Musical Meaning in Beethoven: Markedness, Correlation, and Interpretation*. Bloomington: Indiana University Press, 1994.
———. *Interpreting Musical Gestures, Topics, and Tropes: Mozart, Beethoven, Schubert*. Bloomington: Indiana University Press, 2004.
Haydn, Joseph. *Symphony in D Major: London Symphony: No. 12: Hob. I, 104*. Edited by Hubert Unverricht. Kassel: Bärenreiter, 1995.
Herttrich, Ernst. "Johannes Brahms—Klaviertrio H-Dur Opus 8: Frühfassung und Spätfassung: Ein analytischer Vergleich." In *Musik, Edition, Interpretation: Gedenkschrift Günter Henle*, edited by Martin Bente, 218–36. München: G. Henle Verlag, 1980.
Hill, John Walter. "Thematic Transformation, Folksong, and Nostalgia in Brahms's Horn Trio, op. 40." *The Musical Times* 152/1914 (2011): 20–24.
Hodgson, Antony. *The Music of Joseph Haydn: The Symphonies*. London: Tantivy Press, 1976.
Hoffmann, E. T. A. *The Life and Opinions of the Tomcat Murr, Together with a Fragmentary Biography of Kapellmeister Johannes Kreisler on Random Sheets of Waste Paper*. Translated and annotated by Anthea Bell. London: Penguin Books, 1999.
Hofmann, Renate, and Kurt. *Johannes Brahms Zeittafel zu Leben und Werk*. Publikationen des Institutes für Österreichische Musikdokumenten, 8. Tutzing: Hans Schneider, 1983. Cited in Jan Swafford, *Johannes Brahms: A Biography* (New York: Alfred A. Knopf; Distributed by Random House, 1997), 649, n. 53.
Hopkins, Antony. *The Nine Symphonies of Beethoven*. Seattle: Heinemann Educational Books Ltd and the University of Washington Press, 1981; repr. Aldershot: Scolar Press, 1996.
Hopkins, Robert G. "When a Coda is More Than a Coda: Reflections on Beethoven." In *Explorations in Music, the Arts, and Ideas: Essays in Honor of Leonard B. Meyer*, edited by Eugene Narmour and Ruth A. Solie, 393–410. Stuyvesant, NY: Pendragon Press, 1988.
Horstmann, Angelika. "Die Rezeption der Werke op. 1–10 von Johannes Brahms zwischen 1853 und 1860." In *Brahms und seine Zeit: Bericht über das Symposion 1983 in Hamburg*, edited by Constantin Floros, Hans Joachim Marx, and P. Petersen, 33–44. Hamburg: Laaber-Verlag, 1984.

Horton, John. *Brahms Orchestral Music*. BBC Music Guides. Seattle, WA: University of Washington Press, 1978.
Hull, Kenneth Ross. "Brahms the Allusive: Extra-Compositional Reference in the Instrumental Music of Johannes Brahms." PhD diss., Princeton University, 1989.
———. "Allusive Irony in Brahms's Fourth Symphony." In *Brahms Studies*., vol. 2, edited by David Lee Brodbeck, 135–68. Lincoln, NE: University of Nebraska Press, 1998.
Hussey, William Gregory. "Compositional Modeling, Quotation, and Multiple Influence Analysis in the Works of Johannes Brahms: An Application of Harold Bloom's Theory of Influence to Music." PhD diss., University of Texas, Austin, 1997.
James, Burnett. *Brahms: A Critical Study*. London: Dent, 1972.
Janik, Allan, and Stephen Toulmin. *Wittgenstein's Vienna*. New York: Simon & Schuster, 1973.
Jenner, Gustav. "Zur Entstehung des D-Moll Klavierkonzertes op. 15 von Johannes Brahms." *Die Musik* 12 (1912/13): 32–37.
Joachim, Joseph. *Konzert D-Moll in Ungarischer Weise für Violine und Pianoforte, op. 11*. Leipzig: Breitkopf & Härtel, n.d.
Joachim, Joseph, et al. *Letters from and to Joseph Joachim*. Edited and translated by Nora Bickley. London: Macmillan and Co., 1914; repr. New York: Vienna House, 1972.
Johannes Brahms: Leben und Werk. Edited by Christiane Jacobsen. Wiesbaden: Breitkopf & Härtel, 1983.
Kalbeck, Max. *Johannes Brahms*, Kalbeck, Max. *Johannes Brahms*, 4 vols. Berlin: Deutsche Brahms-Gesellschaft, 1912–21; repr. Tutzing: Hans Schneider, 1976.
Kämper, Dietrich. *Die Klaviersonate nach Beethoven: Von Schubert bis Skrjabin*. Darmstadt: Wissenschaftliche Buchgesellschaft, 1987.
Karnes, Kevin Charles. "Heinrich Schenker and Musical Thought in Late Nineteenth-Century Vienna." PhD diss., Brandeis University, 2001.
Kerman, Joseph. "Notes on Beethoven's Codas." *Beethoven Studies* 3 (1982): 141–60.
Keys, Ivor. *Brahms Chamber Music*. Seattle, WA: University of Washington Press, 1974.
———. *Johannes Brahms*. Portland, OR: Amadeus Press, 1989.
Kirby, F. E. "Brahms and the Piano Sonata." In *Paul A. Pisk: Essays in His Honor*, edited by John Glowacki and Paul Amadeus Pisk, 163–80. [Austin]: College of Fine Arts, 1966.
Kivy, Peter. *The Corded Shell: Reflections on Musical Expression*. Princeton, NJ: Princeton University Press, 1980.
———. *Sound and Semblance: Reflections on Musical Representation*. Princeton, NJ: Princeton University, 1990.
Klenz, William. "Brahms, op. 38: Piracy, Pillage, Plagiarism or Parody?" *The Music Review* 34/1 (1973): 39–50.
Knapp, Raymond. "The Finale of Brahms's Fourth Symphony: The Tale of the Subject." *19th-Century Music* 13/1 (1989): 3–17.
———. *Brahms and the Challenge of the Symphony*. Stuyvesant, NY: Pendragon Press, 1997.
———. "Brahms and the Anxiety of Allusion." *Journal of Musicological Research* 18 (1998): 1–30.
———. "Utopian Agendas: Variation, Allusion, and Referential Meaning in Brahms's Symphonies." In *Brahms Studies*, vol. 3, edited by David Brodbeck, 129–89. Lincoln: University of Nebraska Press, 2001.
Kohler, Joachim. *Nietzsche and Wagner: A Lesson in Subjugation*. Translated by Ronald Taylor. New Haven, CT: Yale University Press, 1998.

Korstvedt, Benjamin. "Brahms and the 'Angel of History': A Critical Reading of the Revision of the Trio, op. 8." Delivered in New York City on March 23, 2012, at the *Brahms in the New Century* conference sponsored by the American Brahms Society.

Korsyn, Kevin. "Towards a New Poetics of Musical Influence." *Music Analysis* 10/1-2 (1991): 3–72.

———. "Brahms Research and Aesthetic Ideology." *Brahms Analysis* 12/1 (1993): 89–103.

Kramer, Lawrence. *Musical Meaning: Toward a Critical History*. Berkeley: University of California Press, 2002.

Kraus, Detlef. "The Andante from op. 5—A Possible Interpretation." In *Johannes Brahms, Composer for the Piano*. Paperbacks in Musicology; 9. Edited by Andrew D. McCredie in collaboration with Richard Schaal, 29–34. Translated by Lillian Lim. Wilhelmshaven: F. Noetzel, 1988.

Kropfinger, Klaus. "Wagner and Brahms." *Musica* 37/1 (1983): 11–17.

Kross, Siegfried. "Brahms and E.T.A. Hoffmann." *19th-Century Music* 5/3 (1982): 193–200.

———. "Thematic Structure and Formal Processes in Brahms's Sonata Movements." In *Brahms Studies: Analytical and Historical Perspectives; Papers Delivered at the International Brahms Conference, Washington, DC, 5-8 May 1983*, edited by George S. Bozarth, 423–44. Oxford: Clarendon Press, 1990.

Kube, Michael. "Brahms' Streichsextette und ihr Gattungsgeschichtlicher Kontext." In *Die Kammermusik von Johannes Brahms: Tradition und Innovation: Bericht über die Tagung Wien 1997*, 149–74. Vienna: Laaber-Verlag, 2001.

Landon, H. C. Robbins. *Haydn Symphonies*. BBC Music Guides. London: British Broadcasting Corporation, 1968.

Latham, Peter. *Brahms*. London: J. M. Dent and Sons, 1966.

Littlewood, Julian. *The Variations of Johannes Brahms*. London: Plumbago Books, 2004.

Litzmann, Berthold. *Clara Schumann: An Artist's Life, Based on Material Found in Diaries and Letters*. Translated and abridged from the 4th ed. by Grace E. Hadow, with a preface by W. H. Hadow. 2 vols. London: MacMillan and Co. and Leipzig: Breitkopf & Härtel, 1913; repr. New York: Vienna House, 1972.

Livingstone, Ernest. "Unifying Elements in Haydn's Symphony No. 104." In *Haydn Studies: Proceedings of the International Haydn Conference, Washington DC, 1975*, edited by Jens Peter Larsen, Howard Serwer, and James Webster, 493–96. New York: W. W. Norton, 1981.

Lubin, Steven. "Transforming Reheard Themes: Brahms and the Legacy of Beethoven's Ninth." *American Brahms Society Newsletter* 17/1 (1999): 1–4.

MacDonald, Hugh. "Cyclic Form." *Grove Music Online*. Accessed March 21, 2004. www.grovemusic.com.

———. "Transformation, Thematic". *Grove Music Online*. Accessed March 21, 2004. www.grovemusic.com.

MacDonald, Malcolm. "'Veiled Symphonies'? The Concertos." In *The Cambridge Companion to Brahms*, edited by Michael Musgrave, 156–70. Cambridge: Cambridge University Press, 1999.

———. *Brahms*. Edited by Stanley Sadie. Oxford: Oxford University Press, 2001. Previously published in New York by Schirmer Books in 1990.

Mahrt, William P. "Brahms and Reminiscence: A Special Use of Classic Conventions." In *Convention in Eighteenth- and Nineteenth-Century Music: Essays in Honor of Leonard*

G. *Ratner*, edited by Wye J. Allanbrook, Janet M. Levy, and William P. Mahrt, 75–112. Stuyvesant, NY: Pendragon Press, 1992.

Marston, Nicholas. "'The Sense of an Ending': Goal-Directedness in Beethoven's Music." In *The Cambridge Companion to Beethoven*, edited by Glenn Stanley, 84–101. Cambridge: Cambridge University Press, 2000.

Mason, Colin. "Brahms' Piano Sonatas." *Music Review* 5 (1944): 112–18.

May, Florence. *The Life of Johannes Brahms*. 2nd ed., enlarged and illustrated. 2 vols. Neptune City, NJ: Paganiniana Publications, Inc., 1981. (First published 1905 by E. Arnold; 2nd ed. published 1948 by William Reeves.)

Mayerovitch, Robert. "Brahms's Stylistic Evolution: A Comparison of the 1854 and 1891 Versions of the B-Major Piano Trio, op. 8." DM diss., Indiana University, 1986.

Mast, Paul. "Brahms's Study, *Oktaven und Quinten U. A.*: With Schenker's Commentary Translated." *Music Forum* 5 (1980): 2–196.

McClary, Susan. "Narrative Agendas in 'Absolute' Music: Identity and Difference in Brahms's Third Symphony." In *Musicology and Difference: Gender and Sexuality in Music Scholarship*, edited by Ruth A. Solie, 326–44. Berkeley: University of California Press, 1993.

McCorkle, Margit L., with assistance from Donald M. McCorkle. *Johannes Brahms: Thematisch-Bibliographisches Werkverzeichnis*. München: G. Henle Verlag, 1984.

Meurs, Norbert. "Das Verstellte Frühwerk. Zum H-Dur Trio op. 8 von Johannes Brahms." *Musica* 37/1 (1983): 34–39.

———. *Neue Bahnen?: Aspekte der Brahms-Rezeption 1853–1868*. Edited by Detlef Altenburg. Cologne: Studio Verlag Schewe, 1996.

Mitschka, Arno. *Der Sonatensatz in den Werken von Johannes Brahms*. Gütersloh: n.p., 1961.

Montgomery, Kip James. "Cyclic Form in the Music of Brahms." PhD diss., State University of New York, Stony Brook, 2002.

Moseley, Roger. "Brief Immortality: Recasting History in the Music of Brahms." PhD diss., University of California, Berkeley, 2004.

———. "Is There Only Juan Brahms?" *Journal of the Royal Musical Association* 131 (2006): 160–75.

———. "Reforming Johannes: Brahms, Kreisler Junior, and the Piano Trio in B, op. 8." *Journal of the Royal Musical Association* 132 (2007): 252–305.

Mozart, Wolfgang Amadeus. *Konzerte für ein oder Mehrere Klaviere und Orchester mit Kadenzen*. Neue Ausgabe sämtlicher Werke. Series V: Konzerte, vol. 6. Edited by Hans Engel and Horst Heussner. Kassel: Bärenreiter, 1961.

Murdoch, William David. *Brahms, with an Analytical Study of the Complete Pianoforte Works*. London: Rich & Cowan Limited, 1933; repr. New York: AMS Press, 1978.

Murray, Michael. Liner notes for Johannes Brahms, *Serenade No. 1 in D Major; Serenade No. 2 in A Major*. Charles Mackerras and the Scottish Chamber Orchestra. © 1999. Original sound recording made by Telarc. SDA 01694 (1 compact disc).

Musgrave, Michael. "*Frei aber froh*: A Reconsideration." *19th-Century Music* 3 (1979–80): 251–58.

———. "Brahms's First Symphony: Thematic Coherence and its Secret Origin." *Music Analysis* 2/2 (1983): 117–33.

———. *The Music of Brahms*. Companions to the Great Composers. London: Routledge & Kegan Paul, 1985.

——— . *A Brahms Reader*. New Haven, CT: Yale University Press, 2000.
Nagel, Wilibald. *Die Klaviersonaten von Johannes Brahms: Technisch-Aesthetische Analysen*. Stuttgart: Carl Grüninger, 1915.
Nass, Martin L. "The Composer's Experience: Variations on Several Themes." In *Psychoanalytic Explorations in Music*, edited by Stuart Feder, Richard L. Karmel, and George H. Pollock, 21–40. Madison, CT: International Universities Press, 1993.
Nattiez, Jean-Jacques. "Can One Speak of Narrativity in Music?" *Journal of the Royal Musical Association* 115 (1990): 240–57.
Newcomb, Anthony. "Once More 'between Absolute and Program Music': Schumann's Second Symphony." *19th-Century Music* 7 (1983–84): 233–50.
——— . "Schumann and Late Eighteenth-Century Narrative Strategies." *19th-Century Music* 11 (1987): 164–74.
——— . "The Hunt for Reminiscences in Nineteenth-Century Germany." In *Music and the Aesthetics of Modernity*, edited by Karol Berger and Anthony Newcomb, 111–35. Cambridge, MA: Harvard University Press, 2005.
Newman, William S. "Some Nineteenth-Century Consequences of Beethoven's 'Hammerklavier' Sonata, Opus 106." *Piano Quarterly* 67 (1969): 12–18 and 68 (1969): 12–17.
——— . *The Sonata in the Classic Era*. 3rd ed. New York: W. W. Norton, 1983.
——— . *The Sonata Since Beethoven*. 3rd ed. New York: W. W. Norton, 1983.
Niemann, Walter. *Brahms*. 4th printing. Translated by Catherine Alison Phillips. New York: Alfred A. Knopf, 1941.
Nietzsche, Friedrich Wilhelm. *Richard Wagner in Bayreuth; Der Fall Wagner; Nietzsche contra Wagner*. Stuttgart: Reclam, 1973.
The Nineteenth-Century Symphony. Edited by D. Kern Holoman. New York: Schirmer Books, 1997.
Notley, Margaret. "Brahms as Liberal: Genre, Style, and Politics in Late Nineteenth-Century Vienna." *19th-Century Music* 17 (1993): 107–23.
——— . "Discourse and Allusion: The Chamber Music of Brahms." In *Nineteenth-Century Chamber Music*, edited by Stephen E. Hefling, 243–85. New York: Schirmer, 1998.
——— . "'With a Beethoven-Like Sublimity': Beethoven in the Works of Other Composers." In *The Cambridge Companion to Beethoven*, edited by Glenn Stanley, 239–54. Cambridge University Press, 2000.
——— . "Plagal Harmony as Other: Asymmetrical Dualism and Instrumental Music by Brahms." *Journal of Musicology* 22/1 (2005): 90–130.
——— . *Lateness and Brahms: Music and Culture in the Twilight of Viennese Liberalism*. AMS Studies in Music. Edited by Mary Hunter. Oxford: Oxford University Press, 2007.
Osmond-Smith, David. "The Retreat from Dynamism: A Study of Brahms's Fourth Symphony." In *Brahms: Biographical, Documentary, and Analytical Studies*, edited by Robert Pascall, 147–65. Cambridge: Cambridge University Press, 1983.
Pacun, David. "Brahms and the Sense of an Ending." *American Brahms Society Newsletter* 22/1 (2004): 1–4.
Pagano, Roberto. "Scarlatti—Section 7: (Guiseppe) Domenico Scarlatti—Subsection 4: Reception." *Grove Music Online*. Accessed February 3, 2006. www.grovemusic.com
Parmer, Dillon. "Brahms the Programmatic? A Critical Assessment." PhD diss., University of Rochester, 1995.

———. "Brahms, Song Quotation, and Secret Programs." *19th-Century Music* 19/2 (1995): 161–90.

———. "Brahms and the Poetic Motto: A Hermeneutic Aid?" *The Journal of Musicology*, 15/3 (1997): 353–89.

Pascall, Robert. "Some Special Uses of Sonata Form by Brahms." *Soundings* 4 (1974): 58–63.

———. "Musikalische Einflüsse auf Brahms." *Österreichische Musikzeitschrift* 38/4–5 (1983): 228–35.

———. "Genre and the Finale of Brahms's Fourth Symphony." *Music Analysis* 8/3 (1989): 233–45.

———. *Brahms Beyond Mastery: His Sarabande and Gavotte, and Its Recompositions*. Royal Musical Association Monographs, 21. Burlington, VT: Ashgate, 2013.

Pestelli, Giorgio. "On the Finale of Brahms's Fourth Symphony." *Brahms-Studien* 15 (2008): 127–48.

Petersen, Peter. "Die Variationen-Finale aus Brahms' e-Moll-Sinfonie und die c-Moll-Chaconne von Beethoven (WoO 80)." *Archiv für Musikwissenschaft* 70 (2013): 105–18.

Petty, Wayne C. "Brahms, Adolf Jensen and the Problem of the Multi-Movement Work." *Music Analysis* 22/1–2 (2003): 105–37.

Plantinga, Leon. *Schumann as Critic*. Reprint Edition. Yale Studies in the History of Music; 4. edited by William G. Waite. New York: Da Capo Press, 1976.

Platt, Heather. "Probing the Meaning of Brahms's Allusions to Haydn." *International Review for the Aesthetics and Sociology of Music* 42/1 (2011): 33–58.

Potter, Pamela M. "Musicology—Section 3: National Traditions of Musicology—Subsection 4: Germany and Austria." *Grove Music Online / Oxford Music Online*. Accessed July 7, 2012. www.oxfordmusiconline.com.

Ratner, Leonard G. *Romantic Music: Sound and Syntax*. New York: Schirmer Books, 1992.

Reich, Nancy B. "Clara Schumann and Johannes Brahms." In *Brahms and His World*, edited by Walter Frisch, 37–47. Princeton. NJ: Princeton University Press, 1990.

———. *Clara Schumann: The Artist and the Woman*. Revised ed. Ithaca, NY: Cornell University Press, 2001.

Réti, Rudolph. *The Thematic Process in Music*. New York: Macmillan, 1951; repr. Westport, CT: Greenwood Press, 1978.

Reynolds, Christopher Alan. "A Choral Symphony by Brahms?" *19th-Century Music* 9/1 (1985): 3–25.

———. *Motives for Allusion: Context and Content in Nineteenth-Century Music*. Cambridge, MA: Harvard University Press, 2003.

———. *Wagner, Schumann, and the Lessons of Beethoven's Ninth*. Berkeley: University of California Press, 2015.

Ricks, Robert. "A Possible Source for a Brahms Ground." *American Brahms Society Newsletter* 23/1 (2005): 1–5.

Riemann, Hugo. *Johannes Brahms: Erläuterung seiner bedeutendsten Werke*. Frankfurt am Main: H. Bechold, 1898.

Rodriguez, Margarita. "Aspects of Completion in Beethoven's Middle Period Codas." PhD diss., Michigan State University, 2012.

Rosen, Charles. "Influence: Plagiarism and Inspiration." *19th-Century Music* 4/2 (1980): 87–100.

———. *Sonata Forms*. Revised ed. New York: Norton: 1988.

———. *The Romantic Generation*. Cambridge, MA: Harvard University Press, 1995.
———. *Beethoven's Piano Sonatas: A Short Companion*. New Haven, CT: Yale University Press, 2002.
Ruf, Wolfgang. "Die zwei Sextette von Brahms: Eine analytische Studie." In *Brahms-Analysen: Referate der Kieler Tagung 1983. Kieler Schriften zur Musikwissenschaft*, edited by Friedhelm Krummacher and Wolfram Steinbeck, vol. 28, 121–33. Kassel: Bärenreiter, 1984.
———. "Kammermusik zwischen Exklusivität und Öffentlichkeit: Zum Sextett op. 18 von Johannes Brahms." In *Leitmotive: Kulturgeschichtliche Studien zur Traditionsbildung: Festschrift für Dietz-Rüdiger Moser zum 60. Geburtstag am 22. März 1999*, edited by Marianne Sammer, et al., 427–34. Kallmünz: M. Lassleben, 1999.
Rule, Marie Rivers. "The Allure of Beethoven's 'Terzen-Ketten': Third-Chains in Studies by Nottebohm and Music by Brahms." PhD diss., University of Illinois at Urbana-Champaign, 2011.
Ryan, Alan. "The Will to Madness: The Story of Friedrich Nietzsche's Fateful Relationship with Richard and Cosima Wagner." *The New York Times* (January 24, 1999). Accessed January 30, 2017. www.nytimes.com/books/99/01/24/reviews/990124.24ryanlt.html
Sams, Eric. Did Schumann Use Ciphers?" *The Musical Times* 106 (1965): 584–91
———. "The Schumann Ciphers," *The Musical Times* 107 (1966): 392–400
———. "Brahms and His Clara Themes." *The Musical Times* 112/1539 (1971): 432–34.
———. "Brahms and His Musical Love Letters." *The Musical Times* 112/1538 (1971): 329–30.
———. *The Songs of Johannes Brahms*. New Haven. CT: Yale University Press, 2000.
Scarlatti, Domenico. *Sonates*. Vol. 4. Edited by Kenneth Gilbert. Paris: Heugel, 1976.
Schauffler, Robert Haven. *The Unknown Brahms*. New York: Dodd, Mead and Co., 1933.
Schering, Arnold. *Beethoven und die Dichtung, mit einer Einleitung zur Geschichte und Ästhetik der Beethovendeutung*. Berlin: Junker und Dünnhaupt, Berlin, 1936; repr. Hildesheim: G. Olms, 1973.
Schipperges, Thomas. *Serenaden zwischen Beethoven und Reger: Beiträge zur Geschichte der Gattung*, Europäische Hochschulschriften, 36. Frankfurt am Main: Lang, 1989.
Schläder, Jürgen. "Zur Funktion der Variantentechnik in den Klaviersonaten F-Moll von Johannes Brahms und H-Moll von Franz Liszt." In *Brahms und seine Zeit: Bericht über das Symposion 1983 in Hamburg*, edited by Constantin Floros, Hans Joachim Marx, and P. Petersen, 171–97. Hamburg: Laaber-Verlag, 1984.
Schoenberg, Arnold. *Style and Idea: Selected Writings of Arnold Schoenberg*. Edited by Leonard Stein and translated by Leo Black. Berkeley: University of California Press, 1975.
Schubert, Franz. *Complete Sonatas for Pianoforte Solo*. Edited by Julius Epstein from the Breitkopf & Härtel Complete Works ed. Mineola, NY: Dover, 1970.
———. *Complete Song Cycles*. Edited by Eusebius Mandyczewski from the Breitkopf & Härtel Complete Works Ed., with translations by Henry S. Drinker. Mineola, NY: Dover, 1970.
Schubert, Giselher. "Themes and Double Themes: The Problem of the Symphonic in Brahms." *19th-Century Music* 18/1 (1994): 10–23.
Schubring, Adolf. "Schumanniana Nr. 8: Die Schumann'sche Schule: Johannes Brahms." *Neue Zeitschrift für Musik* 12–16 (1862): 93–96, 101–4, 109–12, 117–19, 125–28.
———. "Five Early Works by Brahms," translated Walter Frisch. In *Brahms and His World*, edited by Walter Frisch, 103–22. Princeton, NJ: Princeton University Press, 1990.

Schumann, Clara, and Johannes Brahms. *Letters of Clara Schumann and Johannes Brahms, 1853–1896.* Edited by Berthold Litzmann. 2 vols. New York: Longmans, Green, 1927; repr. New York: Vienna House, 1973.

Schumann, Clara, and Robert Schumann. *The Complete Correspondence of Clara and Robert Schumann.* Critical ed. New York: P. Lang, 1994.

Schumann, Robert. "Neue Bahnen." *Neue Zeitschrift für Musik* 39 (October 28, 1853): 185–86.

———. *Kreisleriana*, op. 16. Edited by Clara Schumann. Robert Schumanns Werke, Series VII: Für Pianoforte zu zwei Händen. Vol. 3. Leipzig: Breitkopf & Härtel, 1885.

———. *On Music and Musicians.* Translated by Paul Rosenfeld. Edited by Konrad Wolff. New York: Pantheon, 1946; repr. New York: W. W. Norton & Company, Inc., 1969.

Schumann, Robert, et al. *Briefe: Neue Folge.* Edited by F. Gustav Jansen. 2nd revised ed. Leipzig: Brietkopf & Härtel, 1904.

———. *The Letters of Robert Schumann.* Selected and edited by Karl G. L. Storck. Translated by Hannah Bryant. New York: Dutton, 1907.

Scott, Ann Besser. "Thematic Transmutation in the Music of Brahms: A Matter of Musical Alchemy." *The Journal of Musicological Research* 15/3 (1995): 177–206.

Sheveloff, Joel Leonard. "The Keyboard Music of Domenico Scarlatti: A Re-Evaluation of the Present State of Knowledge in the Light of the Sources." PhD diss., Brandeis University, 1970.

Sholes, Jacquelyn. "'Transcendence,' 'Loss,' and 'Reminiscence': Brahms's Early Finales in the Contexts of Form, Narrative, and Historicism." PhD diss., Brandeis University, 2008.

———. "Lovelorn Lamentation or Histrionic Historicism? Reconsidering Allusion and Extra-Musical Meaning in the 1854 Version of Brahms's B-Major Trio." *19th-Century Music* 34/1 (2010): 61–86.

———. "Brahms, Mathilde Wesendonck, and the Would-Be 'Cremation Cantata,"' *The American Brahms Society Newsletter* 30/2 (Fall 2012), 1–5.

———. "A 'Cremation Cantata'?: The Dramatic Conclusion of the Brahms-Wesendonck Correspondence." *Ars Lyrica* 21 (2012): 155–72.

———. "Gustav Jenner and the Music of Brahms: The Case of the Orchestral Serenades." *Nineteenth-Century Music Review.* Forthcoming.

Simpson, Robert. *Beethoven Symphonies.* University of Washington Press Edited by Gerald Abraham. Seattle, WA: University of Washington Press, 1971.

Sipe, Thomas Owen. "Interpreting Beethoven: History, Aesthetics, and Critical Reception." PhD diss., University of Pennsylvania, 1992.

Sisman, Elaine. "Brahms's Slow Movements: Reinventing the 'Closed' Forms." In *Brahms Studies: Analytical and Historical Perspectives*, edited by George S. Bozarth, 79–103. Oxford: Clarendon, 1990.

Smidak, Emil. *Isaak-Ignaz Moscheles: The Life of the Composer and His Encounters with Beethoven, Liszt, Chopin, and Mendelssohn.* Aldershot, Hampshire: Scolar Press, 1989.

Smith, Peter Howard. "Brahms and Schenker: A Mutual Response to Sonata Form." *Music Theory Spectrum* 16/1 (1994): 77–103.

———. "Liquidation, Augmentation, and Brahms's Recapitulatory Overlaps." *19th-Century Music* 17/3 (1994): 237–61.

———. *Expressive Forms in Brahms's Instrumental Music: Structure and Meaning in His Werther Quartet.* Bloomington: Indiana University Press, 2005.

Solie, Ruth A. "Beethoven as Secular Humanist: Ideology and the Ninth Symphony in Nineteenth-Century Criticism." In *Explorations in Music, the Arts, and Ideas: Essays in Honor of Leonard B. Meyer*, edited by Ruth A. Solie and Eugene Narmour, 1–42. Stuyvesant: Pendragon, 1988.

Solomon, Yonty. "Solo Piano Music—Section 1: The Sonatas and the Fantasie." In *Robert Schumann: The Man and His Music*, edited by Alan Walker, 41–67. London: Barrie & Jenkins, 1972.

Specht, Richard. *Johannes Brahms*. Translated by Eric Blom. London: J. M. Dent and Sons, 1930.

Stanley, Glenn. "Criticism—Section 2: History to 1945—Subsection 1: Germany and Austria—Sub-subsection 2: 19th Century." *Grove Music Online*. Accessed February 7, 2006. www.grovemusic.com

Sutcliffe, W. Dean. *The Keyboard Sonatas of Domenico Scarlatti and Eighteenth-Century Musical Style*. Cambridge: Cambridge University Press, 2003.

Swafford, Jan. *Johannes Brahms: A Biography*. New York: Alfred A. Knopf; Distributed by Random House, 1997.

Talbot, Michael. *The Finale in Western Instrumental Music*. Oxford Monographs on Music. Oxford: Oxford University Press, 2001.

Taylor, Ronald. *Robert Schumann, His Life and Work*. New York: Universe Books, 1982.

Thalmann, Joachim. "Studien zu Brahms' frühesten Kompositionen: Sein Interesse in alter Musik und dessen Niederschlag in seinem Frühwerk." In *Festschrift Arno Forchert zum 60. Geburtstag am 29. Dezember 1985*, edited by G. Allroggen and Detlef Altenburg, 264–70. Kassel: Bärenreiter, 1986.

Thatcher, David S. "Nietzsche and Brahms: A Forgotten Relationship." *Music & Letters* 54/3 (1973): 261–80.

Thematic Catalog of the Collected Works of Brahms. Edited by Joseph Braunstein. Enlarged ed. [New York]: Ars Musica Press, 1956.

Thompson, Christopher Kent. "Brahms and the Problematizing of Traditional Sonata Form." PhD diss., University of Wisconsin, Madison, 1996.

Tovey, Donald Francis. *Essays in Musical Analysis*. 6 vols. London: Oxford University Press, 1935–39.

———. *Essays in Musical Analysis: Chamber Music*. London: Oxford University Press, 1944.

———. *A Companion to Beethoven's Pianoforte Sonatas (Bar-to-Bar Analysis)*. London: The Associated Board of the Royal Schools of Music, 1948.

———. "Brahms's Chamber Music." In *The Main Stream of Music and Other Essays*, edited by Hubert J. Foss, 220–70. New York: Oxford University Press, 1949.

Treitler, Leo. "Reflections on the Communication of Affect and Idea through Music." In *Psychoanalytic Explorations in Music: Second Series*, edited by Stuart Feder, Richard L. Karmel, and George H. Pollock, 43–62. Madison, CT: International Universities Press, 1993.

———. *Reflections on Musical Meaning and Its Representations*. Bloomington: Indiana University Press, 2011.

Truscott, Harold. "Brahms and Sonata Style." *The Music Review* 25 (1964): 186–201.

Unsre Lieblinge: Die schönsten Melodien für das Pianoforte. Edited by Carl Reinecke. Vol. 1. Leipzig: Breitkopf & Härtel, [1869].

Unverricht, Hubert, and Cliff Eisen. "Serenade." *Grove Music Online*. Accessed April 12, 2006. www.grovemusic.com.
Urbantschitsch, Viktor. "Die Entwicklung der Sonatenform bei Brahms." *Studien zur Musikwissenschaft* 14 (1927): 264–85.
Vaillancourt, Michael. "Brahms's Sinfonie-Serenade' and the Politics of Genre." *Journal of Musicology* 26/3 (2009): 379–403.
Wagner, Richard. *On Conducting (Über das Dirigiren): A Treatise on Style in the Execution of Classical Music*. Translated by Edward Dannreuther. London: William Reeves, 1887.
———. *Gesammelte Schriften und Dichtungen*, 3rd ed. 10 vols. Leipzig: E. W. Fritzsch, 1887–88.
———. *Richard Wagner's Prose Works*. Edited and translated by William Ashton Ellis. London: Kegan Paul, Trench, Trübner and Co., Ltd., 1897.
———. *Tannhäuser*. Edited by Felix Mottl. Leipzig: C. F. Peters, n.d.; repr. Mineola, NY: Dover, 1984.
Walker, Alan. "Schumann, Liszt and the C Major Fantasie, op. 17: A Declining Relationship." *Music & Letters* 60/2 (1979): 156–65.
———. *Franz Liszt*. 3 vols. New York: Alfred A. Knopf, 1983.
Walton, Chris. *Wagner's Zurich: The Muse of Place*. Rochester, NY: Camden House, 2007.
Weber, Horst. "Melancholia—Versuch über Brahms' Vierte." In *Neue Musik und Tradition: Festschrift Rudolf Stephan zum 65. Geburtstag*, edited by Joseph Kuckertz, 281–95. Laaber: Laaber-Verlag, 1990.
Webster, James. "Schubert's Sonata Form and Brahms's First Maturity." *19th-Century Music* 2 (1978): 18–35 and 3 (1979): 52–71.
Weingartner, Felix. *Weingartner on Music and Conducting: Three Essays by Felix Weingartner*. Translated by H. M. Schott. New York: Dover, 1969.
Whitesell, Lloyd. "Men with a Past: Music and the 'Anxiety of Influence.'" *19th-Century Music* 18/2 (1994): 152–67.
Wilson, Richard. "Piano Concerto No. 1 in D Minor, op. 15." In *The Complete Brahms: A Guide to the Musical Works of Johannes Brahms*, edited by Leon Botstein, 47–50. New York: W. W. Norton, 1999.
Wintle, Christopher. "The 'Sceptred Pall': Brahms's Progressive Harmony." In *Brahms 2: Biographical, Documentary and Analytical Studies*, edited by Michael Musgrave, 197–222. Cambridge: Cambridge University Press, 1987.
Wolf, Eugene K. "The Recapitulations in Haydn's London Symphonies." *Musical Quarterly* 52 (1966): 71–89.
Wolff, Christoph. "Brahms, Wagner, and the Problem of Historicism in Nineteenth-Century Music." In *Brahms Studies: Analytical and Historical Perspectives*, edited by George S. Bozarth, 7–11. Oxford: Clarendon Press, 1990.
Zaunschirm, Franz. *Der frühe und der späte Brahms: Eine Fallstudie anhand der autographen Korrekturen und gedruckten Fassungen zum Trio Nr. 1 für Klavier, Violine und Violoncello opus 8*. Schiftenreihe zur Musik; 26. Hamburg: Wagner, 1988.

Index

Adler, Guido, 11
Adorno, Theodor Wiesengrund, 225n117
Aeschylus, 208
Agawu, Kofi, 3
Ambros, August Wilhelm, 11
"Anxiety of Influence," Harold Bloom's theory of. *See* Bloom, Harold, "Anxiety of Influence" theory. *See also* Beethoven, Ludwig van: Brahms's anxieties and
Austrian National Library (Österreichische Nationalbibliothek), 64n38

Bach, Carl Philipp Emanuel, 13; Rondo in E Flat, W. 61/1, 230n3
Bach, Johann Sebastian, 180, 181, 182, 186, 189, 203, 228; Cantata No. 93, *Wer nur den lieben Gott lässt walten* (BWV 93), 58–59, 63n21; Cantata No. 150, *Nach dir, Herr, verlanget mich* (BWV 150), 8, 181–82, 186, 188–89, 191, 196, 197, 202, 212, 213, 216n19, 217n21, 224n115, 228; Mass in B Minor (BWV 232), 181; Partita No. 2 in D Minor for Solo Violin (BWV 1004), 181, 216n12, 216n14. *See also* Schumann, Robert, works of: 6 Fugues on "B-A-C-H" (op. 60)
Bailey, Robert, 190
Baldassarre, Antonio, 79
Bargiel, Woldemar, 204
Bayreuth, 206, 207, 223n103
Beckerath, Rudolf von, 214n4
Beethoven, Ludwig van, 2, 7, 9n9, 11, 13, 14, 47, 49, 56, 57, 58, 65n42, 66n52, 89, 98n20, 99n22, 104, 131n1, 131n5, 134–39, 168–74, 177n34, 186, 200, 203, 213, 215n11, 217n21, 220n61, 225n117
  Brahms as heir to, 2, 14, 26, 61, 92–93, 128, 130, 205, 228
  Brahms's anxieties and, 2, 7, 11, 14, 15, 24, 61, 62n14, 63n20, 92–93, 132n14, 168–74, 177n34, 227–28
  Schumann's views on, 2, 3–4, 9n8, 132n14, 208
  Wagner's views on, 202, 205, 207, 208, 221n74
  See also Beethoven, Ludwig van, Brahms's anxieties and; Beethoven, Ludwig van, Schumann's views on; Beethoven, Ludwig van, works of: symphonies, No. 5 in C Minor (op. 67), "Fate Motive" from; Nottebohm, Gustav; Schumann, Robert, critical writings of, "*Neue Bahnen*"
Beethoven, Ludwig van, works of,
  32 Variations in C Minor (WoO 80), 181
  An die ferne Geliebte (op. 98), 68, 69, 70; No. 6, "Nimm sie hin den, diese Lieder," 69, 70, 89, 90, 92, 93, 94, 95, 181, 190
  Fidelio (op. 72), 177n45
  "Ode to Joy." *See* Beethoven, Ludwig van, works of, symphonies, No. 9 in D Minor (op. 125, "Choral")
  piano concertos
    No. 1 in C Major (op. 15), 171
    No. 3 in C Minor (op. 37), 66n52, 134, 135, 136–37
  piano sonatas
    No. 8 in C Minor (op. 13, "Pathétique"), 47, 57, 58, 59
    No. 21 in C Major (op. 53, "Waldstein"), 37–38, 40, 43, 47
    No. 23 in F Minor (op. 57, "Appassionata"), 57, 66n52
    No. 29 in B-flat Major (op. 106, "Hammerklavier"), 37–38, 47, 180, 203, 217n20
  Septet in E-flat Major (op. 20), 104
  symphonies, 4, 208
    No. 1 in C Major (op. 21), 104, 131n1
    No. 2 in D Major (op. 36), 104, 131n1

250 | Index

No. 3 in E-flat Major (op. 55, "Eroica"), 181
No. 4 in B-flat Major (op. 60), 131n1
No. 5 in C Minor (op. 67), 15, 24, 56–57, 58, 180, 181, 215n11, 217n21; "Fate" motive from, 15, 24, 47, 51, 54–58, 60, 65n45, 142, 151, 175n18, 186, 191
No. 6 in F Major (op. 68, "Pastoral"), 104
No. 7 in A Major (op. 92), 69
No. 9 in D Minor (op. 125, "Choral"), 4, 15, 63n16, 170, 171, 174n1, 175n13, 175n18, 175n19, 189, 200, 202, 208; "Ode to Joy," 4, 5, 13, 15, 21. *See also* Beethoven, Ludwig van: Wagner's views on
Violin Concerto in D Major (op. 61), 66n49
Violin Sonata No. 5 in F Major (op. 24, "Spring"), 104
Berlin, 77, 205
Berlin Philharmonic Orchestra, 220n68
Berlioz, Hector, 2, 12, 202, 204
Berry, Paul, 5, 10n18, 99n24, 229, 231n7
Billroth, Theodor, 77, 104, 208
Bloom, Harold, "Anxiety of Influence" theory, 13, 62n14, 171
Bonn, University of, 12
Botstein, Leon, 166
Boyd, Malcolm, 77, 91
Bozarth, George, 60, 66n54, 167, 174, 177n44
Brahms, Johanna Christiane, 27, 33
Brahms, Johannes,
  Baroque music and, 77, 82, 96, 98n10, 98n20, 102n64, 180, 181, 199, 202, 207, 213 (*see also* Bach, Johann Sebastian; Brahms, Johannes: "early" Music and; Brahms, Johannes, works of: gavottes (WoO 3–4); Brahms, Johannes, works of: organ works (WoO 7–10); Brahms, Johannes, works of: sarabandes (WoO 5); Buxtehude, Dieterich; chaconne form; Couperin, François; Handel, George Frideric; Joachim, Joseph: Brahms's counterpoint exchange with; Lully, Jean-Baptiste; Scarlatti, Domenico)
  "Brahms the Progressive" (Schoenberg), 214
  Classicism and, 7, 12, 66n86, 103–4, 128, 130 (*see also* Beethoven, Ludwig van, Brahms as heir to; Haydn, Franz Joseph; Mozart, Wolfgang Amadeus)
  death as theme in work of, 8, 60, 179, 180, 186, 188–91, 197–99, 199–203, 208, 212, 213, 214, 229
  death of, 96, 197, 208, 219n50, 221n69
  developing variation in the music of, 214
  "early" music and, 12, 62n8, 77, 93 (*see also* Brahms, Johannes, Baroque music and; Marenzio, Luca; Minnesänger; Phrygian mode)
  editorial activities of, 13
  "F(rei)-A(ber)-F(roh)" motive and, 33, 224n113
  honorary doctorate, 207
  "lateness" and, 199–202, 225n117
  library of, 7, 13, 78
  Modernism and, 12
  mother's death, 27, 33
  octaves and fifths, collections of parallel, 13, 78
  performances given by, 7, 78, 97n3, 98n20, 134, 205, 207
  Postmodernism and, 12
  See also Beethoven, Ludwig van, Brahms's anxieties and; Beethoven, Ludwig van, Brahms as heir to; folksong; Hoffmann, Ernst Theodore (Wilhelm) "Amadeus" (E. T. A.): Kreisler; Johannes; Joachim, Joseph: Brahms's counterpoint exchange with
Brahms, Johannes, works of,
  4 Balladen und Romanzen for vocal duet (op. 75): No. 1: "Edward," 99n27
  Ballades, op. 10: No. 1: "Edward," 56, 175n12
  capriccios in opp. 76 and 116, 78
  Deutsches Requiem, Ein (op. 45). See Brahms, Johannes, works of, German Requiem
  "F-A-E" Sonata, scherzo for, 56–57, 60, 67n60
  gavottes (WoO 3–4), 96

German Requiem, 47, 99n27, 197, 205
"Liebeslieder-Walzer" (op. 52), 205
organ works (WoO 7–10), 102n64
Overture, "Tragic" (op. 81), 223n109, 175n12
piano concertos,
  No. 1 in D Minor (op. 15), 7, 133–78; Beethoven, relationship to music of, 7, 134–39, 168–73; "horn call" in, 135, 154–65, 166, 167, 169, 170, 171, 174, 176n20; minor mode, transcendence of, 150–54, 163, 169, 172, 174, 176n20; Schumann's, relationship of the work to, 133, 167–68, 170–71, 173–74, 176n26, 176n29, 177n43, 177n45, 177n46; soloist's role in, 134, 135, 139–50, 151, 153–54, 156, 161, 162, 163, 166–68, 169, 170, 171, 172, 174, 176n20
  No. 2 in B-flat major (op. 83), 146, 170
Piano Quartet No. 3 in C Minor (op. 60, "Werther"), 3
piano sonatas, 6, 36
  No. 1 in C Major (op. 1), 7, 37–47, 64n38; Beethoven, relationship to music of, 37–38, 40, 43, 47
  No. 2 in F-sharp Minor (op. 2), 64n38, 90, 91, 100n39
  No. 3 in F Minor (op. 5), 47–61, 66n52, 67n60, 101n53, 176n25; Beethoven, relationship to music of, 47, 51, 54–58, 59, 60, 66n52
sarabandes (WoO 5), 96
Scherzo in E-flat Minor (op. 4), 96
serenades for orchestra, 12
  No. 1 in D Major (op. 11), 7, 103–32; as Classicist work, 7, 12, 103–104; finale's relationship to previous movements, 103, 104–25, 127, 130; Haydn, relationship to music of, 7, 103, 104, 125–30, 131n7, 132n13
Sextet for Strings No. 2 in G Major (op. 36), 32–33
songs (*ordered by opus number*),
  5 Gesänge (op. 72), No. 5, "Unüberwindlich," 78
  6 Lieder (op. 86), No. 2, "Feldeinsamkeit," 188

2 Gesänge (op. 91), No. 1, "Gestillte Sehnsucht," 188
5 Lieder (op. 94), No. 1, "Mit vierzig Jahren," 188
5 Gesänge (op. 104), No. 5, "Im Herbst," 221n77
5 Lieder (op. 105): No. 2, "Immer leiser wird mein Schlummer," 221n77; No. 4, "Auf dem Kirchhofe" 188, 221n77
4 ernste Gesänge (op. 121), 188; No. 2, "Ich wandte mich und sahe," 188; No. 3, "O Tod," 188, 197–99
folksong settings of. *See* folksong
String Quartet No. 3 in B-flat major (op. 67), 6, 33–36; Mozart, relationship to music of, 33, 35
symphonies, 9n6, 215n10
  No. 1 in C minor (op. 68), 6, 14–26, 27, 62n15, 63n16, 103, 179, 224n113, 228; Beethoven, relationship to music of, 4, 5, 13, 14–15, 24, 47, 55, 189, 207, 208, 223n102
  No. 2 in D major (op. 73), 224n113
  No. 3 in F Major (op. 90), 208–12, 223n109, 223n110; Wagner, relationship to music of, 208–12, 223n110, 224n113
  No. 4 in E Minor (op. 98), 2, 179–227, 228; antiquarianism in, 12, 179–80, 213, 225n117 (*see also* chaconne form); associations with death and tragedy, 8, 179–80, 181, 186–91, 197–203, 208, 212, 213–214, 219n40, 224n115, 229; Bach, relationship to music of, 8, 180, 181–82, 186, 188–89, 191, 196, 197–99, 202, 203, 212–13, 216n19, 224n115; reception of, 200–201, 220n68, 221n69; Wagner, relationship to music and life of, 8, 180–81, 191–97, 198–99, 199, 202, 203–8, 212, 213, 219n49, 228 (*see also* Brahms, Johannes, works of, Overture, "Tragic" (op. 181); motives, falling thirds)
trios
  Horn Trio in E-flat major (op. 40), 6, 27–33, 63n21, 99n27, 228

Piano Trio in B Major (op. 8), 2, 5, 7, 68–102; 1854 version, 2, 7, 68–77, 78–93; Beethoven, allusion to (*see* Beethoven, Ludwig van, works of, *An die ferne Geliebte* [op. 98]); revised version (1889), 7, 69, 82, 93–96; Scarlatti, allusion to Domenico (*see* Scarlatti, Domenico); Schubert, allusion to (*see* Schubert, Franz, *Schwanengesang* [D. 957])
Triumphlied, op. 55, 206
Variations and Fugue on a Theme by G. F. Handel (op. 24), 78, 98n20, 204
Variations on a Theme by Haydn (op. 56), 216n12
Variations on a Theme by Robert Schumann (op. 9), 100n41
"Brahms the Progressive" (Schoenberg), 214
Breitkopf & Härtel, 93, 97n3, 203
Breslau, University of, 207
Brinkmann, Rheinhold, 200
Brodbeck, David, 190, 206, 207, 209, 217n21, 223n11, 224n113
Bruch, Max, 204
Bülow, Cosima von. *See* Liszt, Cosima (Francesca Gaetana)
Bülow, Hans von, 63n17, 181, 182, 206, 220n64
Buxtehude, Dieterich, Ciacona in E Minor (BuxWV 160), 181, 224

canon of musical works, concept of, 12, 13
chaconne form, 7–8, 12, 180, 181, 186, 202, 213, 215n12, 216n13, 224n115
Chamisso, Adelbert von, 219n49
Chopin, Frederic, 13, 91, 96
Chrysander, Friedrich, 11, 216n14
"Clara cipher," 191. *See also* Schumann, Robert: "Clara cipher," use of
Collier, Michael, 168
Cologne, 177n44, 199
Cornelius, Peter, 204–5, 222n88
Couperin, François, 13, Passacaille in B Minor (Suite No. 8, Part 8), 181, 216n14
Czerny, Carl, 4, 9n9, 91; Scarlatti sonata edition, 77, 78, 91, 99n22; *School of Practical Composition*, 4

da Silva, Fabio Roberto Gardenal. *See* Silva, Fabio Roberto Gardenal da
Daverio, John, 67n60, 178n46
Detmold, 103
developing variation, 214
Dietrich, Albert, 100n39, 204, 229
"Dort in den Weiden steht ein Haus." *See under* folksong
Dresden, 206
Dürr, Alfred, 216n19
Düsseldorf, 68, 77, 90, 97n2

"Edward" (Scottish ballad), 56, 99n27, 175n12
Endenich. *See* Schumann, Robert: nervous breakdown of
"Es soll sich der Mensch nicht mit der Liebe abgeben." *See under* folksong
"Es soll sich ja keiner mit der Liebe abgeben." *See under* folksong
Euripides, 208
Expressionism, 200

"F-A-E" motive. *See* Joachim, Joseph: "F(rei)-A(ber)-E(insam)" motive and
"F-A-E" Sonata. *See* Brahms, Johannes, works of: "F-A-E" Sonata, scherzo for; Schumann, Robert, works of: "F-A-E" Sonata, Intermezzo for
"F-A-F" motive. *See* Brahms, Johannes: "F(rei)-A(ber)-F(roh)" motive and
falling thirds motive. *See* motives: falling thirds
Faust (Goethe play), 223n109, 225n117
"Fate" motive. *See under* Beethoven, Ludwig van, works of: symphonies: Symphony No. 5 in C Minor (op. 67)
Feder, Stuart, 230
Ferris, David, 91
Finck, Henry Theophilus, 221n73
Finscher, Ludwig, 200
Floros, Constantin, 215n11
Forkel, Johann Nicolaus, 11
folksong, 12, 27, 28–29, 59, 63n21, 66n54, 82, 99n27, 228; "Dort in den Weiden steht ein Haus," 27–28, 63n21, 99n27; "Es soll sich der Mensch nicht mit der Liebe abgeben," 27, 63n21; "Es soll sich ja keiner mit der

Liebe abgeben," 27, 29, 63n21; "Steh' ich in finst'rer Mitternacht," 59
"Frei aber einsam." See Joachim, Joseph: "F(rei)-A(ber)-E(insam)" motive and
"Frei aber froh." See Brahms, Johannes, "F(rei)-A(ber)-F(roh)" motive and
Frisch, Walter, 34, 66n52, 166, 185, 186, 218n29

Gàl, Hans, 166, 180
Gänsbacher, Josef, 33
Garratt, James, 4
Goethe, Johann Wolfgang von, 4, 225n117; *Faust*, 223n109
Göllerich, August, 102n62
Göttingen, 32
Grädener, Carl, 204
Grimm, Julius Otto, 32, 62n11, 173, 177n44, 204

Hamburg, 68
Handel, George Frideric, 11, 13, 180, 207; "Behold and See" (*Messiah*), 215n11. See also Brahms, Johannes, works of: Variations and Fugue on a Theme by G. F. Handel (op. 24)
Hanover, 68, 100n39
Hanslick, Eduard, 12, 201, 207, 227
Hatten, Robert, 3
Hauer, Ottilie, 32
Hauptmann, Moritz, 204
Haydn, Franz Joseph, 11, 221n77: serenades, 103; symphonies (general), 104; Symphony No. 44 in E Minor (Hob. I: 44, *"Trauersinfonie"*), 179, 214n4; Symphony No. 104 in D Major (Hob. I: 104, "London"), 7, 103, 104, 125–30, 131n7, 132n13, 132n14;
Heine, Heinrich, 72
Herzogenberg, Elisabeth von, 77, 189, 200, 220n68, 229
Herzogenberg, Heinrich von, 77, 229
Hill, John Walter, 27, 28, 63n21
Hiller, Ferdinand, 56, 204
Hoffmann, Ernst Theodore (Wilhelm) "Amadeus" (E. T. A.): *Kater Murr*, 167; Kreisler, Johannes, 60, 167

Holland, 90
"Hot Cross Buns," 131n7
Hull, Kenneth Ross, 5, 12, 13, 94, 181, 189–90, 224n116

Jacobsthal, Gustav, 12
Jahn, Otto, 11
Jeitteles, Alois, 69, 72
Jenner, Gustav, 229
Joachim, Joseph, 32, 57, 68, 77, 90, 93, 134, 173, 200, 204, 205, 220n68, 222n93, 229; Brahms's counterpoint exchange with, 13, 93; "F(rei)-A(ber)-E(insam)" motive and, 60; marriage of, 32; Violin Concerto in D Minor, op. 11 ("in the Hungarian Style)," 172–73. See also New German School: manifesto against

Kalbeck, Max, 13, 27, 59, 63n18, 63n21, 79, 96n2, 97n4, 97n7, 99n27, 177n44, 180, 200, 223n109
Kater Murr (Hoffmann novel). See Hoffmann, Ernst Theodore (Wilhelm) "Amadeus" (E.T.A.): *Kater Murr*
key associations: D minor, 139, 175n12; E minor, 179, 180, 214n3
Keys, Ivor, 94
Kiesewetter, Raphael Georg, 11
Kirchner, Theodor, 204, 229
Knapp, Raymond, 177n44, 180, 186, 199, 202, 215n11, 217n20, 217n26, 219n40, 225n118, 227
Köchel, Ludwig von, 11
Korsyn, Kevin, 12
Kramer, Lawrence, 3
Kreisler, Johannes. See Hoffmann, Ernst Theodor (Wilhelm) "Amadeus" (E. T. A.): Kreisler, Johannes
Kretzschmar, Hermann, 97n4, 190
Kross, Siegfried, 167

Lachner, Franz, 229
Leipzig, 68, 91, 146, 208
Ligeti, György, 3
Liszt, Cosima (Francesca Gaetana), 206, 208, 222n99, 223n107
Liszt, Franz, 2, 5, 12, 66n52, 91, 202, 204, 205, 208,

Littlewood, Julian, 189
Lully, Jean-Baptiste, 180, 224n115; *Phaëton*, 181, 224n115

MacDonald, Malcolm, 90, 94, 134, 176n20, 217n21
Mahler, Gustav, 200
Mandyczewski, Eusebius, 97n7
Marenzio, Luca, 99n22
Marx, Adolf Bernhard, 11
May, Florence, 78
Mehlem, 97n2
Meiningen, 200, 201, 207, 214n1, 221n69
Mendelssohn, Felix, 180; *Hebrides, The* (Overture, op. 26), 215n11; Symphony No. 5 in D Major (op. 107, "Reformation"), 132n14
Messiah. See Handel, George Frideric: "Behold and See" (*Messiah*)
Minnesänger, 12, 209
Modernism, 12
Moscheles, Ignaz, 91
Moseley, Roger, 170–71
motives: falling thirds, 182–86, 188–89, 194, 197–98, 202, 213, 215n11, 217n20, 217n21, 217n22, 217n26, 218n36, 220n51. *See also* Beethoven, Ludwig van, works of: symphonies: Symphony No. 5 in C Minor (op. 67): "Fate" motive; Brahms, Johannes: "*F(rei)-A(ber)-F(roh)*" motive and; Brahms, Johannes, works of: piano concertos: No. 1 in D Minor (op. 15): "horn call" in; Joachim, Joseph: "*F(rei)-A(ber)-E(insam)*" motive and
Mozart, Wolfgang Amadeus, 11, 13, 99n22; andantes of, 131n1; *Don Giovanni*, 66n49, 219n42; *Requiem*, 219n42; serenades, 103; String Quartet in B-Flat Major (K. 458, "Hunt"), 33, 35; Symphony No. 40 in G Minor (K. 550), 180
Muffat, Georg, Passacaglia in G minor for Organ, 181
Munich, 205, 207
Mürzzuschlag, 179
Musgrave, Michael, 166, 224n113
musicology, field of, 11–12: Brahms and, 13. *See also* canon of musical works, concept of

Nass, Martin L., 8n5
Naumann, Emil, 204
"Neue Bahnen." *See* Schumann, Robert: critical writings of: "Neue Bahnen"
Neue Zeitschrift für Musik, 11, 47, 90, 222n90
Newcomb, Anthony, 4, 5, 132n14
New German School, 12, 14, 68, 202, 203, 208, 227; manifesto against, 204, 221n84. *See also* Liszt, Franz; Wagner, Richard
New York Philharmonic, 201, 221n72
Niemann, Walter, 90, 149, 175n12, 179
Nietzsche, Friedrich, 206, 222n99
Nikisch, Arthur, 208
Notley, Margaret, 94, 95, 98n21, 225n117
Nottebohm, Gustav, 11, 13, 203, 215n11, 217n21, 221n78

Ochs, Siegfried, 181–82, 186, 208, 212, 224n115
Österreichische Nationalbibliothek, 64n38

Paganini, Niccolò, Caprice in E Major (op. 1/9), 97n10
Palestrina, Giovanni Pierluigi da, 11
Parmer, Dillon, 90, 100n35
Passacaglia. *See* chaconne form
Pestelli, Giorgio, 190
Phrygian mode, 180, 213, 217n21
plagal harmony, 180, 215n10
Planer, Minna, 205–6
Pohl, Carl Ferdinand, 11, 221n77
Postmodernism, 12

Ratner, Leonard, 3
Reger, Max: 7 *Fantasiestücke* (op. 26), No. 5, "Resignation," 213; Organ Suite No. 1 in E Minor (op. 16), 213
Reich, Nancy, 91
Reinecke, Carl, 204
Reynolds, Christopher, 5, 9n9, 13, 62n16, 92, 101n49, 132n14, 173, 174n1, 208, 230
Ricks, Robert, 181, 224n115
Riemann, Hugo, 11, 214n3
Rietz, Julius, 204
Rosen, Charles, 134–35, 227
Rubinstein, Anton, 201; Symphony No. 2 in C Major (op. 42, "Ocean"), 181
Rule, Marie Rivers, 217n21

Sams, Eric, 99n27, 120n36, 178n46
Santini, Fortunato, 78
Scarlatti, Domenico, 7, 68–69, 72–89, 91, 92–93, 97n10, 98n12, 98n20, 99n22, 100n31: Brahms's engagement with the music of, 77–78; Fugue in G Minor (K. 30, "Cat's Fugue"), 91; performance of during the nineteenth century, 91, 92; sonatas for keyboard (general), 77, 91, 99n22; Sonata in C Major (K. 159), 68, 72–77, 73, 75, 78–89, 91, 92, 96, 97n10, 98n12; Sonata in G Major (K. 180), 78. *See also* Czerny, Carl: Scarlatti sonata edition
Schenker, Heinrich, 3, 102n62
Schoenberg, Arnold, 217n28; "Brahms the Progressive," 214
Scholz, Bernhard, 204
Schön, Friedrich, 207
Schopenhauer, Arthur, 4
Schubert, Franz, 7, 11, 13, 63n20, 66n52, 92, 98n20, 104, 205; *Schwanengesang* (D. 957), 68, 71–72, 87, 92, 93; Symphony No. 8 in B Minor (D. 759, "Unfinished"), 181
Schubring, Adolf, 2, 8n3, 66n54
Schumann, Clara Wieck, 2, 7, 56, 61, 63n22, 68, 69, 77, 78, 89, 90, 91, 92, 94, 95, 97n3, 99n24, 100n41, 133, 167, 173, 174, 177n45, 177n46, 181, 190, 191, 204, 206, 212, 220n68, 224n114, 230; marriage to Robert Schumann, 69, 92, 190, 191; Scarlatti, associations with music of, 91, 92. *See also* "Clara cipher"; Schumann, Robert: "Clara cipher," use of
Schumann, Gustav, 204
Schumann, Robert, 2, 5, 55–56, 63n20, 68, 69, 77, 90, 92, 93, 94, 100n39, 104, 131n5, 132n14, 133, 167, 170–71, 173, 174, 176, 177n43, 177n46, 181, 204, 230
Beethoven, views on, 2, 3, 4, 9n8, 132n14, 208
Brahms, as editor of works of, 13
Brahms, mentorship of, 2, 3–4, 9n8, 55, 56, 61, 68, 77, 90, 93, 133, 170–71, 174, 230 (*see also* Schumann, Robert: critical writings of: "*Neue Bahnen*")
"Clara cipher," use of, 173, 178n46, 181
critical writings of, 56, 66n47; "*Neue Bahnen*," 2, 47, 61, 90, 96n1, 130, 205, 228

(*see also* Beethoven, Ludwig van, Schumann's views on; Schumann, Robert, *Neue Zeitschrift für Musik*, founding and editing of)
death of, 133, 191
marriage to Clara Wieck, 69, 92, 190, 191
nervous breakdown of, 7, 68, 90, 94, 133, 173, 174
Neue Zeitschrift für Musik, founding and editing of, 11
Schumann, Robert, works of,
6 Fugues on "B-A-C-H" (op. 60), 100n30
"F-A-E" Sonata, Intermezzo for, 67n60
Genoveva (op. 81), 100n36
Fantasie in C Major (op. 17), 68, 69, 71, 72, 89, 92, 93, 94, 98n20, 101, 181
Kreisleriana (op. 16), 167, 168, 173
songs,
Frauenliebe und leben (op. 42), No. 6, "Süsser Freund," 101n49, 181, 190, 219n49
Lieder und Gesänge aus 'Wilhelm Meister' (op. 98a), No. 7, "Singet nicht in Trauertönen," 101n49
String Quartet No. 2 in F Major (op. 41/2), 101n49
symphonies,
No. 1 in B-flat Major (op. 38, "Spring"), 176n26
No. 2 in C Major (op. 61), 101n49, 132n14
No. 3 in E-flat major (op. 97, "Rhenish"), 190
No. 4 in D Minor (op. 120), 170
Siebold, Agathe von, 31–32, 33
Silva, Fabio Roberto Gardenal da, 94, 99n27, 100n31
Simrock, Fritz, 93, 94, 95, 200, 214n1, 219n50
Smetana, Bedřich: Czech Dances, 131n7
Smith, Peter, 3
Sophocles, 179, 208
Specht, Richard, 208
Speidel, Ludwig, 199, 201, 212
Spitta, Philipp, 11, 182
Standhartner, Josef, 204
"Steh' ich in finst'rer Mitternacht." *See under* folksong

Sternau, C. O., 58; "Der Abend dämmert," 58, 59–60, 66n54; "Bitte," 59–60
Stockhausen, Julius, 229
Strasbourg, University of, 12
Swafford, Jan, 139, 179, 200, 225n116
symphony, status of following Beethoven, 14, 15, 199, 202, 204, 208

Tausig, Carl, 204
Thomas, Theodore, 221n73
Tovey, Donald Francis, 99n28, 172, 175n9, 179, 180
Treitler, Leo, 2, 3

University of Bonn, 12
University of Breslau, 207
University of Strasbourg, 12
University of Vienna, 12
Urbantschitsch, Viktor, 130n1

Vaillancourt, Michael, 132n13, 231n6
Venice, 206
Vienna, 64n38, 98n20, 200, 204, 207, 221n69, 223n107
Vienna, University of, 12

Wagner, Cosima. *See* Liszt, Cosima (Francesca Gaetana)
Wagner, Minna. *See* Planer, Minna
Wagner, Richard, 2, 12, 191, 194, 196, 199, 202, 203, 204, 208, 212, 213, 223, 224n113, 225n118, 227, 228
  antisemitism of, 205, 207
  Brahms, relationship with, 2, 8, 181, 202, 203–8, 212, 223n112, 224n113, 227; criticisms of Brahms in print, 205, 207–8, 224n113
  Bülow, Hans von, relationship with, 206, 207
  death of, 203, 207, 208, 212, 213
  Nietszche, Friedrich, relationship with, 206, 222n99

Planer, Minna, marriage to, 205–6
symphony after Beethoven, views on, 14, 202, 204, 208 (*see also* Beethoven, Ludwig van, Wagner's views on)
Wesendoncks, relationship with the, 205–6
Wagner, Richard, works of,
  Faust Overture, 208
  Der fliegende Holländer, 208
  Götterdämmerung, 224n113
  Das Rheingold, 205, 207
  Sonata für das Album von Frau M. W., 206
  Tannhäuser:"Beglückt dar nun dich, o Heimat" ("Pilgrim's Chorus"), 8, 181, 191–97, 194, 202, 212, 213, 219n49, 224n115; overture, 191, 194, 195–96, 202; "Venusberg" music from *"Naht euch dem Strande"* ("Chorus of the Sirens"), 204–5, 207, 208, 209, 210, 212, 213, 219n49, 223n112, 224n115
  Tristan und Isolde, 205, 206, 208, 212
  Wesendonck Lieder, 206
Webern, Anton, Passacaglia for Orchestra (op. 1), 213
Webster, James, 57
Weingartner, Felix, 202
Weitzmann, Carl Friedrich, 221n84
Wendt, Gustav, 179
"Wer nur den lieben Gott lässt walten." *See* Bach, Johann Sebastian: Cantata No. 93, *Wer nur den lieben Gott lässt walten* (BWV 93)
Wesendonck, Mathilde, 205–6, 207, 222n98
Wesendonck, Otto, 205–6
Wieck, Clara. *See* Schumann, Clara Wieck
Wiesbaden, 208
Wüllner, Franz, 204

Zemlinsky, Alexander von: Symphony in B-Flat Major, 213
Zurich, 104, 131n6, 206

JACQUELYN E. C. SHOLES serves on the faculty in the Department of Musicology and Ethnomusicology at Boston University.

www.ingramcontent.com/pod-product-compliance
Lightning Source LLC
Chambersburg PA
CBHW050900240426
43673CB00050B/1946